IMAGES
of Rail

DELAWARE VALLEY RAILWAY
1901–1937

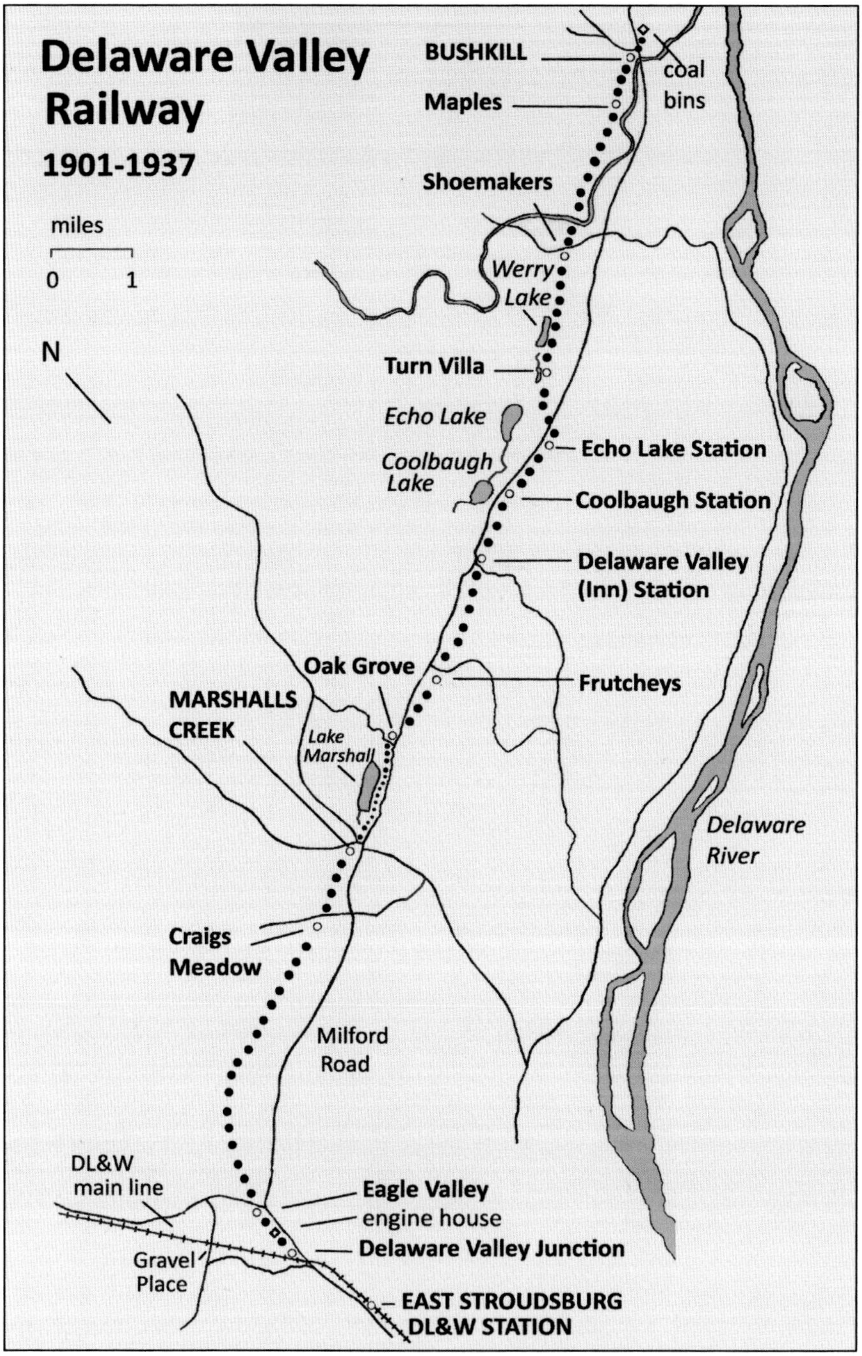

The 12-mile route of the Delaware Valley Railway included 14 stations and stops, several sidings, and a few service areas such as the enginehouse in East Stroudsburg and the coal bins in Bushkill. Elevation varied from 422 feet in East Stroudsburg to 511 feet in Coolbaugh and 370 feet in Bushkill. (Authors' collection.)

On the Cover: Vacationers await the Delaware Valley Railway at Turn Villa Station in 1911. (John W. Hudson II and Depot Square Publishing, Loveland, Ohio.)

IMAGES
of Rail

DELAWARE VALLEY RAILWAY 1901–1937

Michelle Jacques with John Beljean
Foreword by Kim Williams

ARCADIA
PUBLISHING

ISBN 978-1-4671-2615-1

Published by Arcadia Publishing
Charleston, South Carolina

Printed in the United States of America

Library of Congress Control Number: 2016959295

For all general information, please contact Arcadia Publishing:
Telephone 843-853-2070
Fax 843-853-0044
E-mail sales@arcadiapublishing.com
For customer service and orders:
Toll-Free 1-888-313-2665

Visit us on the Internet at www.arcadiapublishing.com

This book is dedicated to the people of the valley who built, ran, rode, and have remembered the Delaware Valley Railway.

Contents

Foreword

My mom—and my grandmother—often said, "I'm glad I was young when I was." I could not understand that statement when I was a youth. I was too busy experiencing the gladness of being young within my own generation. Now that I'm an old codger, guess what? I am glad that I was young when I was. At this point, I clearly understand what my mom and grandmother meant.

My grandmother was young before school buses were used. And she was a country girl whose home was a big farmhouse almost 10 miles from the nearest settlement of more than 50 people. Her high school was in town. How did she and other teenagers in the townships in that 10-mile area get to high school? They rode a train—the Delaware Valley dinkey!

The big house that she lived in with her five siblings and her mom and dad (my great-grandparents) was advertised by the Delaware, Lackawanna & Western in 1909 and 1910 as Christian Colabaugh's Locust Farm House: "accommodates 15; rates: $6.00 to $8.00 per week; open June 1 to November 1; milk, butter, eggs and vegetables from the farm; conveyance at train when notified; one mile from station."

I can just imagine my grandmother and her brothers and sisters in summertime sleeping in a tent in the backyard when my great-grandfather's house was full of paying boarders. I almost wish I was young when she was!

The area between East Stroudsburg and Bushkill had many "guest homes" in the early 1900s. The Delaware Valley Railway was instrumental in transporting thousands of folks on the last leg of their journey to the kind of scenic and laid-back vacation destinations that were so popular at the turn of the 20th century.

The railway was far from perfect, but imperfections are not uncommon in fairy tales. And that is what the dinkey's existence seems like now—a fairy tale. Yet it was real! The following pages might make you, too, wish that you had lived in the valley and camped in the backyard with the Colabaugh kids.

—Kim Williams
Middle Smithfield Township Historical Commission

ACKNOWLEDGMENTS

We are grateful to the following individuals for sharing their collections, memories, and time: Kendrick Bisset, Pat Francis, Hermann Fruck, Beryl Hellgren, John W. Hudson II, Bob Huffman, Ken Johns, Susan Kopczynski, the Kulick family, Michele and Chris Kuna, Pam Lavelle, W. Fred and Diane May, Rob McLaughlin, Ed Regina, Kathleen and Kevin Sandt, Ed Schmidheiser, Mr. and Mrs. Ralph Vecchio, and the staff of Pocono Palace, Rainbow Mountain Resort, St. Paul's Lutheran Church of Smithfield, and Smithfield Township. For innumerable exchanges of ideas, images, and materials, for offering the foreword, and for scrupulous research and proofing of text, we are deeply indebted to Kim Williams.

"The Passing of the Dinkey" by Horace G. Walters (chapter 7) is a manuscript in the collections of the Monroe County Historical Association and is printed here with the association's kind permission.

Images appear courtesy of individual collectors and of the following Pennsylvania institutions: Bushkill Lehman Township Historical Society (BLTHS), Delaware Water Gap National Recreation Area (DEWA), Eastern Monroe Public Library (EMPL), Kemp Library of East Stroudsburg University, East Stroudsburg Community Alliance, East Stroudsburg Railroad Tower Society, Middle Smithfield Township Historical Commission, Monroe County Historical Association (MCHA), Monroe County Recorder of Deeds and County Archives (MCRD), Paradise Township Historical Society, Pennsylvania Department of Transportation (PennDOT), Pennsylvania Historical & Museum Commission (PHMC), Pike County Historical Society (PCHist), Pike County Recorder of Deeds, Railroad Museum of Pennsylvania (RRMPa), Slate Belt Heritage Center, and Steamtown National Historic Site (STEA). Images were also obtained from Anderson University and Church of God Archives, Anderson, Indiana; Depot Square Publishing Collection, Loveland, Ohio; Montana Historical Society Research Center Photograph Archives, Helena, Montana, and Railpace Newsmagazine, Greentown, Pennsylvania. We thank the staff of these organizations for their assistance.

Online collections consulted include the Library of Congress at www.loc.gov (LOC) and the US Geological Survey at www.usgs.gov (USGS), and the Delaware Public Archives (DPA) aerial photographs in chapter 8 were taken in 1939 through the US Department of Agriculture, Agricultural Adjustment Administration and accessed online in 2016 at www.pennpilot.psu.edu (PSU).

Introduction

"Railroad fever along the Delaware," reported the *Milford Herald* in 1876, "reaches about 90 degrees in the shade." The next year, the *American Railroad Journal* stated that the project for "a railroad up the Delaware Valley is being revived." A Stroudsburg–to–Port Jervis line would link the Lackawanna and Lehigh coalfields to New England and "open the picturesque scenery of the upper Delaware to pleasure seekers." By the 1890s, steam locomotives and electric trolleys were crisscrossing the dreamscape from Kingston, New York, to Saylorsburg, Pennsylvania, and from Resica Falls in the valley to Culvers Gap in New Jersey.

Trains had first called in Monroe County in 1856, when the county was just 20 years old. The Delaware, Lackawanna & Western (DL&W) out of New York stopped at the busy resort village of Delaware Water Gap, then continued to the DL&W Station in East Stroudsburg and through the Poconos to Scranton.

Travelers from Philadelphia could connect to the DL&W in East Stroudsburg via the Pennsylvania Railroad through Wilmington, Delaware, and Mauch Chunk, Pennsylvania. Coal from the anthracite region around Wilkes-Barre and Scranton could roll into Philadelphia by the reverse route. To reach the coalfields of eastern Pennsylvania, in 1882, the New York, Susquehanna & Western (NYS&W) established a route to the DL&W's Gravel Place in Stroud Township; its small freight station in Stroudsburg is still standing.

The age of rail had reached the threshold of the eastern Poconos. Yet, though the resort industry was already established along the Delaware River, transportation up and down the valley was still, as the railway's prospectus lamented, "by private conveyance and the antiquarian stage coach."

While not all the fevered dreams of promoters became reality, the railway was no hallucination. It bought rights, laid track, ran engines, moved passengers, hauled freight, and boosted the economy of Monroe County for more than a generation. Among the smallest of small "roads," in its time it took its place among 1,000 small lines running over the nation's 200,000 miles of track.

Railway Chronology

1893–1896: Various plans are announced for an electric railway between Stroudsburg and Bushkill and between Stroudsburg and Port Jervis. More than eight miles are graded (East Stroudsburg to Coolbaugh), but no railway is built.

1894–1899: Three rail companies are successively formed to run from Wind Gap and Saylorsburg to Matamoras. Only five miles from Wind Gap to Saylorsburg are built.

1899: Delaware Valley Railroad Company (DVRR) is organized, acquiring the rights of the previous rail companies and electric lines.

1899–1900: DVRR obtains a mortgage and issues bonds.

1901: DVRR hires a contractor, purchases an engine, and begins construction. The first train runs as far as Coolbaugh on August 22.

1902: The bridge over Bush Kill is completed in January, and the first train runs to Bushkill. Extensions to Port Jervis and Saylorsburg are announced but never built.

1903: Despite turning a profit, DVRR sells on November 10 for $80,000 to Milton Yetter, an East Stroudsburg businessman.

1904: Delaware Valley Railway Company (the railway) incorporates on January 9, and stock is issued. The heyday of the railway begins, with modest surpluses each year until World War I. Passenger revenue begins to exceed freight.

1911: Milton Yetter dies on August 28 at the age of 62.

1916: With roads improving, tourists travel more by taxi and bus. Losses set in.

1924: The railway charters Delaware Valley Transportation Company (DVT) to compete with bus transportation. In 1927, bus service substitutes for one train run.

1928: The railway suspends all passenger rail service and runs DVT buses instead. The railway's employee roll is down to five, plus day hires as needed.

1931: The railway purchases a truck to haul less-than-carload freight. A modest fleet of vehicles carries packages and small freight. There is only one full-time employee.

1936: The railway clears $238 and carries only one carload of coal and one of gasoline.

1937: The railway clears only $40 in its first two months and petitions the Interstate Commerce Commission to abandon the line. Permission is granted on September 2, 1937. Russell E. Jones, acting for bondholders, purchases the assets for $30,600.

1938: Tracks are removed between March and June. Disposition of assets and reversion of rights-of-way to landowners begins, concluding between 1962 and 1969 under W. Jack Wallie.

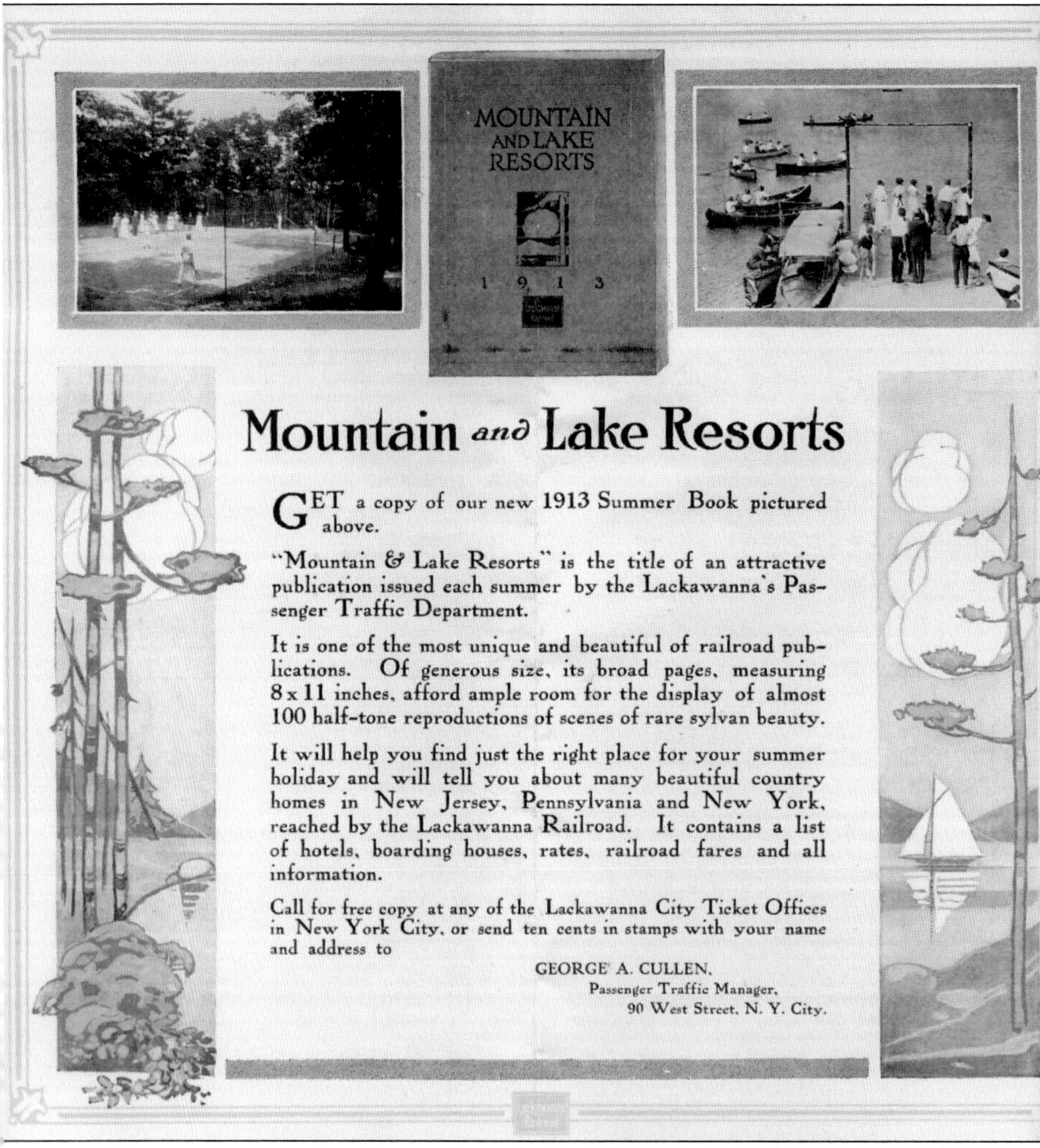

"Almost any point in the valley can be reached in half an hour's trip from Stroudsburg by the Delaware Valley Railroad," crowed the Lackawanna Railroad in its passenger guide, *Mountain and Lake Resorts along the Lackawanna Railroad*. "The hotels . . . are filled with those who seek a quiet, restful country life." This blurb inside a rail timetable promoted the 100-page guide and promised the turn of the century's ideal—a relaxing vacation away from city heat, noise, and bad air. With listings published by the railroad, even small guesthouses could draw in big-city vacationers. (BLTHS.)

One

The Railway Era

In Monroe County, the valley of the Delaware River runs northeast to southwest and is linked firmly to Bushkill, just across the Pike County line to the northeast, and Stroudsburg and East Stroudsburg to the southwest. Through the valley on the Pennsylvania side runs Milford Road, descendant of a centuries-old Indian path from the Hudson River and New England to Philadelphia.

Clustered along the road in the railway era were small communities, surrounded by farms and dotted by natural and artificial lakes—Craigs Meadows, Marshalls Creek, Frutcheys, Coolbaugh, Shoemakers, and Bushkill (in both Monroe and Pike Counties). By 1900, many farmhouses had turned to the resort industry by taking in summer guests. With names like villa, cottage, inn, and retreat, they usually served fewer than 40 people. Some were merely enlarged farmhouses, with cash-paying summer boarders adding to the farmer's income and his wife and children doing the cooking and serving.

First chartered with capital from New York and Philadelphia to be an electric line from Saylorsburg to Port Jervis, New York, the Delaware Valley Railway also took on the name *Delaware Valley Railroad* in 1901 with a steam charter to carry freight. The first train ran northeast to Coolbaugh in August 1901, and trains reached Bushkill the next year, but revenue was insufficient to service its debt, and the line was sold to new and local investors and once again styled "Delaware Valley Railway." This time, the venture took root.

In the valley, the age of rail was now the railway era and the heyday of the Delaware Valley Railway had begun. Guesthouses expanded into grand inns serving 100 or more guests. Tourist brochures extolled the beauty and healthfulness of the area. Goods rolled into Bushkill and Marshalls Creek to be transported, and visitors and residents rode the dinkey up and down the line. The railway's single track linked the valley to East Stroudsburg, and from East Stroudsburg, tracks beyond counting linked the valley to the nation at large.

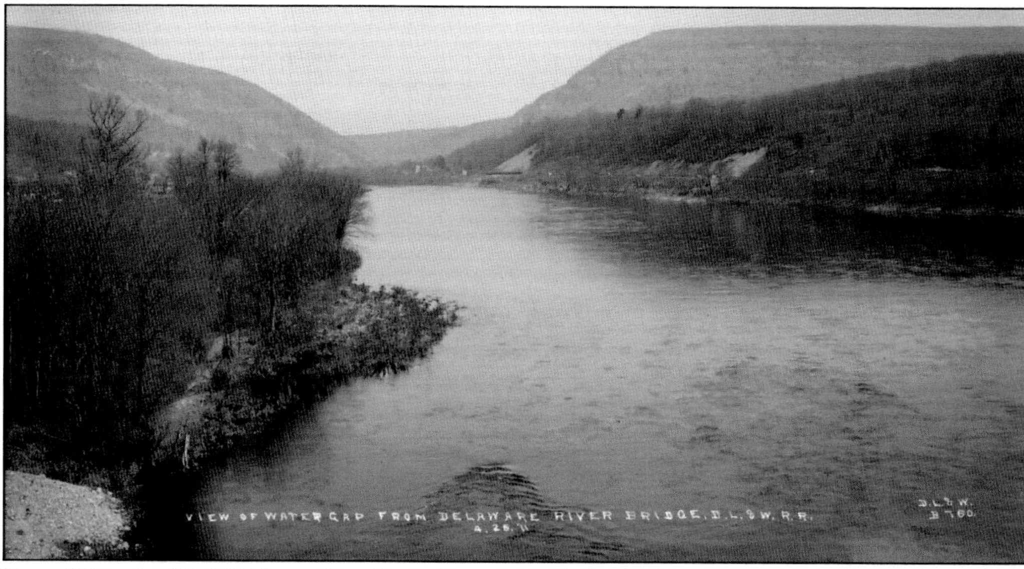

From 1911, the DL&W from New York City crossed the Delaware River on the viaduct of the Lackawanna Cutoff near Portland, Pennsylvania, giving passengers this dramatic view of the water gap. By reducing curves and climbs, the cutoff route trimmed travel from New York by 11 miles and 27 minutes. (LOC.)

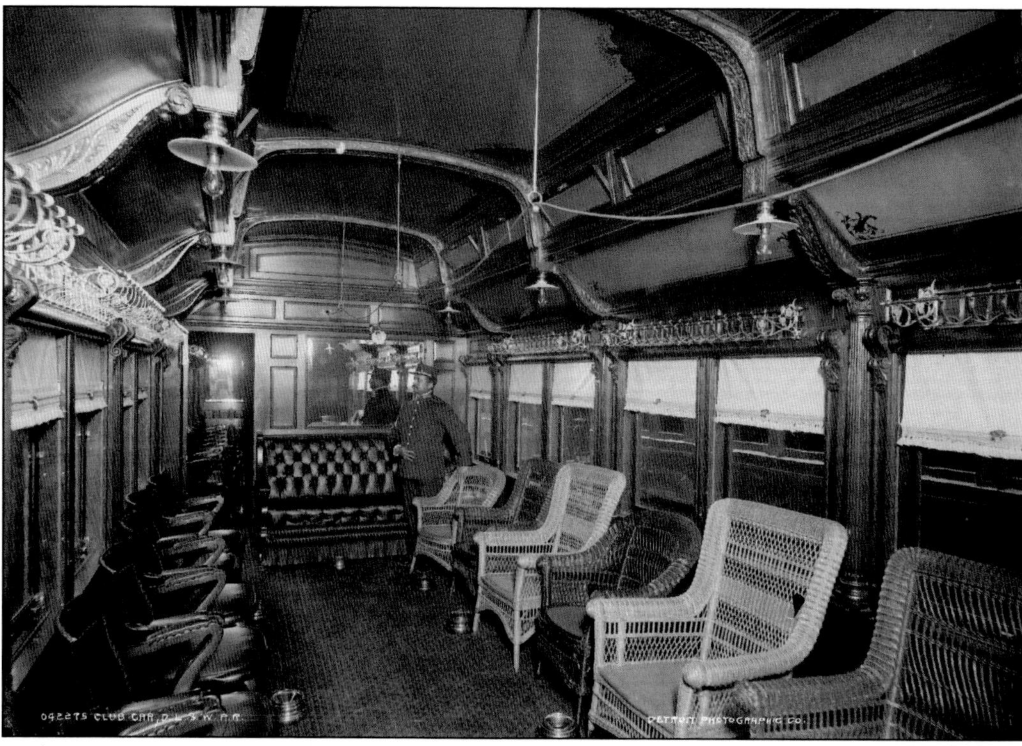

Lackawanna passengers could take in the scenery in style in club cars like this on the DL&W line in 1900. Club and parlor cars out of New York and Philadelphia might be attached to a railway run, but the railway itself through the years had only passenger coaches, freight cars, and a mail/luggage/smoker "combine." (LOC.)

DELAWARE VALLEY RAILROAD.

TIME TABLE IN EFFECT JUNE 1st, 1902.

EASTWARD	DAILY Except Sunday			
	2	4	6	8
	A.M.	A.M.	P.M.	P.M.
Lv. East Stroudsburg. D. L. & W. Station	6.45	9.20	12.55	5.00
" Delaware Valley Junction	f6.47	f9.22	f12.57	f5.02
" Craig's Meadows	f6.57	f9.32	f1.07	f5.12
" Marshall's Creek	6.59	9.34	1.09	5.14
" Oak Grove	f7.01	f9.36	f1.11	f5.16
" Frutcheys	f7.04	f9.39	f1.14	f5.19
" Coolbaugh	7.07	9.42	1.17	5.22
" Turn Villa	f7.11	f9.46	f1.21	f5.26
" Shoemakers	7.15	9.50	1.25	5.30
Ar. Bushkill	7.20	9.55	1.30	5.35

WESTWARD	DAILY Except Sunday				Sunday Only	Monday Only
	3	5	7	9	11	15
	A.M.	A.M.	P.M.	P.M.	P.M.	A.M.
Lv Bushkill	8.00	10.45	3.40	6.00	7.00	6.00
" Shoemakers	8.05	10.5	3.45	6.05	7.05	6.05
" Turn Villa	f8.09	f10.54	f3.49	f6.09	f7.09	f6.09
" Coolbaugh	8.13	10.58	3.53	6.13	7.13	6.13
" Frutcheys	f8.16	f11.01	f3.56	f6.16	f7.16	f6.16
" Oak Grove	f8.19	f11.04	f3.59	f6.19	f7.19	f6.19
" Marshall's Creek	8.21	11.06	4.01	6.21	7.21	6.21
" Craig's Meadows	f8.23	f11.08	f4.03	f6.23	f7.23	f6.23
" Delaware Valley Junction	f8.33	f11.18	f4.13	f6.33	f7.33	f6.33
Ar. East Stroudsburg. D. L. & W Station	8.35	11.20	4.15	6.35	7.35	6.35

THROUGH TRAIN CONNECTIONS.

DELAWARE, LACKAWANNA AND WESTERN RAILROAD.

WESTWARD			STATIONS.	EASTWARD			
5	3	21		26	2	6	24
P.M.	A.M.	A.M.		P.M.	P.M.	P.M.	P.M.
			Lve . . . New York . . . Arr.				
†1 40	†10 00	†4 30	Barclay Street	12 30	3 30	7 35	10 25
1 45	10 00	4 30	Christopher Street	12 25	3 25	7 35	10 20
4 56	12 29	8 47	Arr. . . Stroudsburg . . Lve.	9 28	11 52	4 54	7 45
5 00	12 55	9 20	Lve . . Stroudsburg . . Arr	8 35	11 20	4 15	7 35
5 35	1 30	9 55	Arr . . . Bushkill . . . Lve	†8 00	†10 45	†3 40	‡7 00

PENNSYLVANIA RAILROAD.

Westward		STATIONS.	Eastward			
554	558		567	569	573	577
A.M.	Noon		A.M.	P.M.	P.M.	P.M.
†9 06	12 00	Lv. . Phila. Broad St. Station . . Arr.	10 01	1 06	3 23	8 22
1 30	5 35	Arr. . . . . . . Bushkill . . . . Lv.	s6 00	†8 00	†10 45	†3 40

† Daily except Sunday. f Stops on signal, or on notice to conductor.
‡ Runs Sunday only, s Monday morning only, on and after June 8.
A.M. time, light type. P.M. time, heavy type.

THE HOBSON PRESS EASTON, PA.

The railway's 1902 timetable lists 10 stops and connections to New York and Philadelphia. Subsequent timetables show stops at Eagle Valley in 1903 and at Delaware Valley, Echo Lake, and Maples, all by 1915. (BLTHS.)

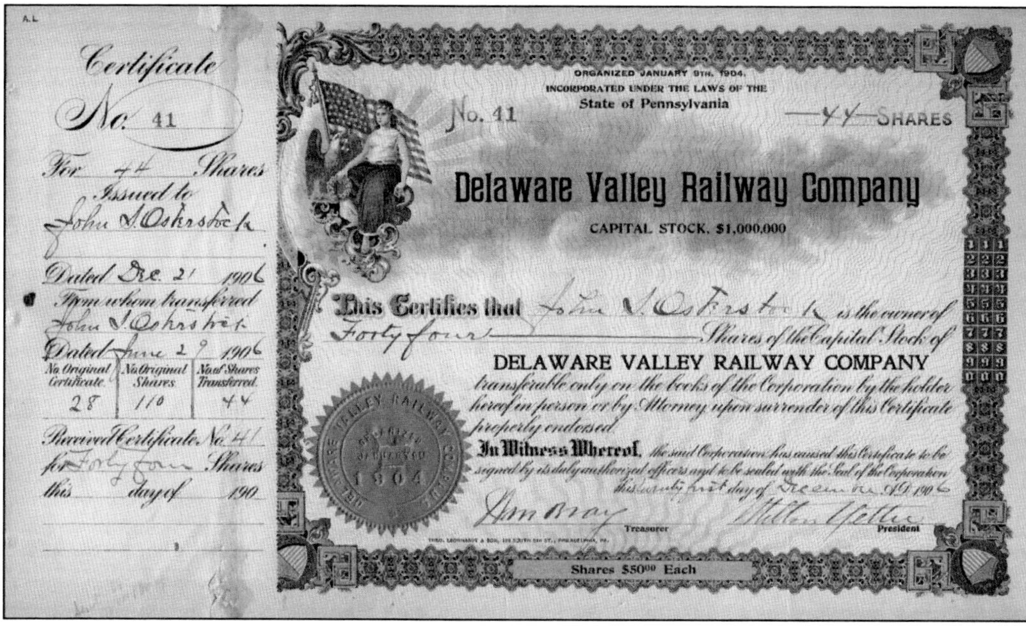

Stock for the new Delaware Valley Railway Company was issued in 1904. These 44 shares were transferred in 1906. It is uncertain what the cost of the shares was; at the railway's dissolution, shareholders would see only 50¢ on the dollar. (East Stroudsburg Railroad Tower Society.)

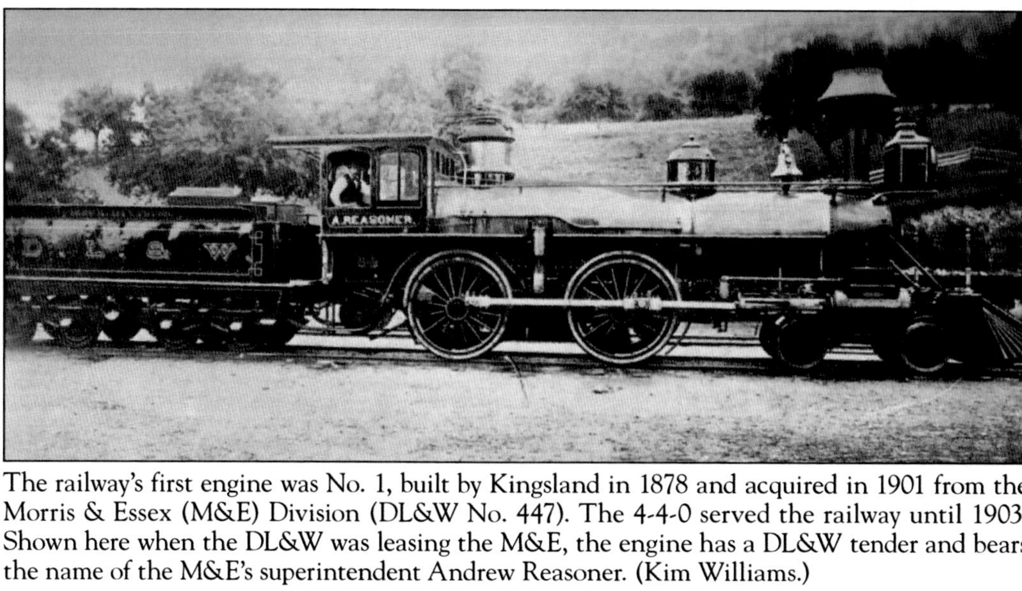

The railway's first engine was No. 1, built by Kingsland in 1878 and acquired in 1901 from the Morris & Essex (M&E) Division (DL&W No. 447). The 4-4-0 served the railway until 1903. Shown here when the DL&W was leasing the M&E, the engine has a DL&W tender and bears the name of the M&E's superintendent Andrew Reasoner. (Kim Williams.)

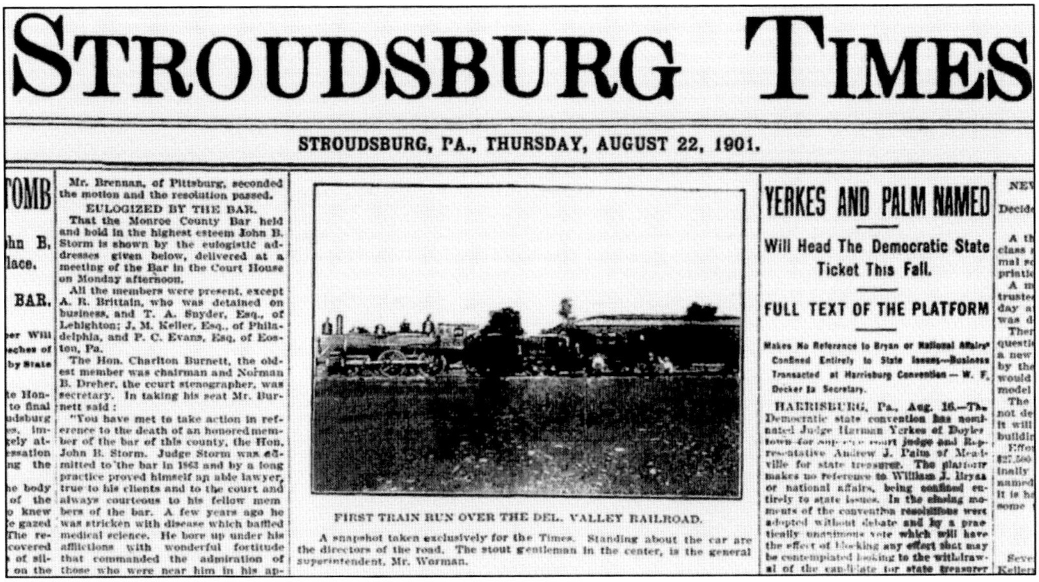

STROUDSBURG TIMES

STROUDSBURG, PA., THURSDAY, AUGUST 22, 1901.

Mr. Brennan, of Pittsburg, seconded the motion and the resolution passed.

EULOGIZED BY THE BAR.

That the Monroe County Bar held and hold in the highest esteem John B. Storm is shown by the eulogistic addresses given below, delivered at a meeting of the Bar in the Court House on Monday afternoon.

All the members were present, except A. R. Brittain, who was detained on business, and T. A. Snyder, Esq., of Lehighton; J. M. Keller, Esq., of Philadelphia, and P. C. Evans, Esq. of Easton, Pa.

The Hon. Charlton Burnett, the oldest member was chairman and Norman B. Dreher, the court stenographer, was secretary. In taking his seat Mr. Burnett said:

"You have met to take action in reference to the death of an honored member of the bar of this county, the Hon. John B. Storm. Judge Storm was admitted to the bar in 1863 and by a long practice proved himself an able lawyer, true to his clients and to the court and always courteous to his fellow members of the bar. A few years ago he was stricken with disease which baffled medical science. He bore up under his afflictions with wonderful fortitude that commanded the admiration of those who were near him in his ap-

FIRST TRAIN RUN OVER THE DEL. VALLEY RAILROAD.

A snapshot taken exclusively for the Times. Standing about the car are the directors of the road. The stout gentleman in the center, is the general superintendent, Mr. Worman.

YERKES AND PALM NAMED

Will Head The Democratic State Ticket This Fall.

FULL TEXT OF THE PLATFORM

Makes No Reference to Bryan or National Affairs—Confined Entirely to State Issues—Business Transacted at Harrisburg Convention—W. F. Decker Is Secretary.

HARRISBURG, Pa., Aug. 16.—The Democratic state convention has nominated Judge Harman Yerkes of Doylestown for superior court judge and Representative Andrew J. Palm of Meadville for state treasurer. The platform makes no reference to William J. Bryan or national affairs, being confined entirely to state issues. In the closing moments of the convention resolutions were adopted without debate and by a practically unanimous vote which will have the effect of blocking any effort that may be contemplated looking to the withdrawal of the candidate for state treasurer

By August 1901, Engine No. 1 could take the railway's directors as far as Coolbaugh, and the foray was first-page news in Stroudsburg. The line reached the western bank of Bush Kill at Shoemakers by late 1901 and the village of Bushkill early in 1902. Running time to Bushkill was 35 minutes. (*Stroudsburg Times*.)

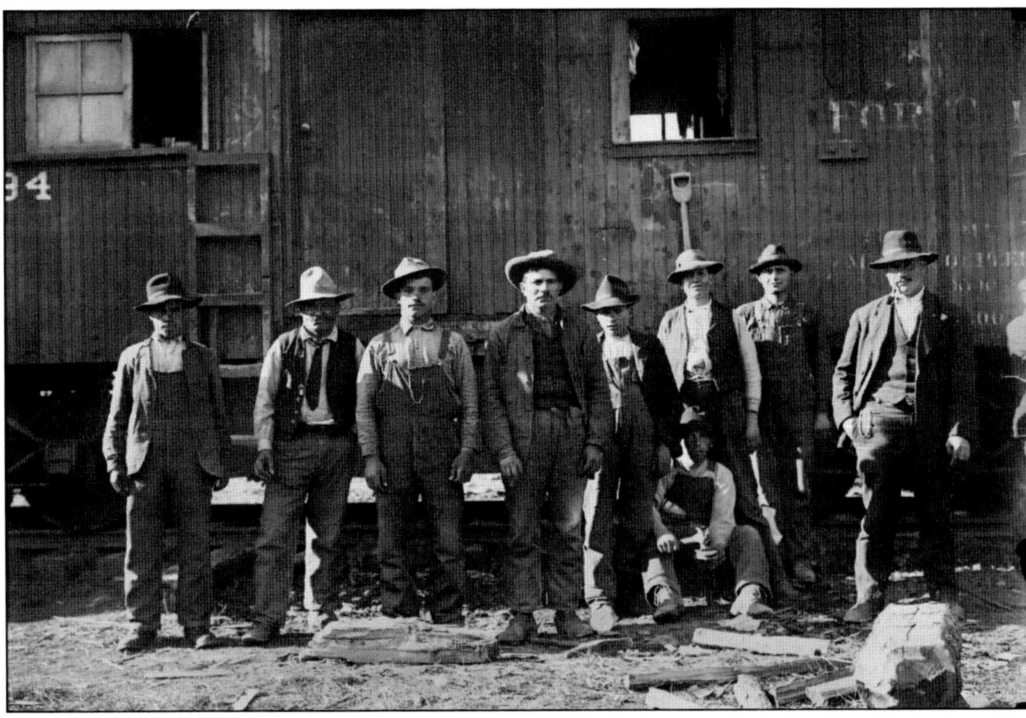

Rail workers did not appear on page 1. These Italian and Greek rail workers, posing in 1910, stand in for all the immigrants who joined muscle with American laborers to make the railway dream a reality. (Montana Historical Society Research Center Photograph Archives, photograph by Evelyn Cameron.)

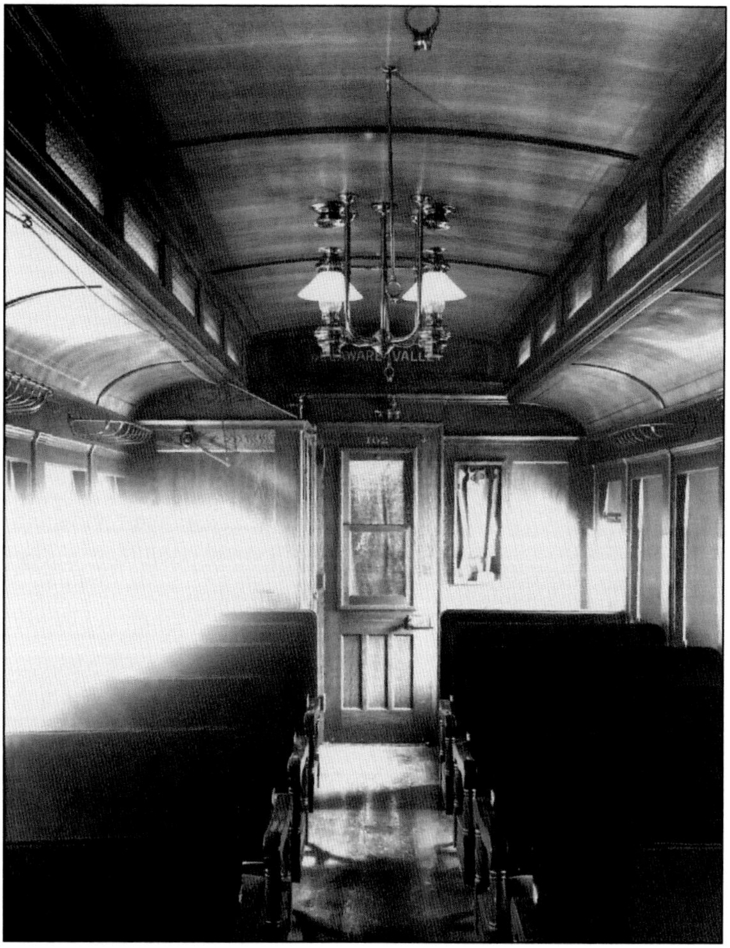

The railway started with two used passenger cars and a "combine" in July 1901. In May 1909, a new combine car, No.102, was delivered from Jackson and Sharp. Wood paneling, chandeliers, and clerestory windows were standard for the day. "It is a very fine car . . . with wide seats and unusually easy riding," reported the *Stroudsburg Times*. It "travels majestically up the line." (DPA.)

Combine No. 102 served as baggage, mail, and smoker car. It must have been wider than the previous railway combine, as a platform adjustment had to be made at Bushkill. Jackson and Sharp Company was founded in the 1860s and within a generation was the largest producer of railcars in the United States. (DPA.)

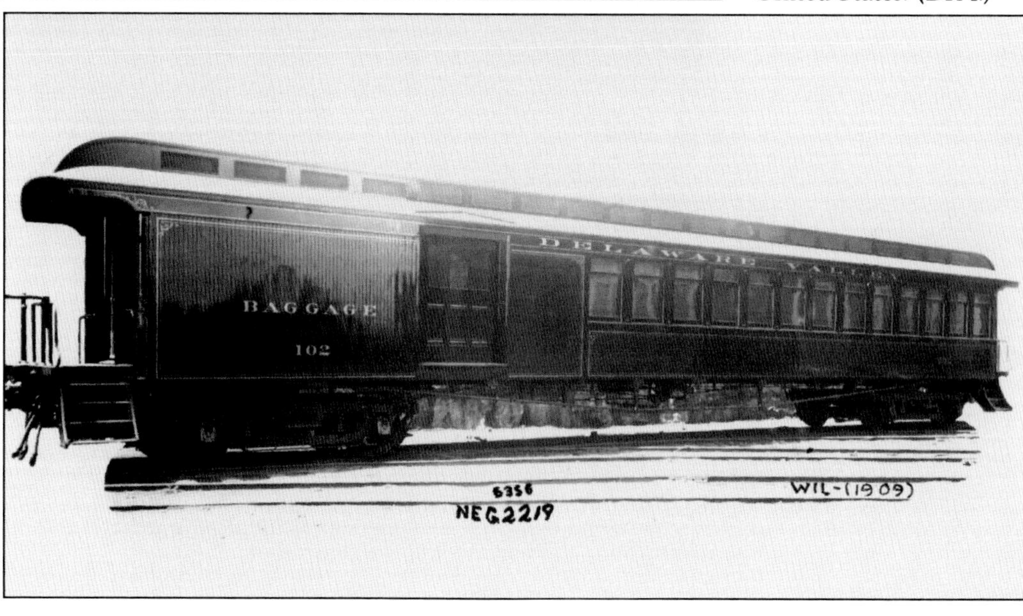

Two

Riding the Railway

As the proposed link between Saylorsburg and East Stroudsburg became less likely, more than ever the selling point of the railway was the growing resort business spilling northward from the crowded streets of Delaware Water Gap into the Delaware Valley.

The c. 1901 railway prospectus, using hotel registers for data, claims that 75,000 passengers a year travelled the valley for summer recreation. It also states that 25,000 people lived in the valley and would produce another 75,000 yearly fares, and that 15,000 tons of coal a year needed to be brought in and 400 cans of milk needed to be brought out.

According to the prospectus, all this traffic would pass through the valley via the proposed rail line from East Stroudsburg to Milford and via ferry and bridge connections to and from the New Jersey bank of the river. The railway projected $170,000 in passenger fares and excursions per year and $65,000 in freight and mail revenue.

A prospectus is always an optimistic document, and these numbers were clearly never achieved. However, for most residents of the valley, the railway was not about tourism or the balance sheet. For them, the dinkey was a school bus for children, a ride to the "New York" stores in East Stroudsburg, a wagon to haul cans of milk and crates of fruit to a hotel, a hopper to haul grain to the mill and ground-up feed back home, or even a cattle car to bring in a new calf. It was cash for trees cut down in winter to spend for coal to heat the home. It was the way to family reunions at Bushkill Falls and church picnics at Echo Lake. It brought teen sweethearts together, and it brought the mail—100 pounds a day. The railway was an offering of the modern and industrial world to a rural way of life where electricity, telephones, refrigeration, and automobiles were still new.

In the 12 months ending May 30, 1903, the railway moved 17,000 passengers up and down this rural valley, both residents and visitors. In time, 6 out of every 10 railway dollars would come from passengers. Here is where they went and what they saw.

Delaware Valley Railway
Official Summer Time Table

WEST BOUND READ DOWN					IN EFFECT	EAST BOUND READ UP					
5	11	9	3	1	JUNE 13, 1925	2	4	10	8	6	12
* P M	‡ A M	* P M	† A M	† A M		† A M	† A M	‡ A M	* P M	† P M	‡ P M
5 00	8 00	12 35	10 00	7 00	Lv. EAST STROUDSBURG Ar.	8 50	11 35	9 35	4 20	6 15	7 35
f 5 12	f 8 12	f12 47	f10 12	f 7 12	Craig's Meadows	f 8 38	f11 23	f 9 23	f 4 08	f 6 03	f 7 23
f 5 14	f 8 14	f12 49	f10 14	f 7 14	Marshall's Creek	f 8 36	f11 21	f 9 21	f 4 06	f 6 01	f 7 21
f 5 16	f 8 16	f12 51	f10 16	f 7 16	Oak Grove	f 8 34	f11 19	f 9 19	f 4 04	f 5 50	f 7 19
f 5 19	f 8 19	f12 54	f10 19	f 7 19	Frutcheys	f 8 31	f11 16	f 9 16	f 4 01	f 5 56	f 7 16
f 5 21	f 8 21	f12 56	f10 21	f 7 21	Delaware Valley	f 8 29	f11 14	f 9 14	f 3 59	f 5 54	
f 5 22	f 8 22	f12 57	f10 22	f 7 22	Coolbaugh	f 8 28	f11 13	f 9 13	f 3 58	f 5 53	f 7 13
f 5 24	f 8 24	f12 59	f10 24	f 7 24	Echo Lake	f 8 26	f11 11	f 9 11	f 3 56	f 5 51	f 7 11
f 5 26	f 8 26	f 1 01	f10 26	f 7 26	Turn Villa	f 8 24	f11 09	f 9 09	f 3 54	f 5 49	f 7 09
f 5 30	f 8 30	f 1 05	f10 30	f 7 30	Winona (or Shoemakers)	f 8 20	f11 05	f 9 05	f 3 50	f 5 45	f 7 05
f 5 33	f 8 34	f 1 08	f10 33	f 7 34	Maples	f 8 16	f11 03	f 9 01	f 3 46	f 5 42	
5 35	8 35	1 10	10 35	7 35	Ar. BUSHKILL Lv.	8 15	11 00	9 00	3 45	5 40	7 00
* P M	‡ A M	* P M	† A M	† A M		† A M	† A M	‡ A M	* P M	† P M	‡ P M

* Daily. † Daily except Sunday. ‡ Sunday only. f All trains stop on signal or notice to conductor

Bushkill, Pa. N. N. GUILLOT, Gen. Supt.

DELAWARE VALLEY RAILWAY
ONE WAY TICKET
WHOLE BUSHKILL HALF
To Stations Punched on Margin

- Maples
- Shoemaker's
- Turn Villa
- Echo Lake
- Coolbaugh
- Frutchey's
- Oak Grove
- Marshall's Creek
- Craig's Meadows
- Del. Valley Junc.
- East Stroudsburg

SERIES B

№ 14511

The 1925 passenger timetable (above) shows all stops except the Delaware Valley Junction station near Milford Crossing and the short-lived Eagle Valley stop in East Stroudsburg, which was perhaps just a gravel platform. (Authors' collection.)

The undated ticket (left) shows the same stations with the exception of Delaware Valley (Inn), later the Regina. The concrete foundation for the Delaware Valley Inn stop was 60 feet long—equivalent to Bushkill's—but its "station" in the 1920s was part of an old railcar. (Authors' collection.)

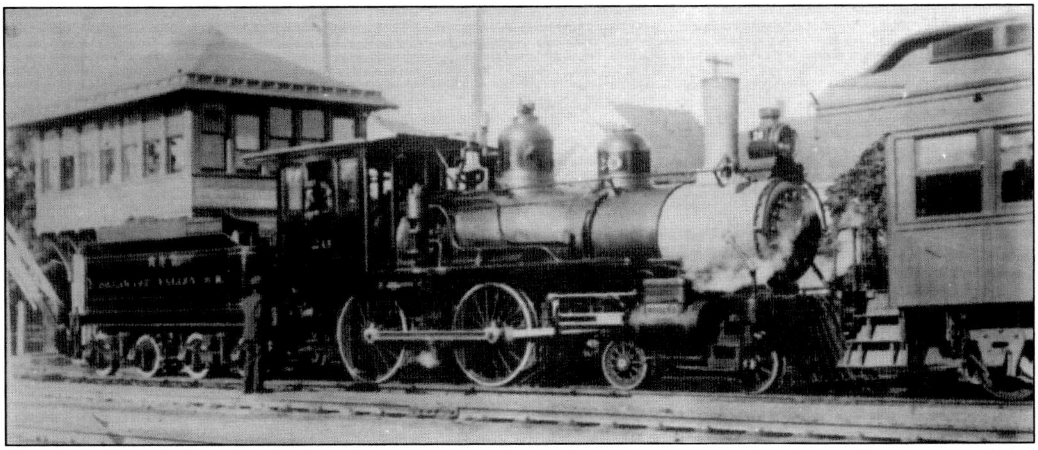

The train's most important riders were the crewmen. The engineer who drove the train and the conductor who handled all passenger and freight transactions were most visible, but the railway's steam engines also needed a fireman to stoke the engine and a brakeman to throw the switches along the line. The crew, in turn, relied on the labor of yard workers to keep the engines running. (PMHC/RRMPa.)

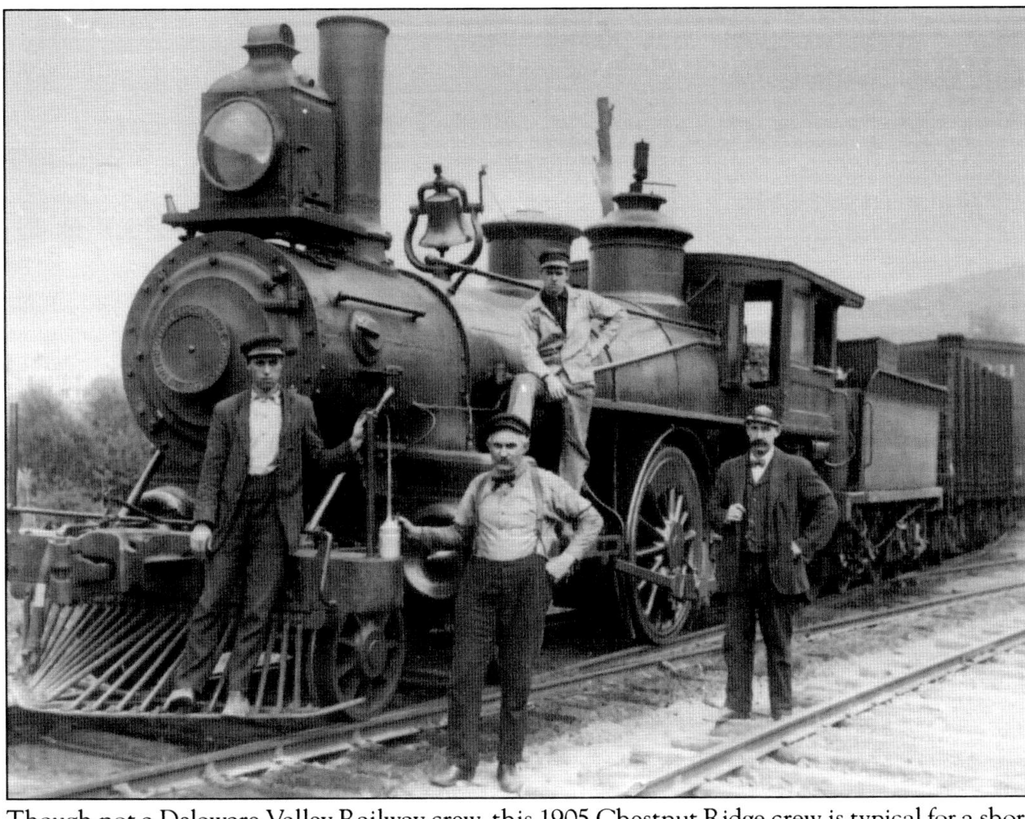

Though not a Delaware Valley Railway crew, this 1905 Chestnut Ridge crew is typical for a short line, hauling bricks, summer visitors, and factory workers through Little Gap. From left to right are brakeman Jim Mackes, engineer Walter Bush with fireman Bob Bush behind, and conductor John Palmer. With one track and few sidings, the Delaware Valley Railway's lone brakeman of record is also remembered as baggage man. (MCHA.)

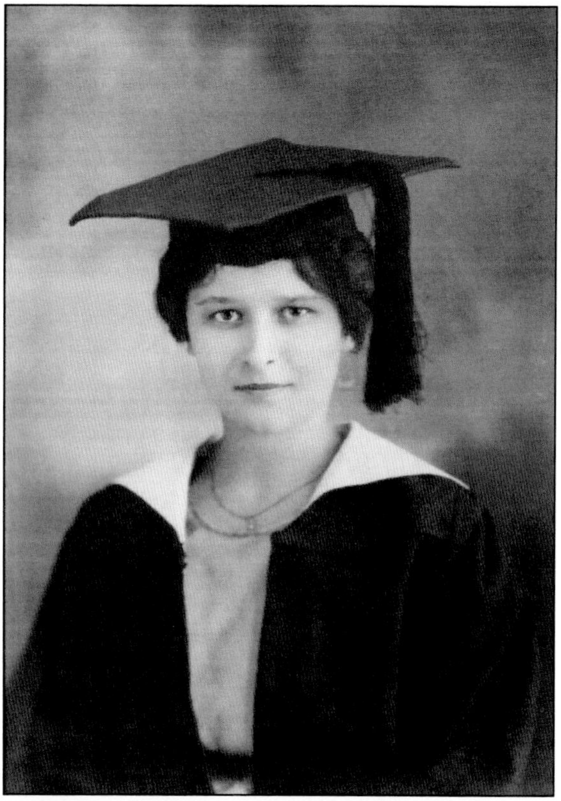

The dinkey brought Mary Colabaugh (left) from her home in Coolbaugh to East Stroudsburg High School to earn her 1920 diploma. The high school, then newly expanded, was next to the Maplehurst Inn on Milford Road, close to Delaware Valley Junction station. (Kim Williams.)

Along the railway route were schoolhouses, many with just one room: Posten School at Eagle Valley, Craigs Meadow, Frutcheys, Central School near Hidden Lake, Sand Hill at Shoemakers, and Maple Grove School at Bushkill (below), to name a few. Pupils rode for free, with schools picking up the fare. (PCHist.)

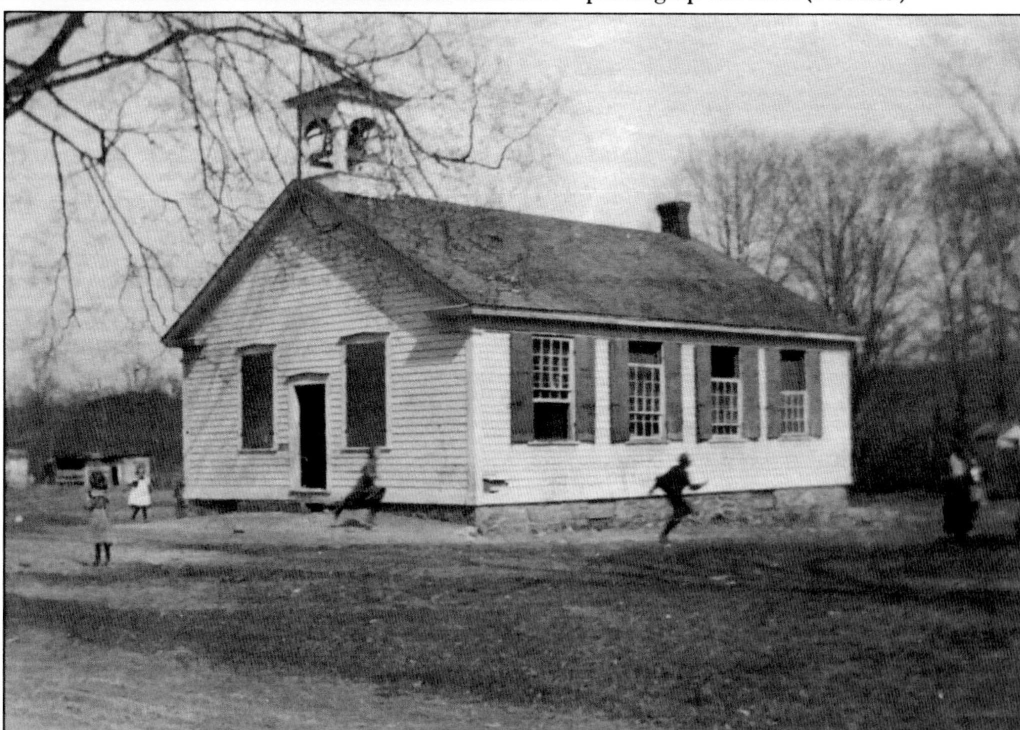

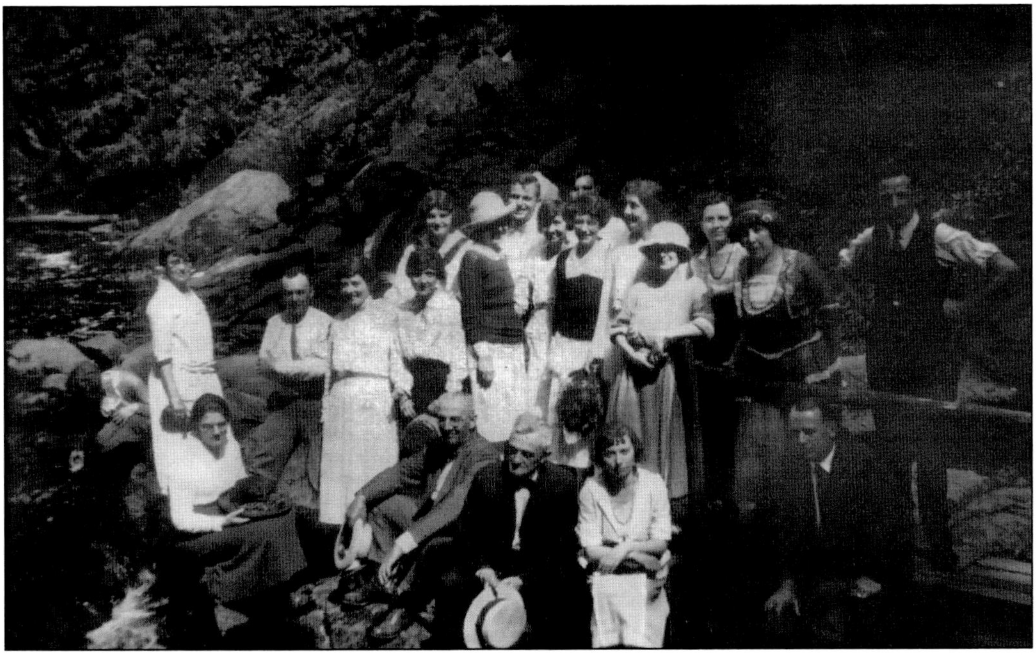

Valley residents used the dinkey to go on church, school, and family outings. Echo Lake, with its boating and swimming, and Bushkill Falls were popular destinations. In 1910, the railway ran an extra trip to get everyone home to Craigs Meadow from a church supper at Marshalls Falls House. (Authors' collection.)

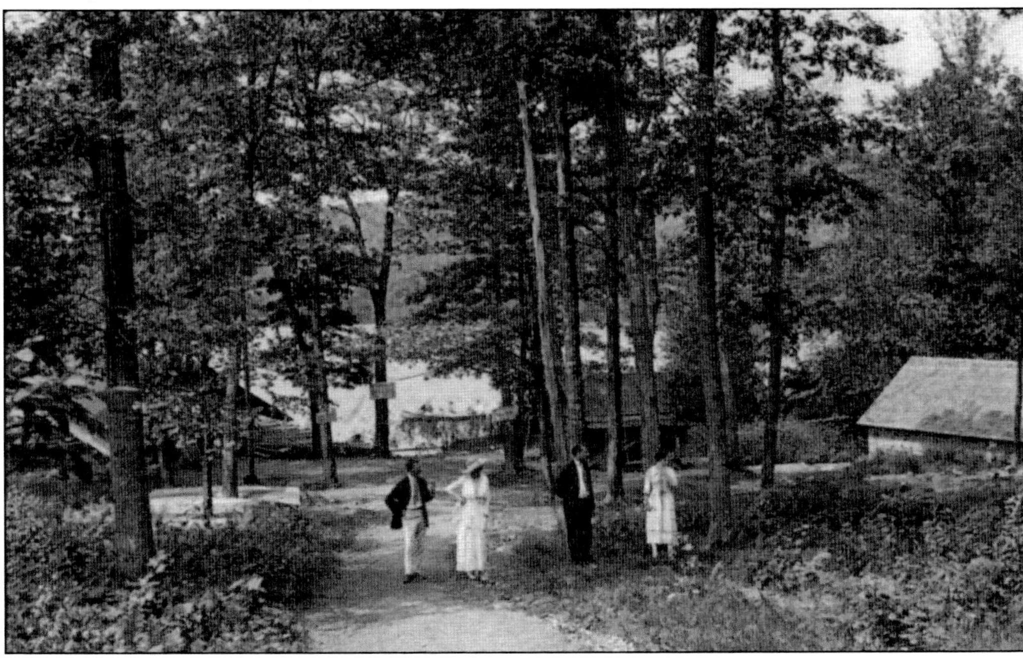

Forest Park was established in 1892 and by the railway era accommodated 330 visitors, with buses bringing in guests from Bushkill station. In 1919, two New York labor unions bought the property: 750 acres became Unity House, and an additional 2,000 acres became (Camp) Tamiment, both hugely successful through World War II. (Authors' collection.)

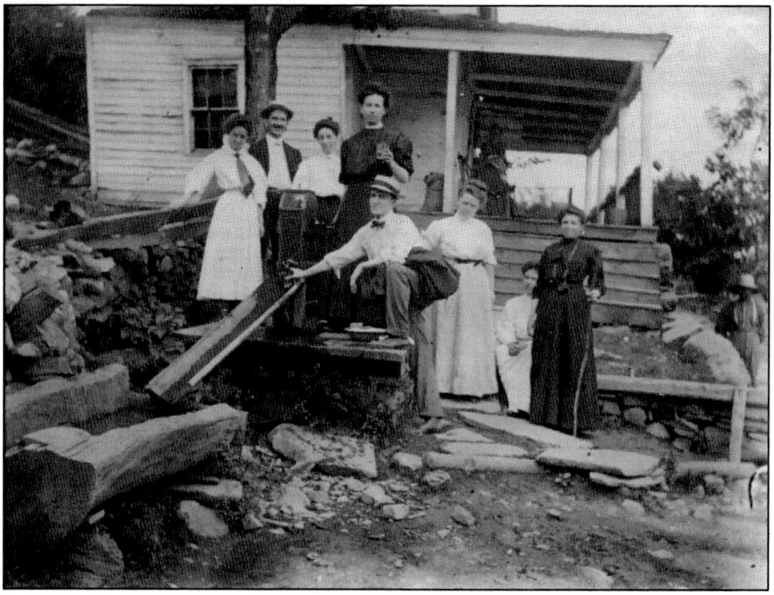

Overlooking Sambo Creek a half mile north of Delaware Valley Junction, Brookside Farm on King Street in East Stroudsburg offered rural charms, like pumping one's own glass of water, that seem to have appealed to city guests. But across the road were the DL&W main line and the International Boiler Works plant. (MCHA.)

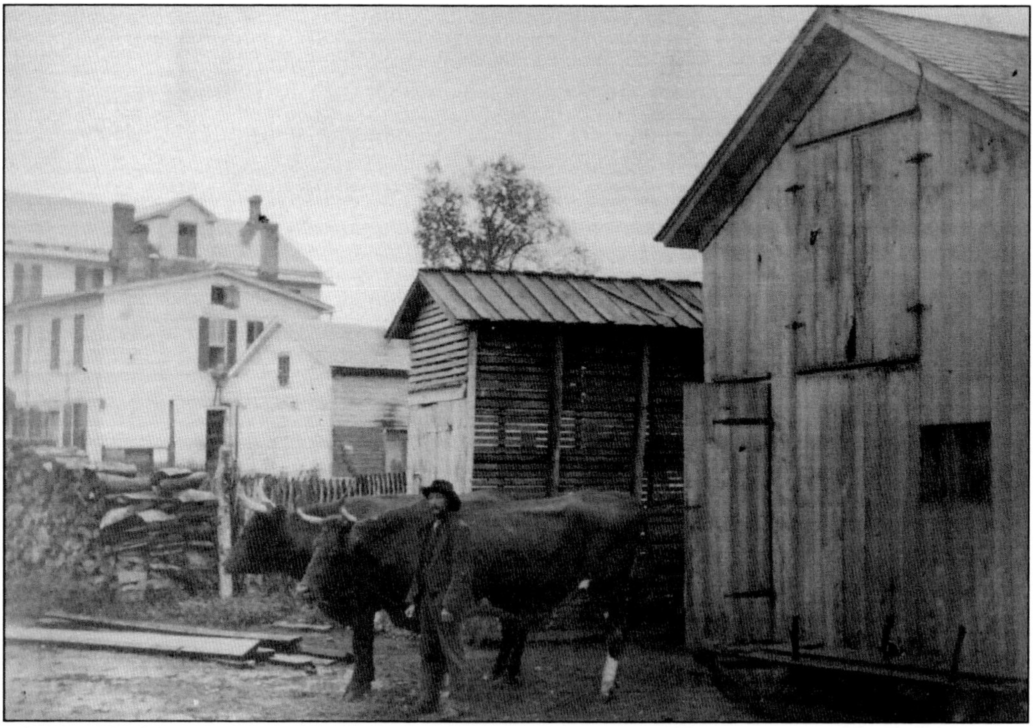

This Bushkill farm is close to, and perhaps part of, a large establishment. A hotel realized benefits from having its own farm for fresh produce and dairy products for the guests' meals. The hotel might also advertise the pastoral setting valued by turn-of-the-20th-century guests. Echo Lake House, in fact, touted its Jersey milk cows. (PCHist.)

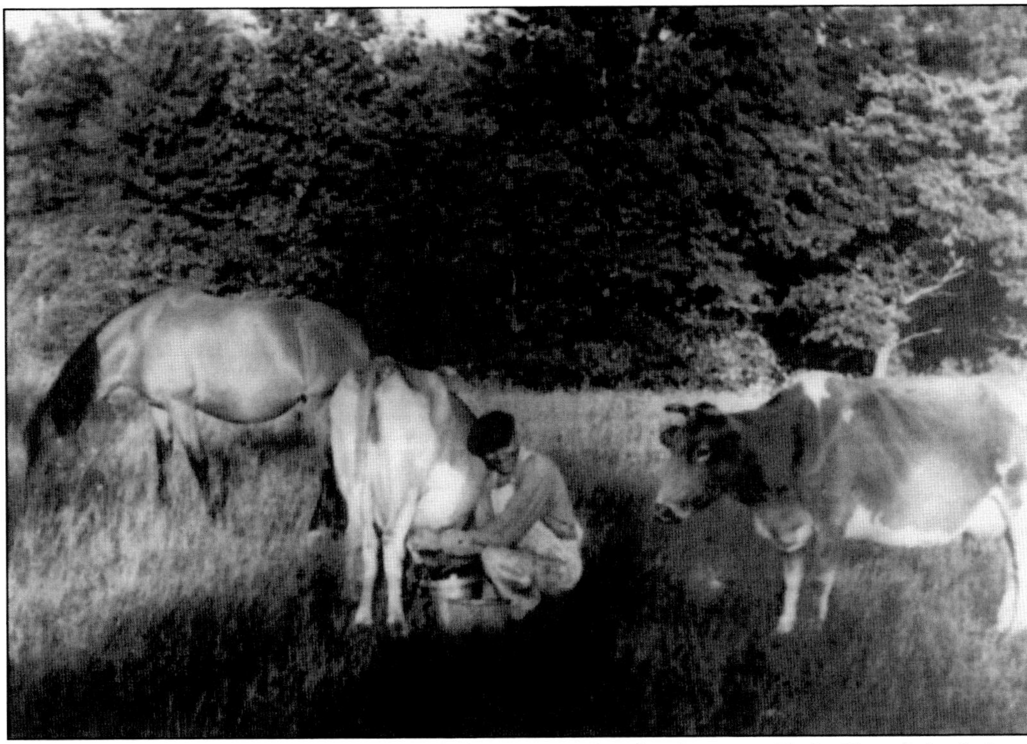

"We had glasses of milk like some people have water," a daughter recalled of her father's dairy farm. Small farmers like George Koerner, shown here with friends at Paradise, could have a few "good milkers" supply the family, satisfy the boarders, and still provide surplus for ready cash. (Paradise Historical Society.)

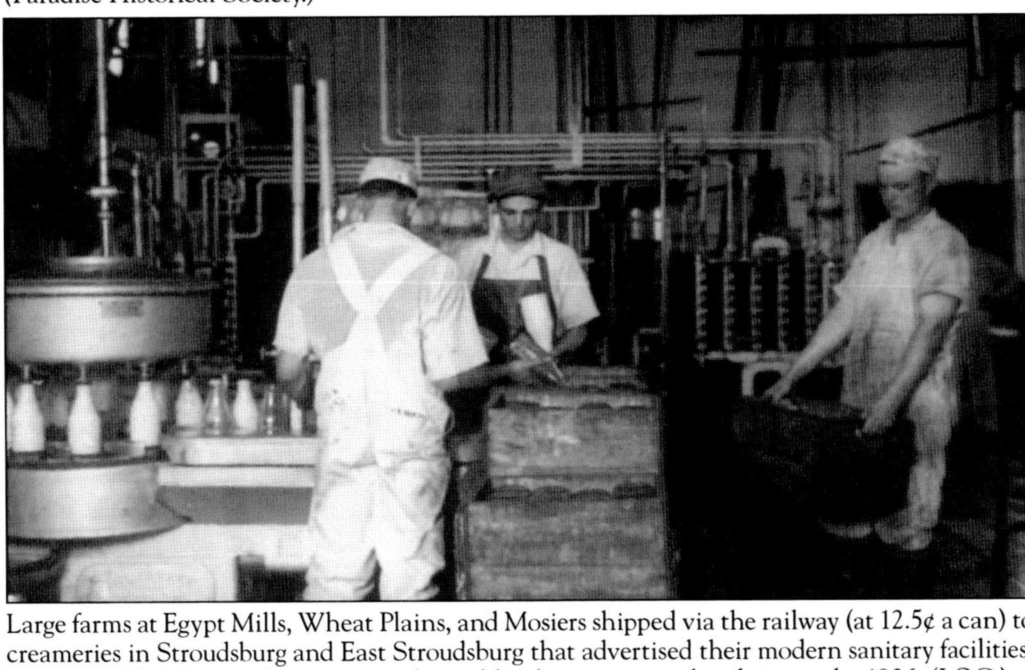

Large farms at Egypt Mills, Wheat Plains, and Mosiers shipped via the railway (at 12.5¢ a can) to creameries in Stroudsburg and East Stroudsburg that advertised their modern sanitary facilities. Automated bottling and capping machines like this one were already in use by 1906. (LOC.)

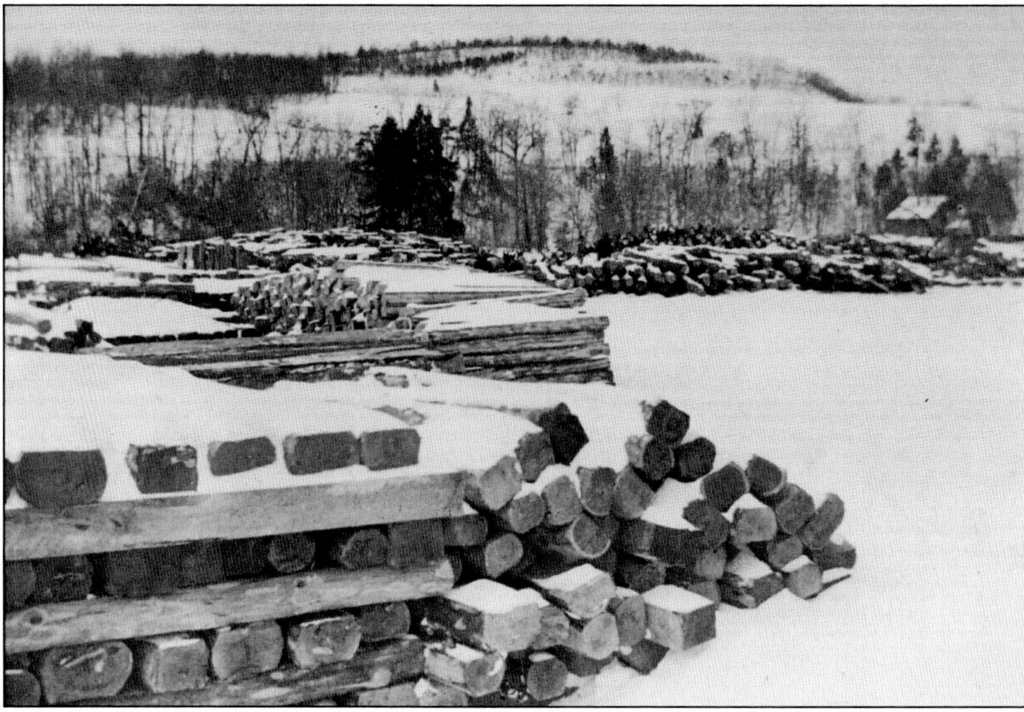

George Nyce's three-acre lumberyard (pictured) had an eight-car siding alongside the station at Bushkill and was one of the railway's biggest customers. There was also a lumberyard with a large siding in the center of the village of Marshalls Creek. (PCHist.)

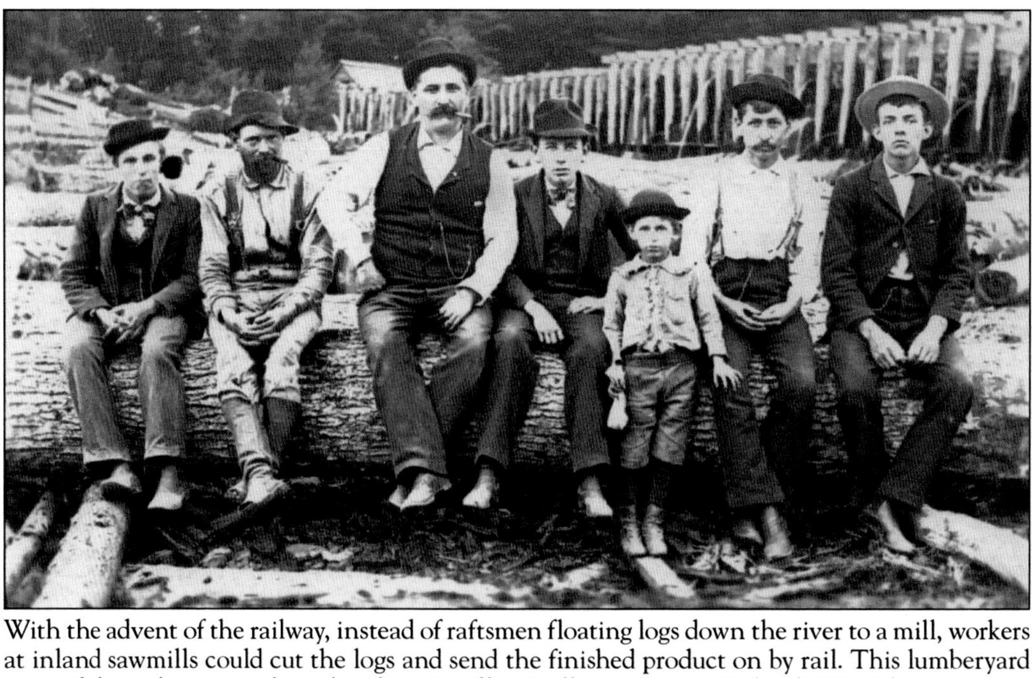

With the advent of the railway, instead of raftsmen floating logs down the river to a mill, workers at inland sawmills could cut the logs and send the finished product on by rail. This lumberyard crew of the railway era takes a break at Stauffer's Mill near Pocono Lake. (MCHA.)

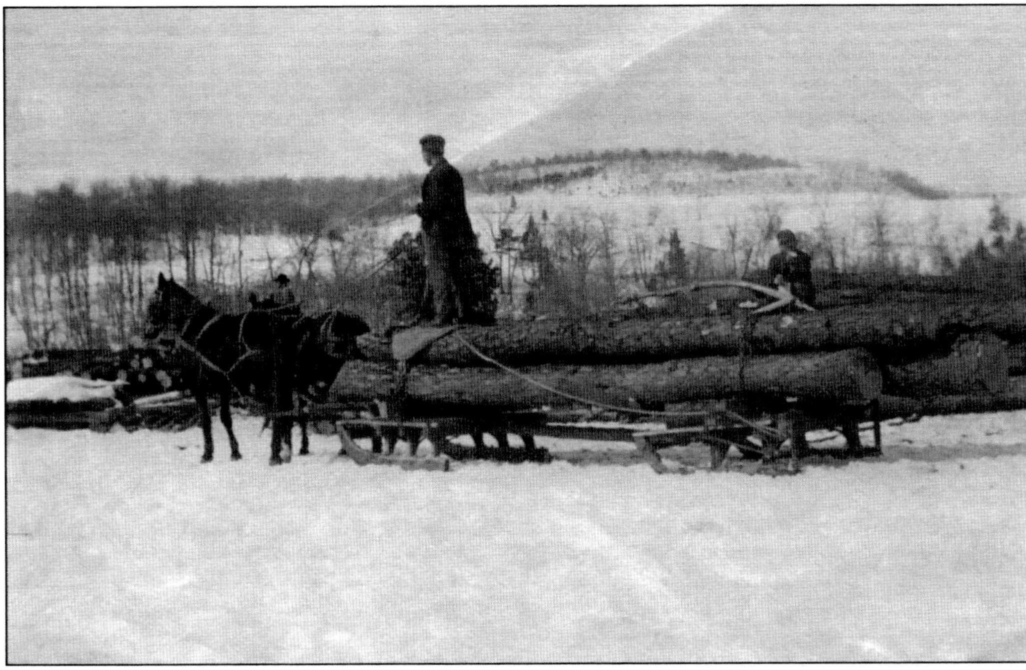

Small-scale logging provided cash for the farmer and his workers and exercise for his teams over the winter months. Sawing tree trunks into poles, mine props, and railroad ties continued year-round until valley forests were eventually depleted. (PCHist.)

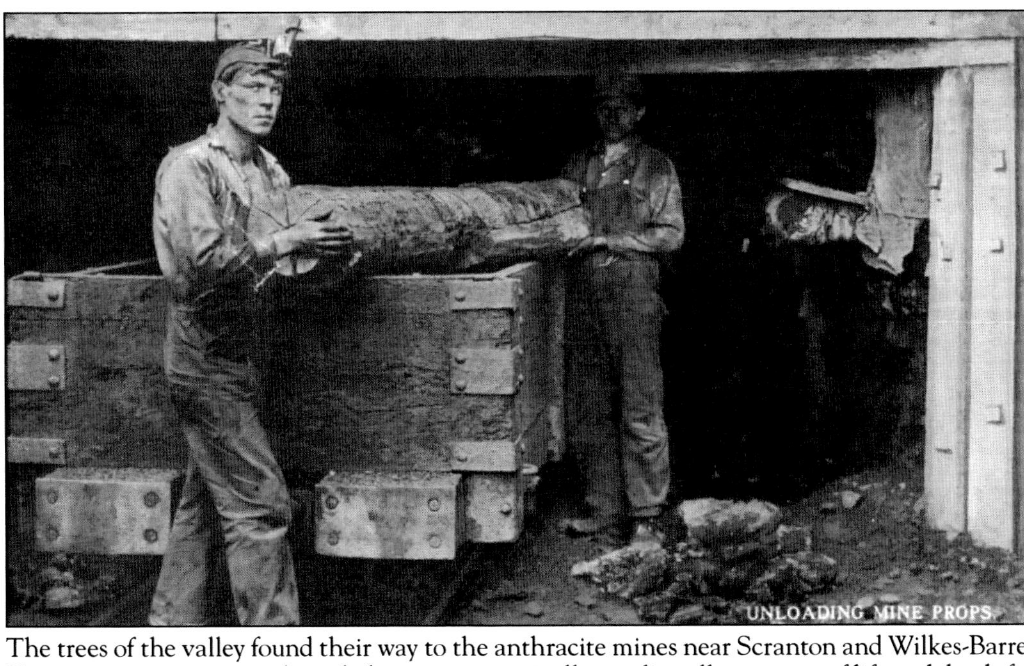

The trees of the valley found their way to the anthracite mines near Scranton and Wilkes-Barre. Having a prop cut correctly and placing it strategically was literally a matter of life and death for the miners. (Authors' collection.)

P. S. C. PA., No. F12
Cancelling P. S. C. PA., No. F10
I. C. C. No. F8

No supplement to this tariff will be issued except for the purpose of cancellation.

DELAWARE VALLEY RAILWAY COMPANY
Freight – Local Class and Commodity Rate Tariff

Class Rates in Cents Per 100 Lbs.

Rate Reference Number	1 Class	2 Class	3 Class	4 Class	5 Class	6 Class
1	14	13	12	11	7	6
2	17	14	12	11	10	6
3	18	14	13	12	10	6
4	19	17	13	12	10	6

Minimum Charge 50 cts.
Consolidated Classification No. 1, I. C. C. No. 45, P. S. C. Pa. O. C. No. 45
"Governed except as otherwise provided herein by the Official Classification (I. C. C. O. C. No. 45, issued and filed by R. N. Collyer, Agent) and supprements thereto."

RATE REFERENCE TABLE

	Mileage	East Stroudsburg	Delaware Valley Junction	Craig's Meadows	Marshall's Creek	Oak Grove	Coolbaugh's	Shoemaker's	Bushkill
East Stroudsburg	.00								
Delaware Valley Junction	.78	1							
Craig's Meadows	4.19	1	1						
Marshall's Creek	4.99	2	2	1					
Oak Grove	5.78	2	2	1	1				
Coolbaugh's	8.05	3	3	1	1	1			
Shoemaker's	10.78	3	3	2	2	2	1		
Bushkill	12.71	4	3	3	3	2	1	1	

The following freight rates will be effective on and after November 1, 1926, to or from East Stroudsburg, Pa., and to or from stations named on line.

	Bushkill	Coolbaugh	Marshall's Creek
* Lagging	$18.00 per car	$18.00 per car	$18.00 per car
* Bark	18.00 " "	18.00 " "	18.00 " "
* 6 in. props	18.00 " "	18.00 " "	18.00 " "
* 8 in. props	18.00 " "	18.00 " "	18.00 " "
* 9 in. props	18.00 " "	18.00 " "	18.00 " "
* 10 in. props	18.00 " "	18.00 " "	18.00 " "
* 12 in. props and up	18.00 " "	18.00 " "	18.00 " "
* Mine Ties	18.00 " "	18.00 " "	18.00 " "
†† Sawed Lumber	$18.00 per car	$18.00 per car	$18.00 per car
†† Switch Ties	$ 6.00 per set	$ 5.70 per set	$ 5.70 per set
†† Cord Wood	$12.00 per car	$12.00 per car	$12.00 per car
†† Pulp Wood	$18.00 " "	$18.00 " "	$18.00 " "
†† Christmas Trees	$24.72 " "	$24.72 " "	$24.72 " "
* Railroad Ties	6 cts. each Per car $18.00	6 cts. each Per car $18.00	6 cts. each Per car $18.00
* Telegraph and Telephone Poles	$19.50 per car If 2 cars used ½ rate additional.	$19.50 per car If 2 cars used ½ rate additional.	$19.50 per car If 2 cars used ½ rate additional.
Coal and Lime	(r) 50 cts. per ton Per car $18.00	(r) 50 cts. per ton Per car $18.00	(r) 50 cts. per ton Per car $18.00
Ice	$12.00 per car	$12.00 per car	$12.00 per car
Cement	(r) $1.00 per ton	(r) $1.00 per ton	(r) $1.00 per ton
Sand, Gravel and Crushed Stone	(r) 50 cts. per ton	(r) 50 cts. per ton	(r) 50 cts. per ton

Petroleum and Petroleum Products, Ind. Oil Switch, East Stroudsburg, per car, (r) $8.00.
Minimum Car 40,000 lbs.
* 49 cts. per ton above minimum weight.
†† 85 cts. per ton above minimum weight.
Switching Charge, $4.90.

(r) Indicates Reduction.
WM. M. SEGUINE, President,
Kenvil, N. J.
October 1, 1926

N. N. GUILLOTT,
Gen. Frt. Agt.
Effective Nov. 1, 1926

This freight tariff, effective November 1926, predates a time of transition for the railway. In 1927, the railway would start bus service to move its people. In 1931, it would use vans and trucks to transport less-than-carload freight. (Authors' collection.)

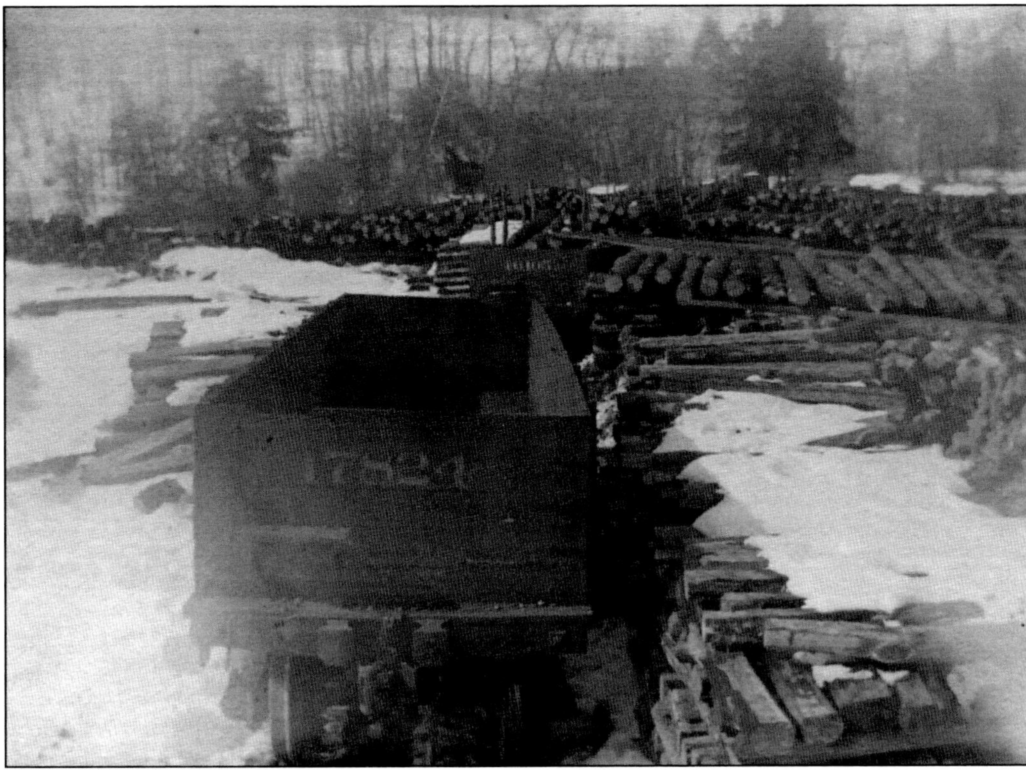

The railway started off with secondhand coaches and boxcars, but in June 1902, it ordered five new freight cars from the Sterlingworth Railway Supply Company in Easton, Pennsylvania. They were probably made all of wood. This secondhand, all-purpose gondola awaits loading at Nyce's lumberyard in Bushkill. (PCHist.)

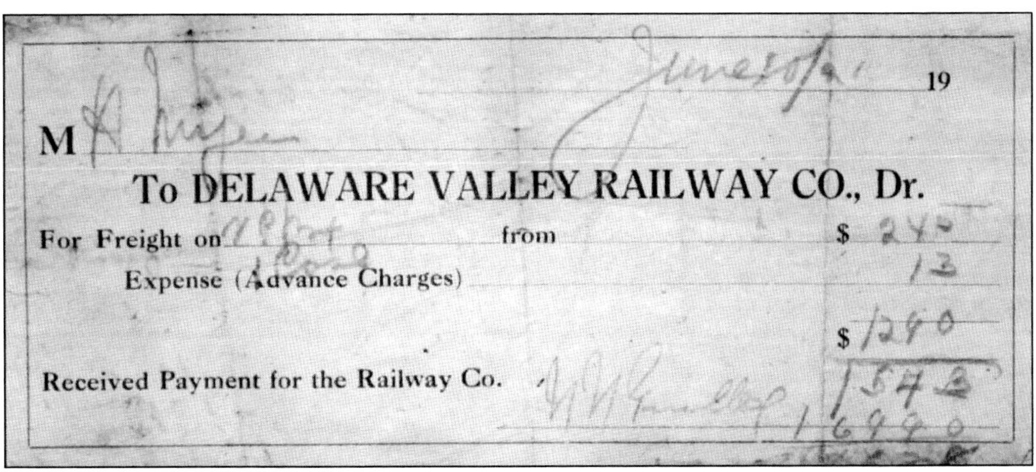

19

M

To DELAWARE VALLEY RAILWAY CO., Dr.

For Freight on from $

Expense (Advance Charges)

$

Received Payment for the Railway Co.

Stationmaster and coalyard manager Norman Guillot signed this June 1921 receipt for a shipment of coal. Judging from the rates in 1926, about four or five tons had come in. Guillot was later superintendent of the railway. (BLTHS.)

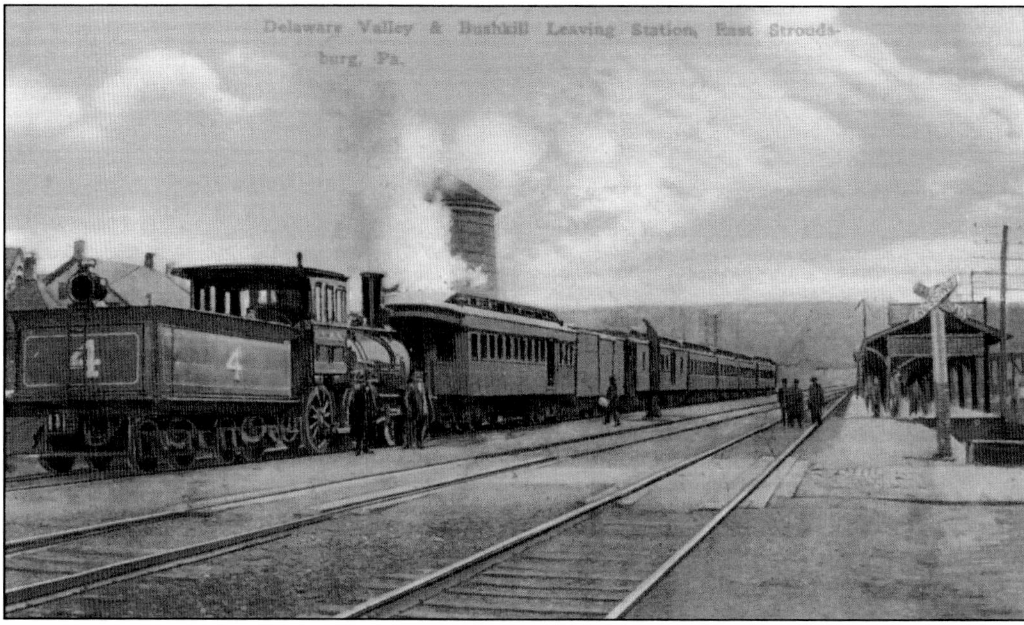

Railway Engine No. 4 awaits departure from the East Stroudsburg station with through-cars for Bushkill added from New York via the DL&W or from Philadelphia via the Pennsylvania Railroad. Built by Cooke in 1884 as No. 1582, the 4-4-0 was acquired by the railway from the Bangor & Portland in 1903 (B&P No. 4) and served until about 1915. (Authors' collection.)

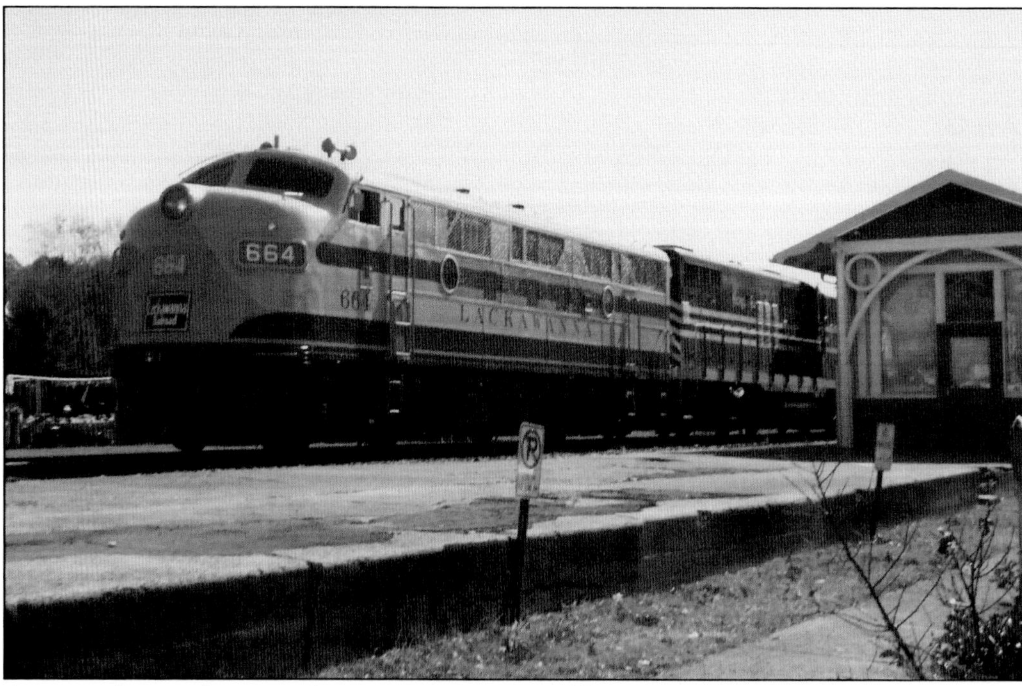

A century later, only one track remains at East Stroudsburg. An early station building still stands at the right; the main hall has been moved to the other side of the track. Diesel Engine No. 664 pulls an excursion train from Scranton back from its destination at the village of Delaware Water Gap. (Authors' collection.)

Three

East Stroudsburg

In 1915, an East Stroudsburg publisher printed *The Bells Ringing the Message of Progress in Monroe County and Tributary Country*. Part advertisement and part "semi-history"—a 140-page early infomercial in print—it claims that Monroe was "where Industry and Recreation meet."

No part of Monroe more exemplified this claim than East Stroudsburg itself, where the Delaware Valley Railway set out up the valley. Clustered around the station were general, drug, and mercantile stores. Heading north, the right-of-way was lined with manufacturers, glass and furniture makers, brewers and bottlers, a tannery, and silk and flour mills. Yet hard alongside these were tourist homes and grand hotels that advertised their restful atmosphere, quiet trout streams, and tables set with produce and dairy products right from the premises.

Due to resistance in Stroudsburg to the noise and mess of a railroad in town, nearly all the rail traffic that might have gone to Stroudsburg had found its way to Dansbury, or "East Stroudsburg," instead. The teachers' college grew on the hill overlooking town, and the high school expanded in 1915, both now serving students from "up valley" who commuted to class by rail. In the railway era, these three square miles were home to 2,600 people, and a significant portion of the labor force had jobs at the glassworks of Milton Yetter, president of the railway from 1904.

This was a landscape on the edge of small-town urbanization. Customers could shop for "New York" wares at the department stores across from the rail station; one could walk down the main street with a fishing rod and creel; visitors equipped with picnic basket, straw hats, and parasols could drive a rented livery by a meadow of sheep. Big-city vacationers rubbed shoulders with factory hands. Dairy cows blockaded the small lanes, while the railway stopped traffic on the larger, but still unpaved, thoroughfares.

The railway leased space in the impressive DL&W Station and, for $1,200 a year, the right to use the DL&W track to Delaware Valley Junction. Under new and local ownership in 1904, railway revenue began to show a modest profit, and the future was bright.

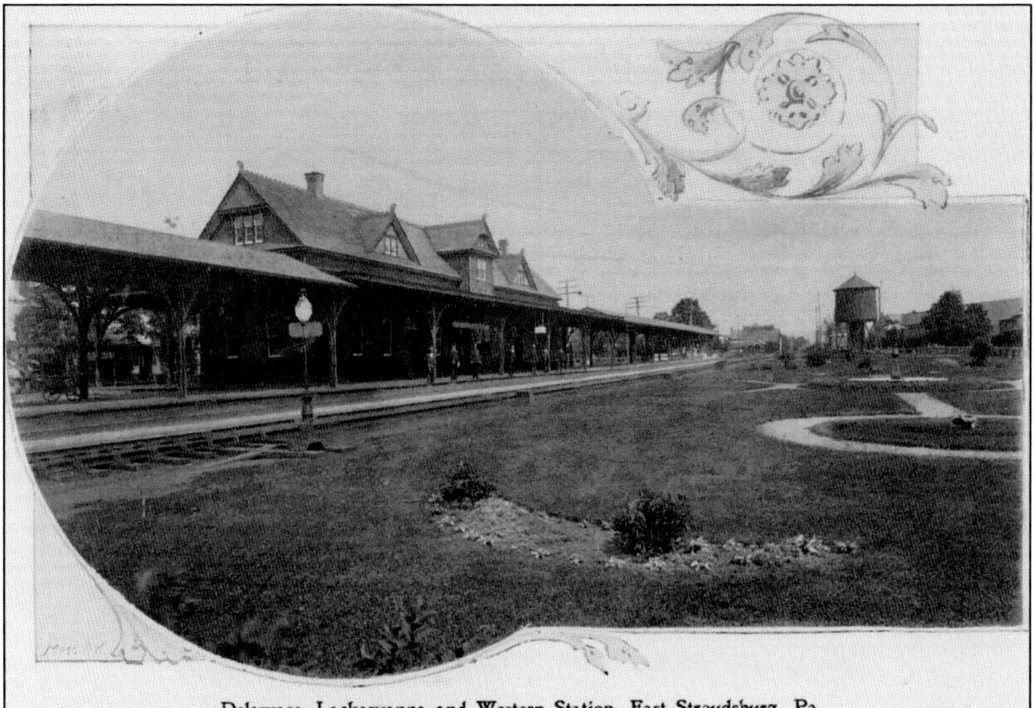

Delaware, Lackawanna and Western Station, East Stroudsburg, Pa.

The DL&W's second East Stroudsburg station was built in 1864. Since the 1850s, freight trains had rumbled through from Scranton laden with anthracite, and by the railway era, passenger connections were bringing in resort customers by the literal carload. This 1897 view shows the old wooden water tower and limited trackage of the time. (EMPL.)

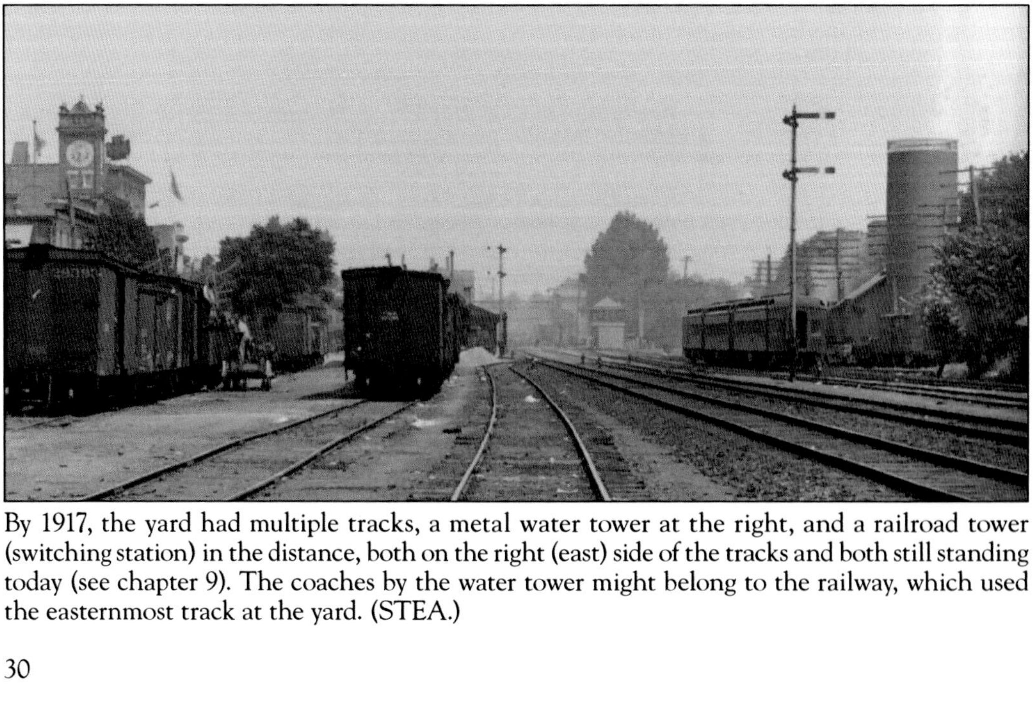

By 1917, the yard had multiple tracks, a metal water tower at the right, and a railroad tower (switching station) in the distance, both on the right (east) side of the tracks and both still standing today (see chapter 9). The coaches by the water tower might belong to the railway, which used the easternmost track at the yard. (STEA.)

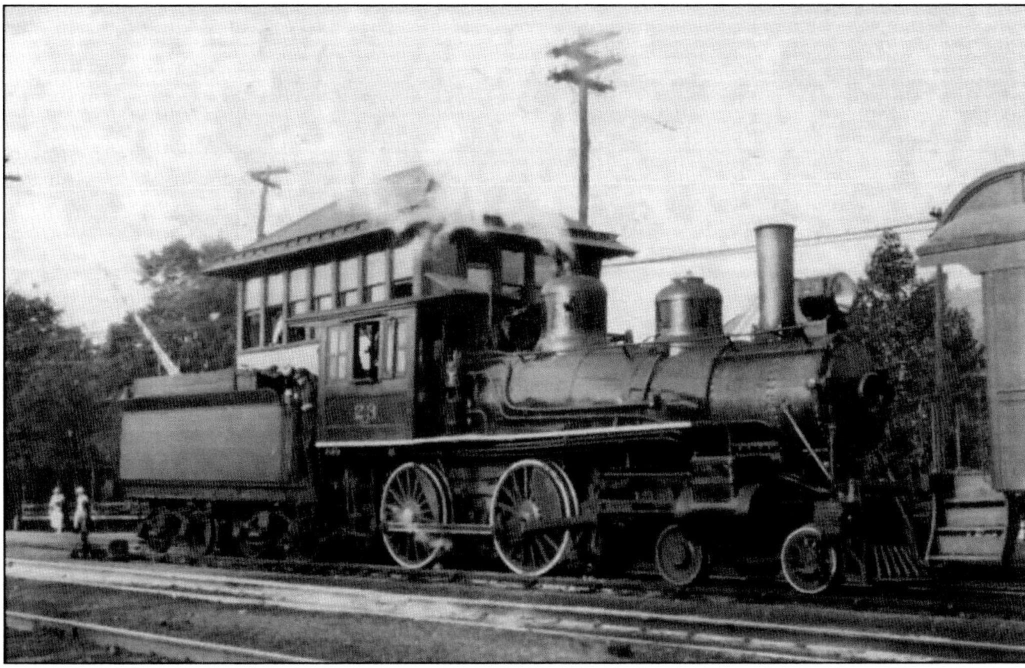

No. 23 is not listed on all the railway's rosters but is remembered by engineers for bringing in the through-cars for Bushkill on summer weekends. Built by Rogers as No. 4982 in 1894, the 4-4-0 was acquired by the railway from the NYS&W around 1923 (NYS&W No. 20) and served until about 1926, when it was probably returned to NYS&W. (MCHA.)

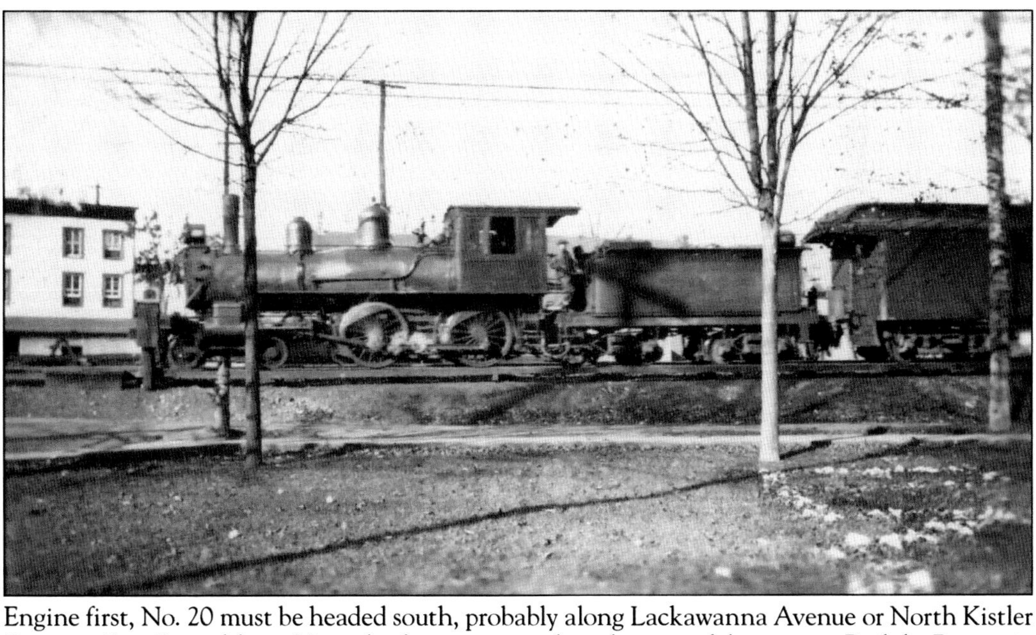

Engine first, No. 20 must be headed south, probably along Lackawanna Avenue or North Kistler Street in East Stroudsburg. Note the fireman at work at the rear of the engine. Built by Rogers in 1892 as No. 4718, the 4-4-0 was acquired from the NYS&W around 1915 (NYS&W No. 20) and served through 1923 or 1926. (MCHA.)

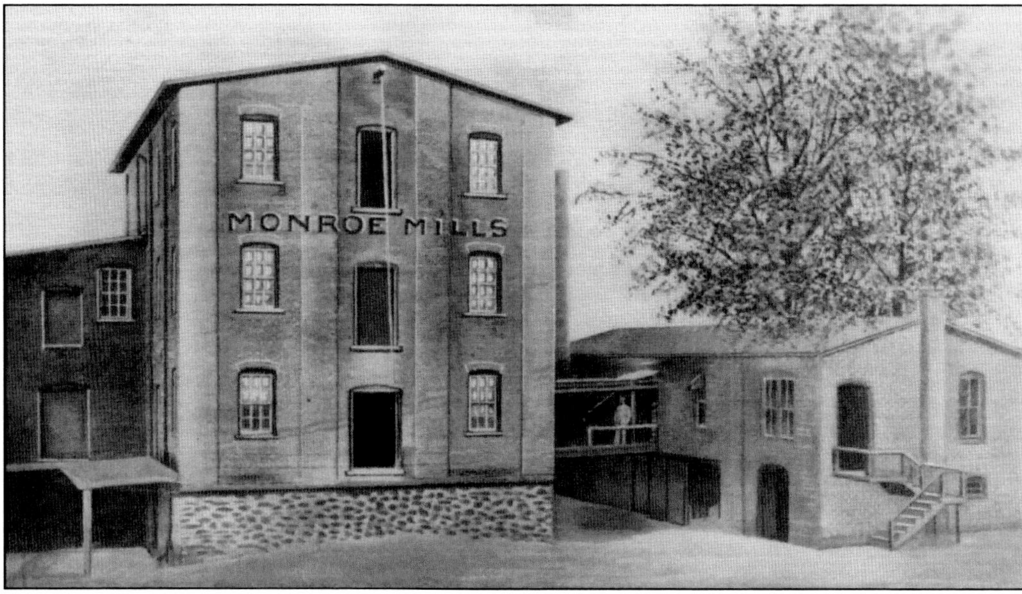

Monroe (Wyckoff) Mills was in the business of grinding feed and grain. It stood at today's Lackawanna Avenue and Kistler Street at the east edge of the DL&W right-of-way until the 1960s. A brick wall there today, covered in concrete (see chapter 9), is probably the foundation of Monroe Mills. (LOC.)

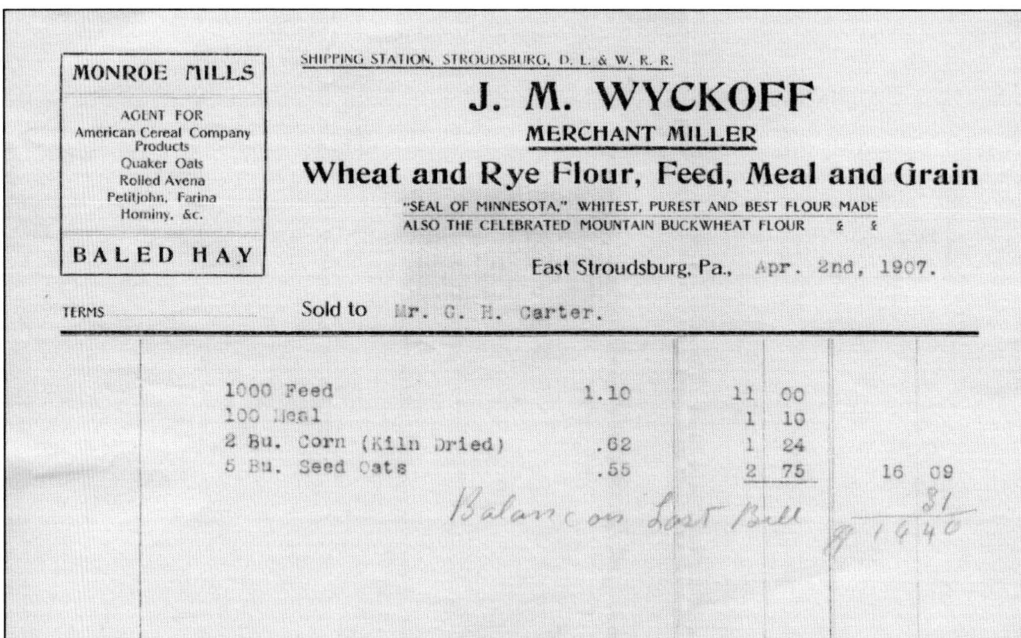

MONROE MILLS

AGENT FOR
American Cereal Company Products
Quaker Oats
Rolled Avena
Petitjohn, Farina
Hominy, &c.

BALED HAY

SHIPPING STATION, STROUDSBURG, D. L. & W. R. R.

J. M. WYCKOFF

MERCHANT MILLER

Wheat and Rye Flour, Feed, Meal and Grain

"SEAL OF MINNESOTA," WHITEST, PUREST AND BEST FLOUR MADE
ALSO THE CELEBRATED MOUNTAIN BUCKWHEAT FLOUR

East Stroudsburg, Pa., Apr. 2nd, 1907.

TERMS

Sold to Mr. C. H. Carter.

1000 Feed	1.10	11 00	
100 Meal		1 10	
2 Bu. Corn (Kiln Dried)	.62	1 24	
5 Bu. Seed Oats	.55	2 75	16 09
Balance on Last Bill			81
			16 90

Sitting along the easternmost track used by the railway, the mill took in grain southbound from valley farms and sent the flour and feed north back up railway's route. The DL&W right-of-way touched on mill land; an agreement was drawn up for the encroachment. (Authors' collection.)

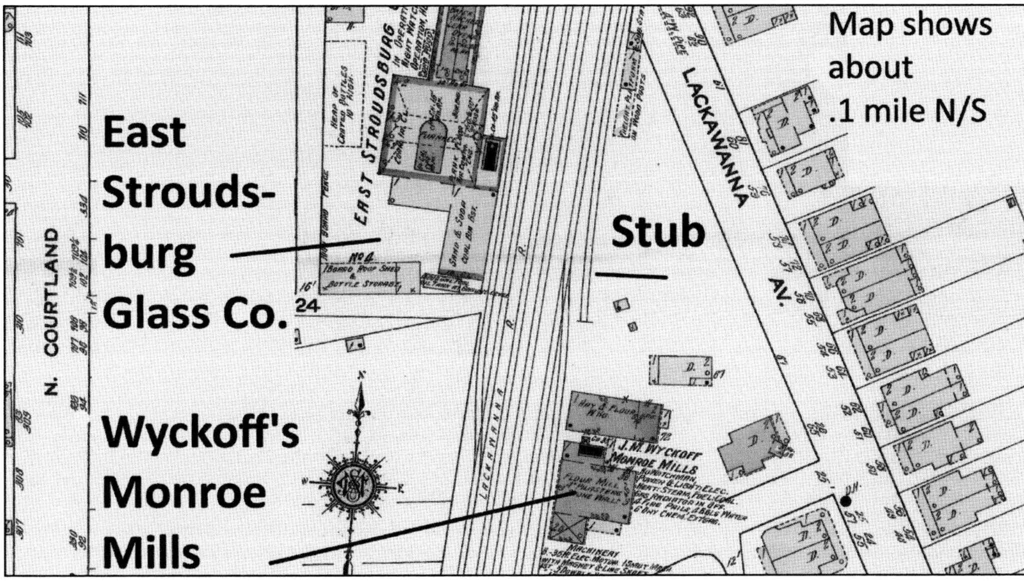

In this 1912 Sanborn Insurance map, north of Monroe Mills is the stub that the railway may have used for its layovers. Across the right-of-way, Milton Yetter's East Stroudsburg Glass Company was a major employer in the borough, manufacturing bottles and wicker-wrapped demijohns. (PSU.)

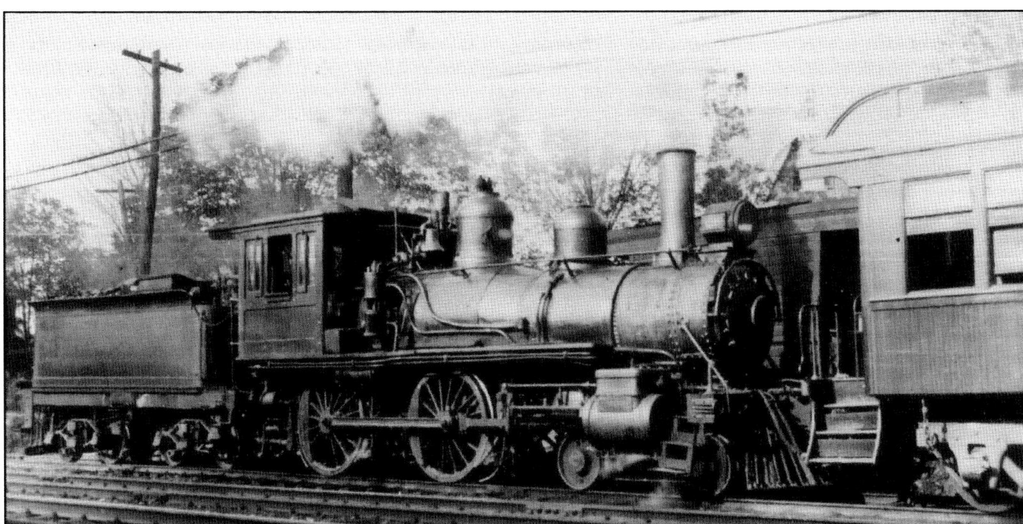
The railway's second locomotive, Engine No. 20, waits in East Stroudsburg, perhaps on the layover stub north of Monroe Mills. Houses lined Lackawanna Avenue, and soot from the idling engine was the dismay of local women hanging out the wash. (MCHA.)

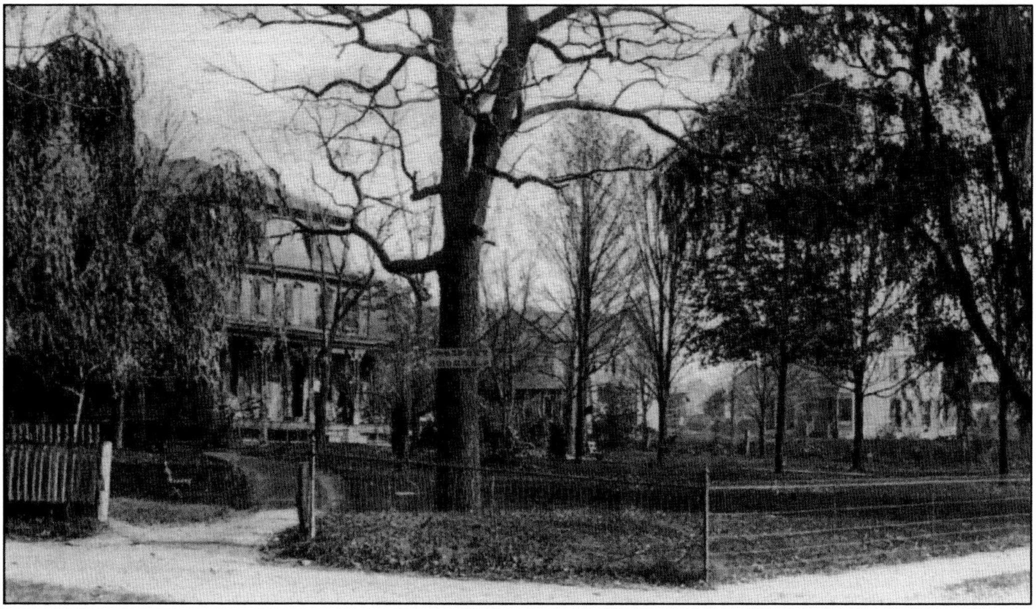

Its ads mentioned light, air, high ground, and shady lawns, but not the rumble of passing locomotives. Enlarged from its 1880s beginnings, Prospect House held 80 guests and stood in its gardens along the right-of-way at Broad and Dearr Streets. The tracks run in front of the small slope in the background. (Authors' collection.)

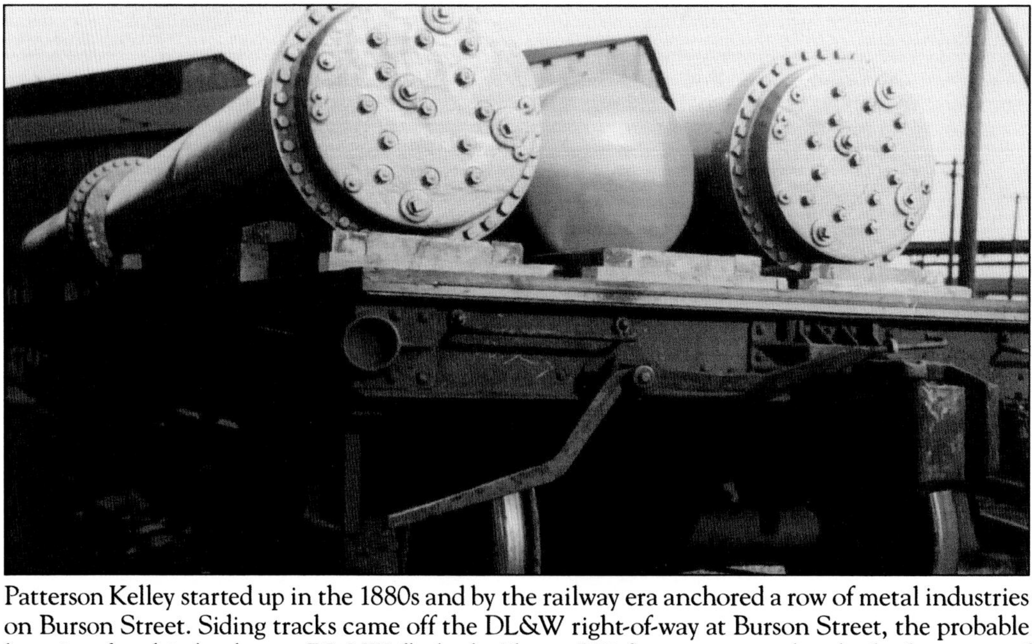

Patterson Kelley started up in the 1880s and by the railway era anchored a row of metal industries on Burson Street. Siding tracks came off the DL&W right-of-way at Burson Street, the probable location for this load on a DL&W flatbed. About 500 feet west was the shady driveway of Maplehurst. (MCHA.)

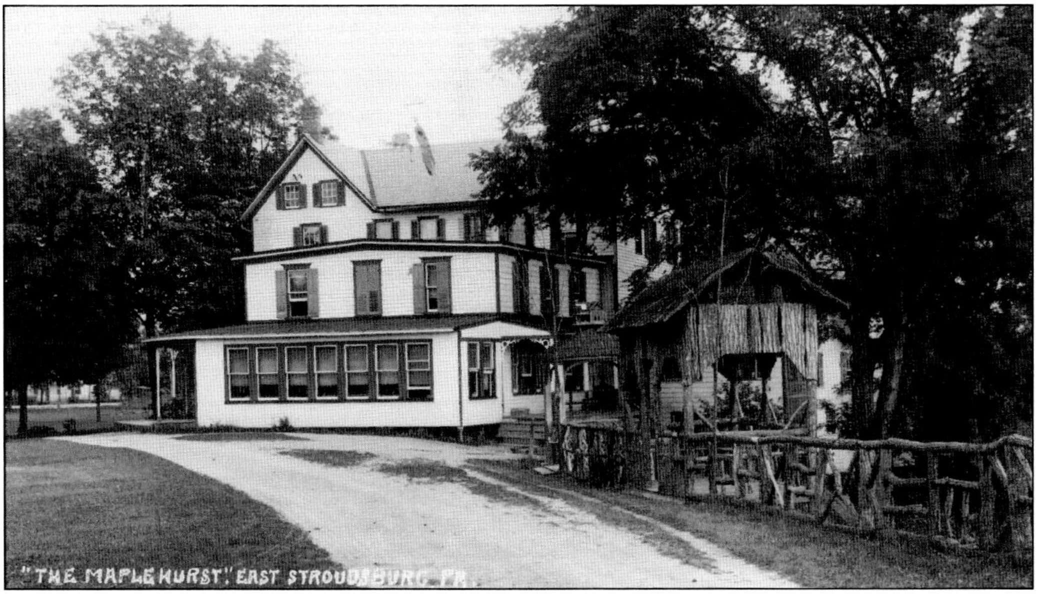

Maplehurst, on Milford Road, was just west of the Burson Street sidings and provided the amenities of a large resort with an in-town location. Accommodating 125, it had its own farm for fresh produce and over the years offered a ball field, putting range, dance barn, and "sanitary concrete swimming pool." (MCHA.)

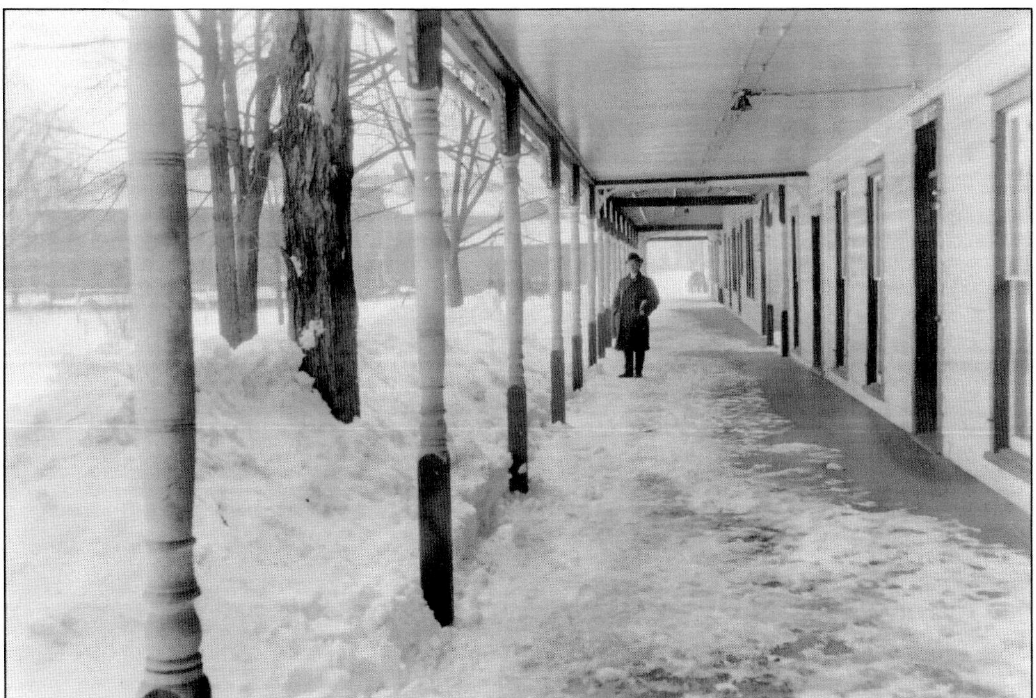

Maplehurst was among the few hotels to brave the winter weather and the slow season for guests. In the background is East Stroudsburg High School, then in the Bunnell Building, to which students from the upper end of the county commuted. In the 1960s, the high school expanded onto most of Maplehurst grounds. (MCHA.)

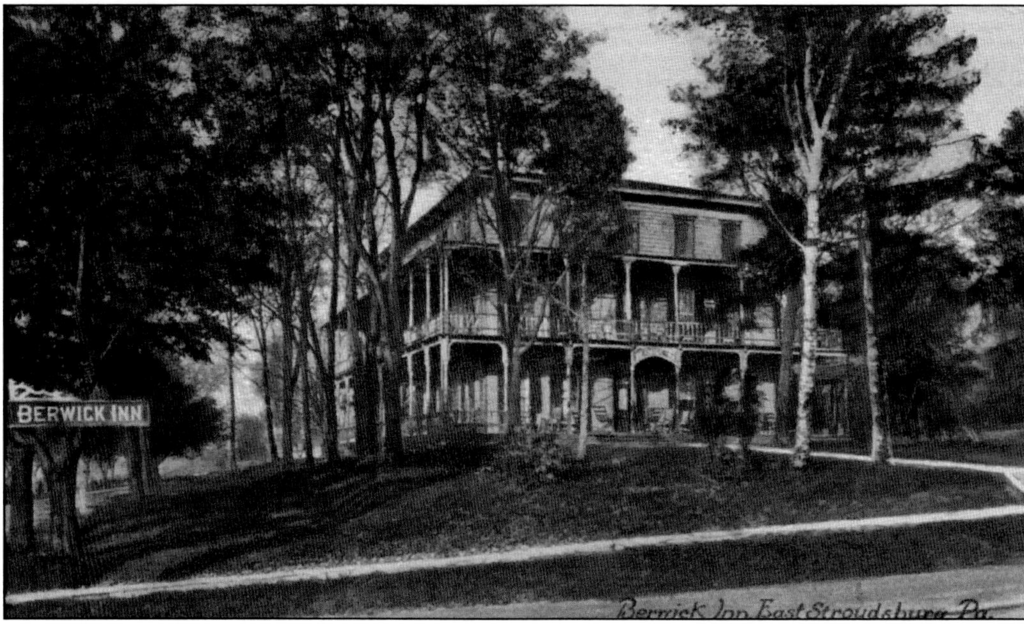

Berwick Inn stood on the height between Milford Crossing and Brodhead Creek, with its own farm for fresh produce and two trout streams for those who wished to catch their own dinner. One might buy some flowers from a vendor at Delaware Valley Junction for a special fellow guest before trudging up the hill. (Authors' collection.)

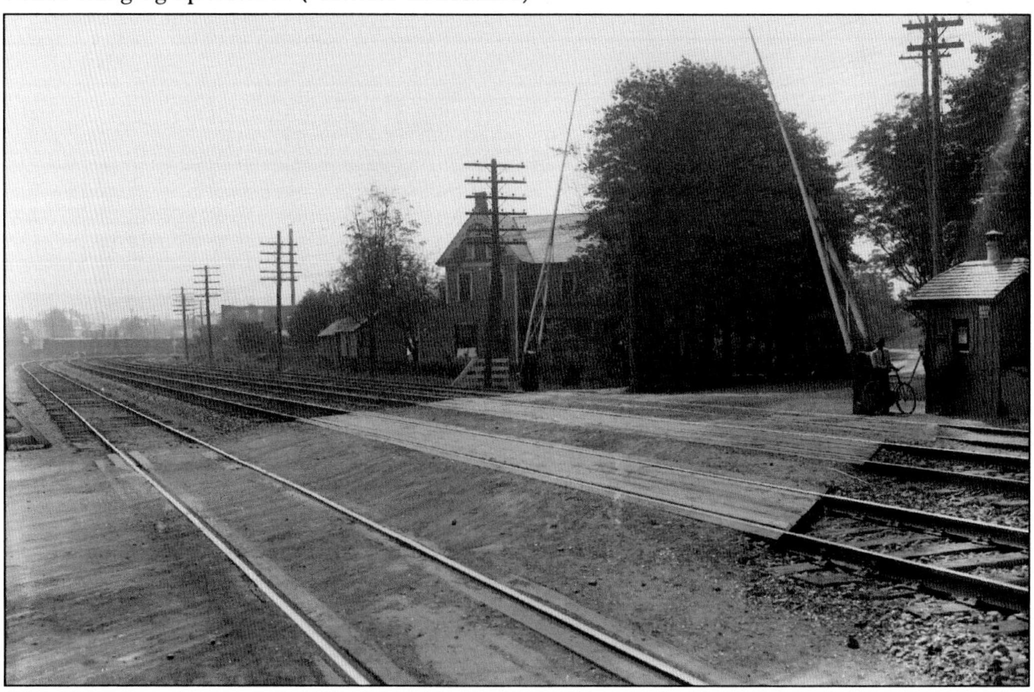

The DL&W tracks crossed Milford Road (today's North Courtland Street, Business Route 209) at Milford Crossing. Seen from about the signal bridge at Delaware Valley Junction, the road in the foreground is Milford Road. Just beyond the open gates is a northbound trolley in the shade of the trees. Today, Cramer's hardware store stands on this corner. The view looks southeast. (STEA.)

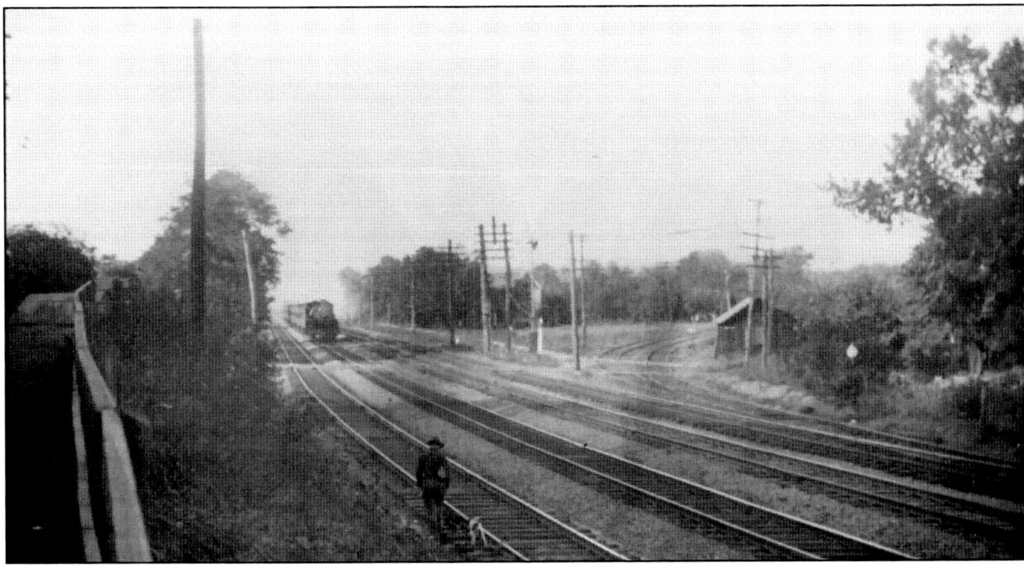

In this view looking northwest, the DL&W's multiple tracks run northwest (left) toward the rail yard at Gravel Place. The railway, though, swings hard north (right) off the DL&W's east track, stopping immediately at the Delaware Valley Junction station, the small wooden structure at the right. King Street is at the far left. (PHMC/RRMPa.)

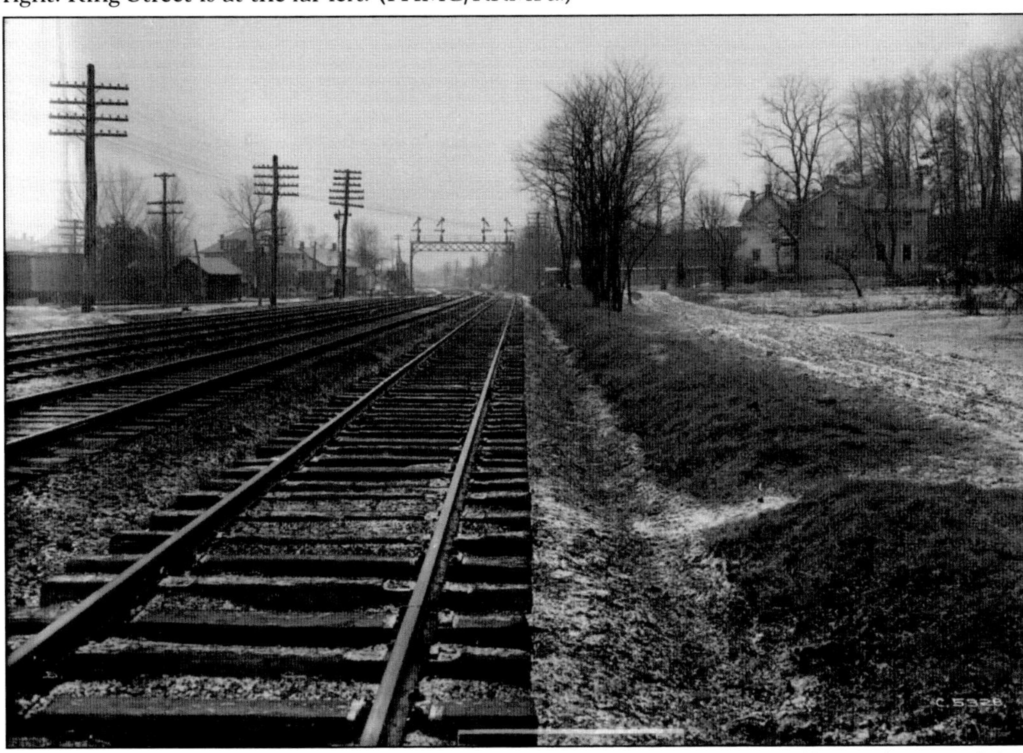

In this view looking southeast on the DL&W main line, the Delaware Valley Railway track has just cut off to the north (left) at the signal bridge. The one-story structure between the poles at the left is the Delaware Valley Junction station, and there appears to be a boxcar on a second track at the far left. King Street runs alongside on the right. (STEA.)

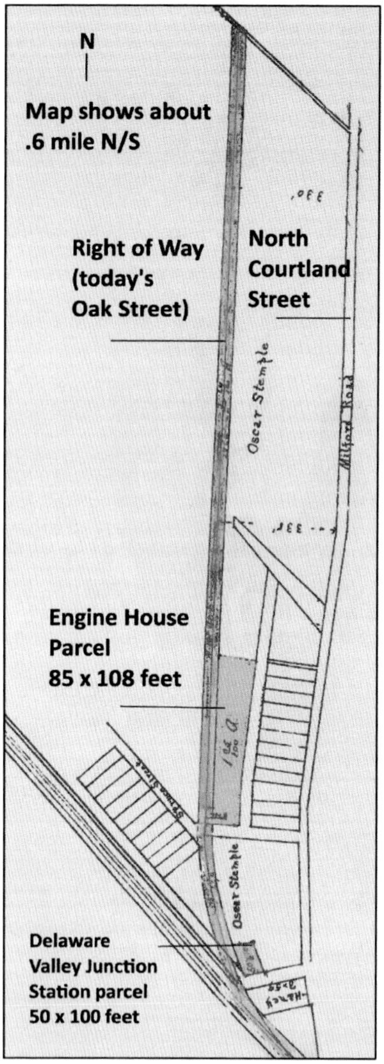

The railway's enginehouse still stands along today's Oak Street (see chapter 9). At 62 by 23 feet, with a south door 16 feet high by 12 feet wide, the one-stall house could fit the railway's "American" engines. It was perhaps too low to accommodate the railway's camelback engine (with the cab astride the boiler), as the roof was later raised about three feet. (MCRD.)

Shown here before its railway days, Engine No. 902 was the railway's only camelback, or "Mother Hubbard." Built by Dickson as No. 328 in 1882, the 4-4-0 was acquired by the railway from the DL&W in 1926 (DL&W No. 902). Serving until 1928, it apparently lay idle at Bushkill until 1933 and was then scrapped. The manufacture of new camelbacks was banned in 1927, as they were judged unsafe. (MCHA.)

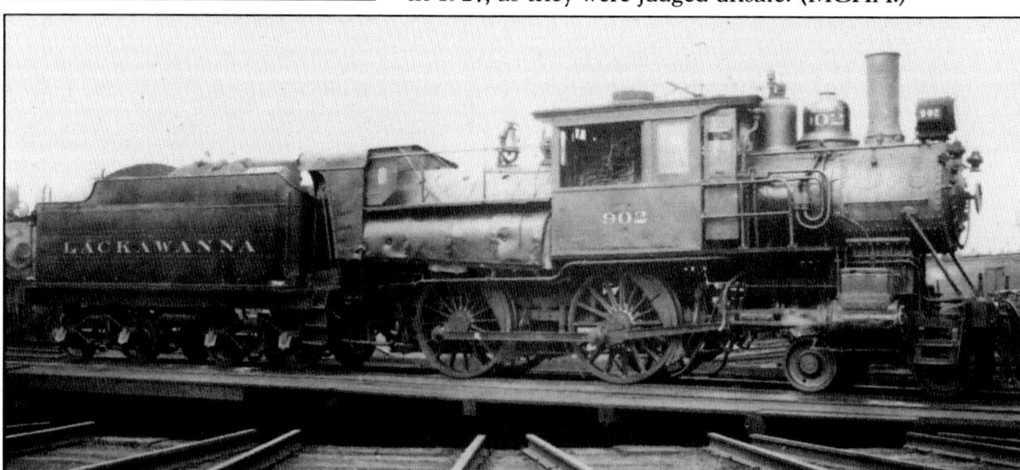

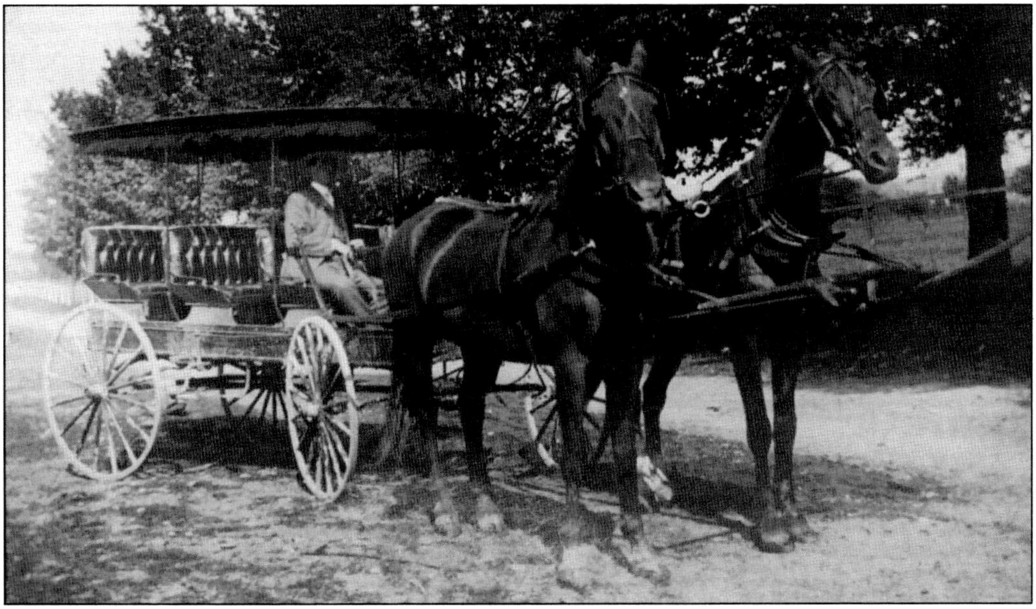

Inns would meet their guests at the station with horse and carriage. In rural areas, this could be a fairly rustic affair, but in-town travelers could hope for a stylish ride with a livery like this from Old Homestead Cottage. In Bushkill, auto-taxis for Dingmans Ferry and Milford, another Milton Yetter enterprise, would meet the railway train. (MCHA.)

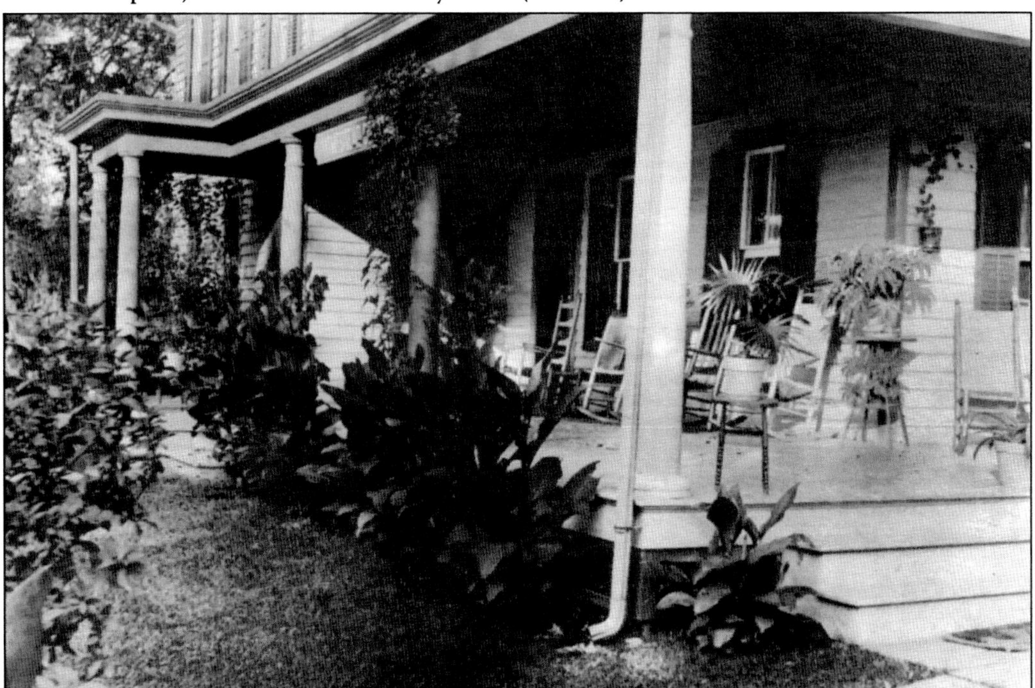

Billed by DL&W as "pretty and homelike," Old Homestead Cottage stood on Brodhead Creek in East Stroudsburg. Besides the snappy livery, amenities included croquet and a piano. In 1909, the Lackawanna Passenger Department listed 16 inns accommodating from 8 to 40 guests in Stroudsburg and East Stroudsburg. (Authors' collection.)

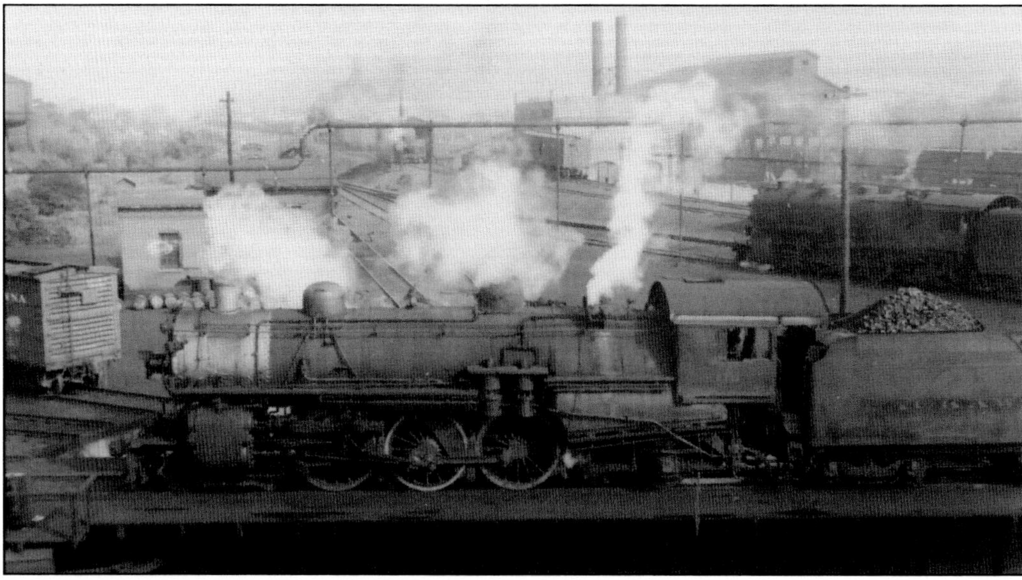

For major repairs, the railway relied on the DL&W at its large Gravel Place facility, two miles north of Delaware Valley Junction along the DL&W main line. This 1928 view is from the top of the roundhouse. Only some of Gravel Place remains today. (MCHA.)

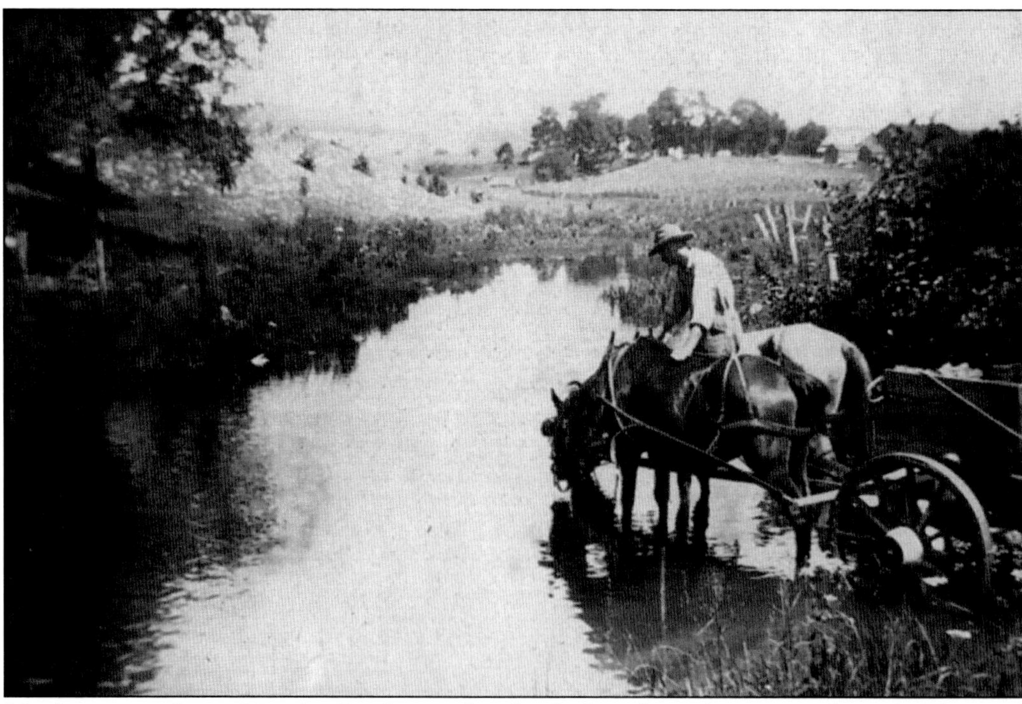

The boggy meadows of Sambo Creek were farmland when the railway came through. The creek originates in the woods of Brushy Mountain and empties into Brodhead Creek in the flats that were behind Berwick and Maplehurst Inns. Since 1914, the creek has been slaking the thirst of two-footed residents of East Stroudsburg as well. (MCHA.)

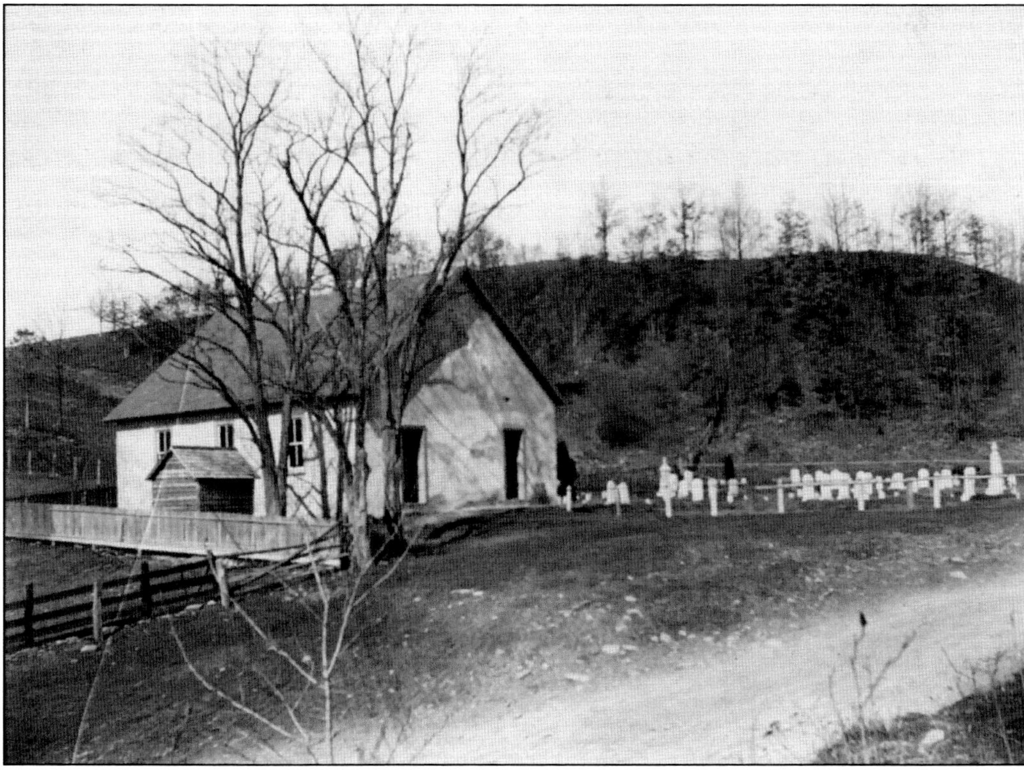

For 1903, the railway listed a stop at Eagle Valley, where the road to Spragueville (Analomink) branched northwest off Milford Road. From the side of that road (now Paradise Trail or Route 447), the 1840s Beakleyville Baptist Church overlooked farm fields and the meanders of Sambo Creek. (MCHA.)

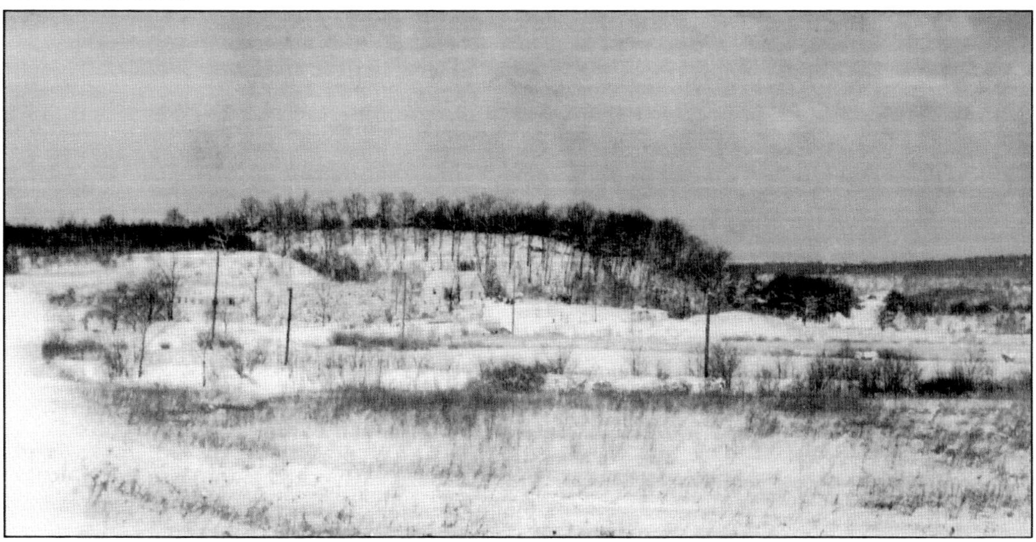

The railway crossed the road to Spragueville below the Beakleyville Church (center). This was the scene of the railway's only fatal collision, when in March 1918, Amzi Strunk drove his wagon across the track and was struck by the morning run. Strunk and one horse died; the other horse ran off. A portion of this scene is on page 94. (MCHA.)

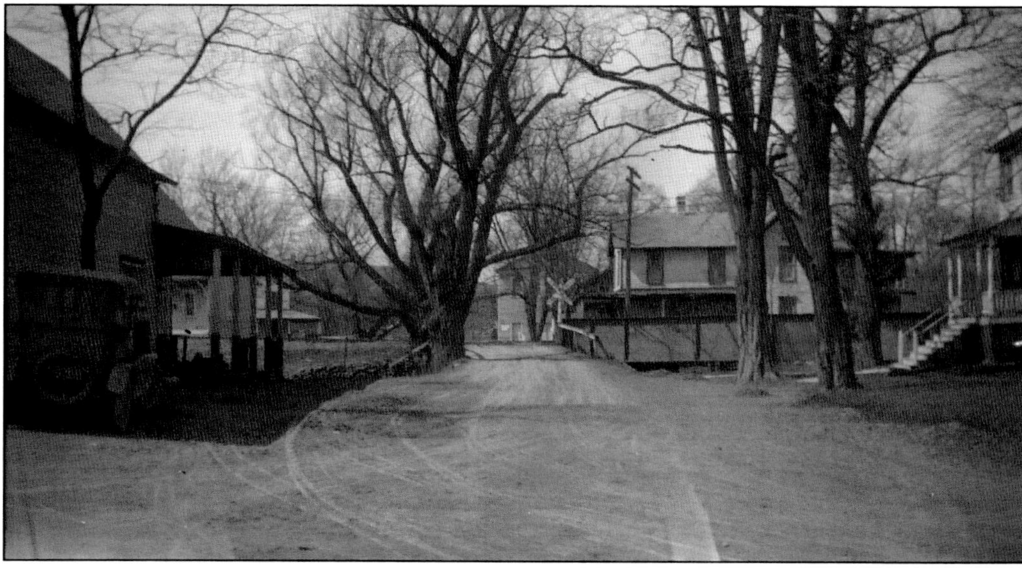

The Marshalls Creek station can be glimpsed through the porch of the Huffman store building (left) around 1922. The mill (later the firehouse) is at the split in the road in the distance, past the cross-buck sign at the track and through-bridge. Marshalls Creek Road turns left at the mill, and the road to Resica Falls is a right turn. (PHMC/RRMPa.)

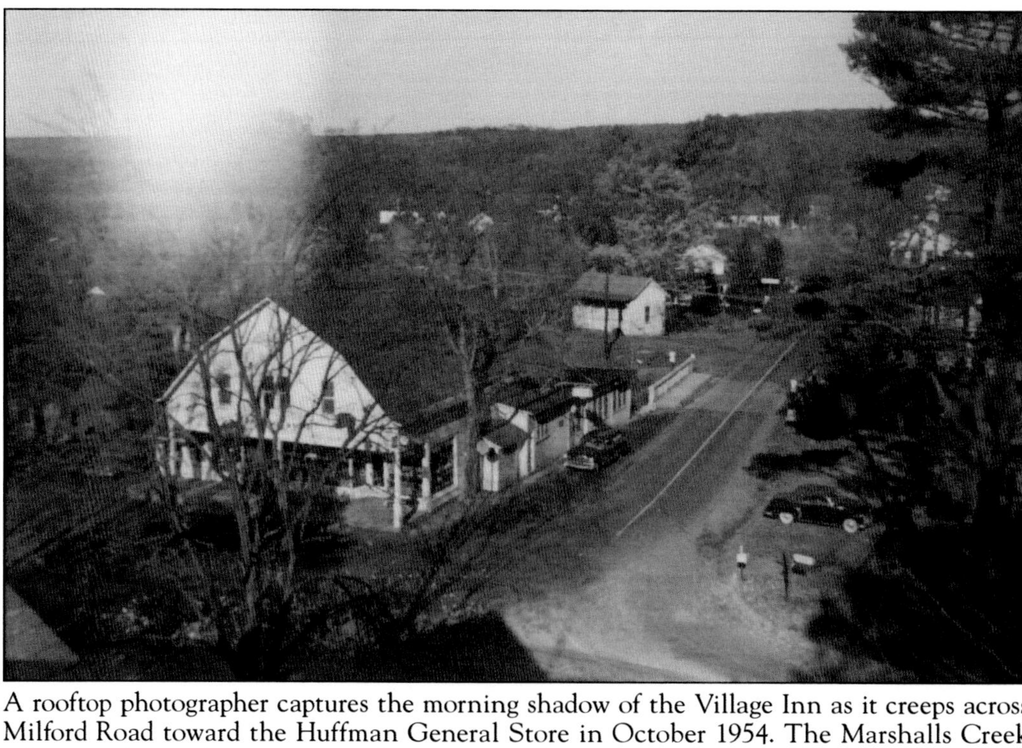

A rooftop photographer captures the morning shadow of the Village Inn as it creeps across Milford Road toward the Huffman General Store in October 1954. The Marshalls Creek railway station, without passengers for a generation, sits behind the store, on the left of the road. (Bob Huffman.)

Four

Stroud and Smithfield Townships, Oak Grove

As the borough of East Stroudsburg expanded, it incorporated rural township land. Otherwise, the borders of Stroud, Smithfield, and Middle Smithfield Townships today are much as they were then. Smithfield especially enjoyed a reputation for beauty based on its streams and scenic drives. The railway needed bridges over Marshalls and Pond Creeks in the heart of the village of Marshalls Creek. Brodhead Creek was just to the west of the right-of-way.

The area had its share of less hospitable land as well. Leaving Eagle Valley, the railway scaled a rocky ridge in Stroud Township (today's Eagle Ridge) on an embankment. The grant by D. Porter Angle stipulated that a "cattle pass" be built under the railroad to give access to his field. Charles Kaul's grant of a right-of-way required the railway to build a 600-foot ditch through the bog meadow to his home in the area that became Lake Valhalla. The railway traveler had a good seat to take in this varied terrain.

Revolutionary War general Thomas Craig (1739–1832) never settled in his meadows, but in 1835, Dr. Philip Bush settled in Smithfield at Craigs Corners. He and his wife had seven children, and not surprisingly, by the late 1880s, the area was also known as Bushville. The names of Bush, Kaul, Posten, and Brutzman, all grantors of right-of-way, date from 1800 to 1835 in this area.

The village of Marshalls Creek, the first real community center out of East Stroudsburg, had both scenery and prosperity: waterfalls a short drive from the station, two mills in town, the Huffman General Store, a lumberyard, ice harvesting in winter, and hotels and a lake within walking distance of the railway station.

At the north end of Lake Marshall and just over the border into Middle Smithfield, Oak Grove House boasted a railway stop on its grounds, virtually at its door. The railway crossed back to the southeast side of Milford Road just after Oak Grove. Ramblers here along today's Mount Nebo Road enjoyed sunsets over Big Pocono to the west or views to the water gap to the east. Today, Mount Nebo's Rainbow Mountain Resort, with its beautiful view westward, remains to give a flavor of the scenery once enjoyed at the hotels clustered around Lake Marshall.

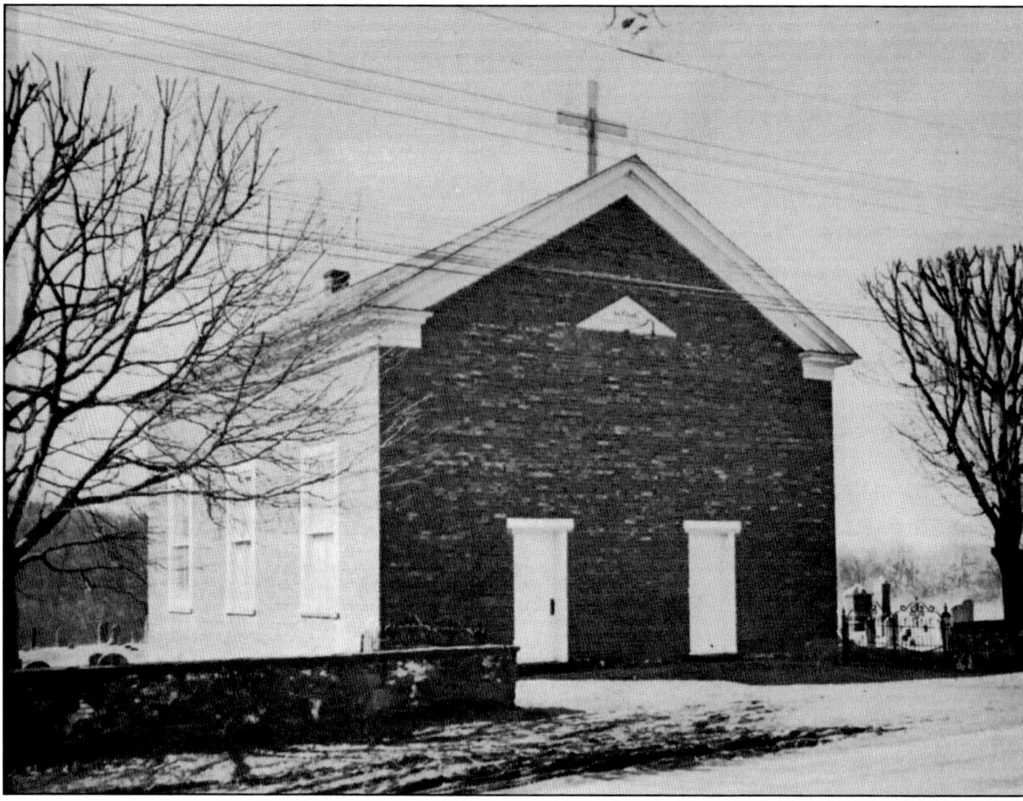

St. Paul's Lutheran Church of Smithfield built this church on Craigs Meadow Road in 1854, and it remains a landmark for travelers even today. The railway ran in the distance on the right, at the far end of the graveyard. The stop, probably no more than a gravel platform, may have been at the end of the graveyard's 1870 stone wall. (EMPL.)

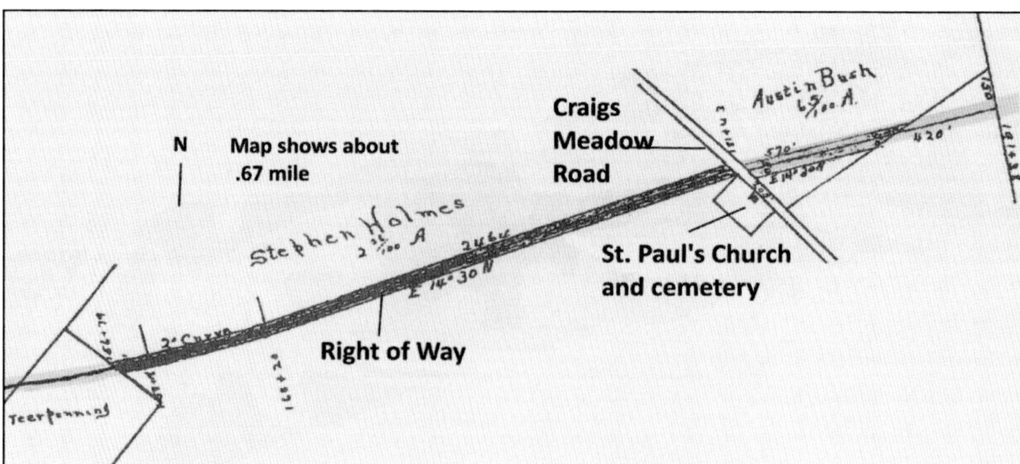

This 1901 deed maps shows the right-of-way through today's Birch Acres community and just nicking the corner of St. Paul's graveyard (see chapter 8). The train then crossed onto land that became a golf course of Mountain Manor, a 400-acre resort operating from 1932 to 2005. The golf course continued to 2011 and is still intact today. (MCRD.)

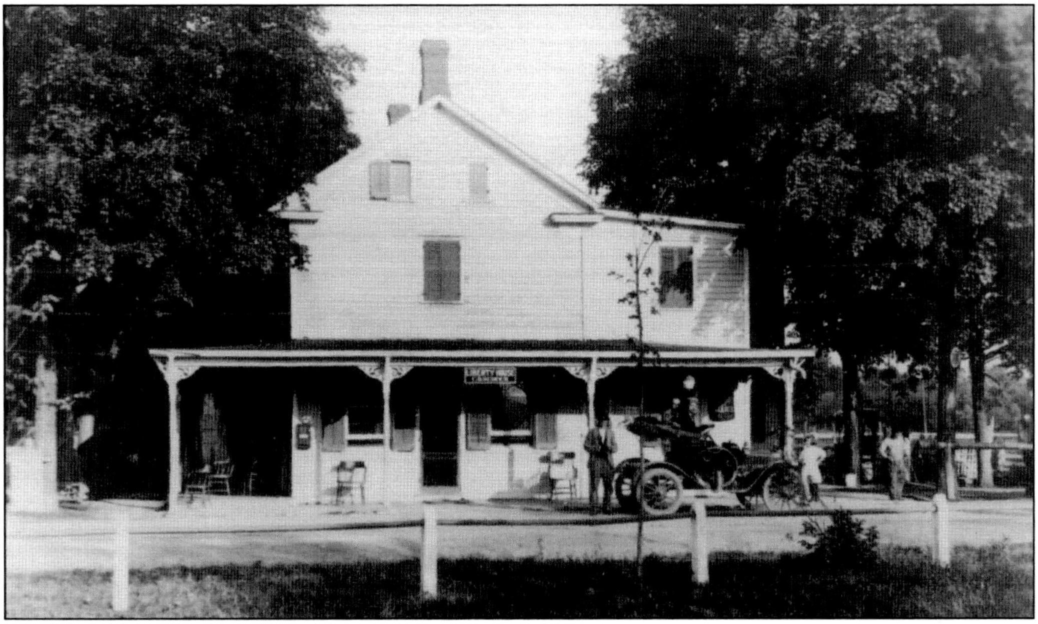

Liberty House (the former Simeon Bush home) stood south of the intersection of today's Franklin Hill and Milford Roads and advertised gas "on tap." A dozen homes, two churches, and a one-room school dotted Craigs Corners here, a quarter mile south of the railway stop. (Authors' collection.)

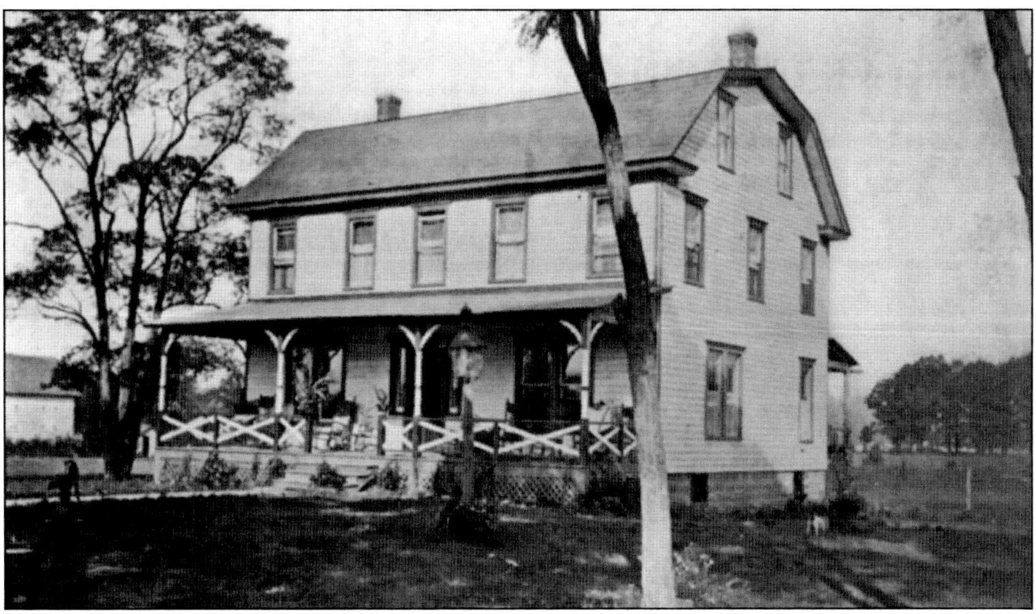

Bonny Mead House, at the Craigs Meadows stop, accommodated 40 on Milford Road, "the best bicycle route in the state." It described itself as "farm of 120 acres at the head of the Sambo Valley." By the summer of 1909, another Bonny Mead, the New Bonny Mead (pictured), was opening to full bookings. (Authors' collection.)

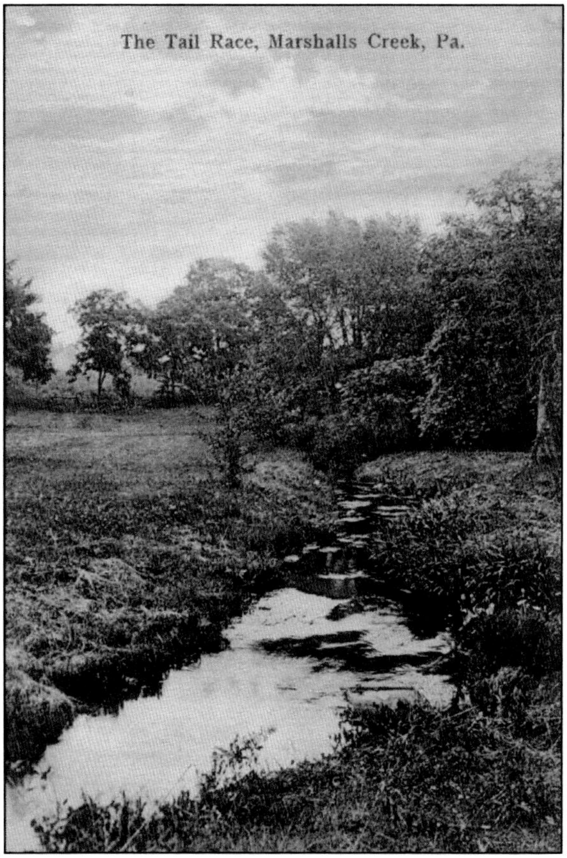

Just before entering the village of Marshalls Creek, the railway passed over a mill's tailrace, shown here in 1911. The railway stopped in the center of the village of Marshalls Creek, which included a flour mill, a feed mill, a lumberyard, a general store, and a hotel. The train then crossed Pond Creek on a through plate-girder bridge. (MCHA.)

The right-of-way deed map of 1901 shows the site of the future station, marked "B. shop." The store (now the 1836 Saloon), a few houses, and the railway station remain from that era (see chapter 9). One mill has become the firehouse. (MCRD.)

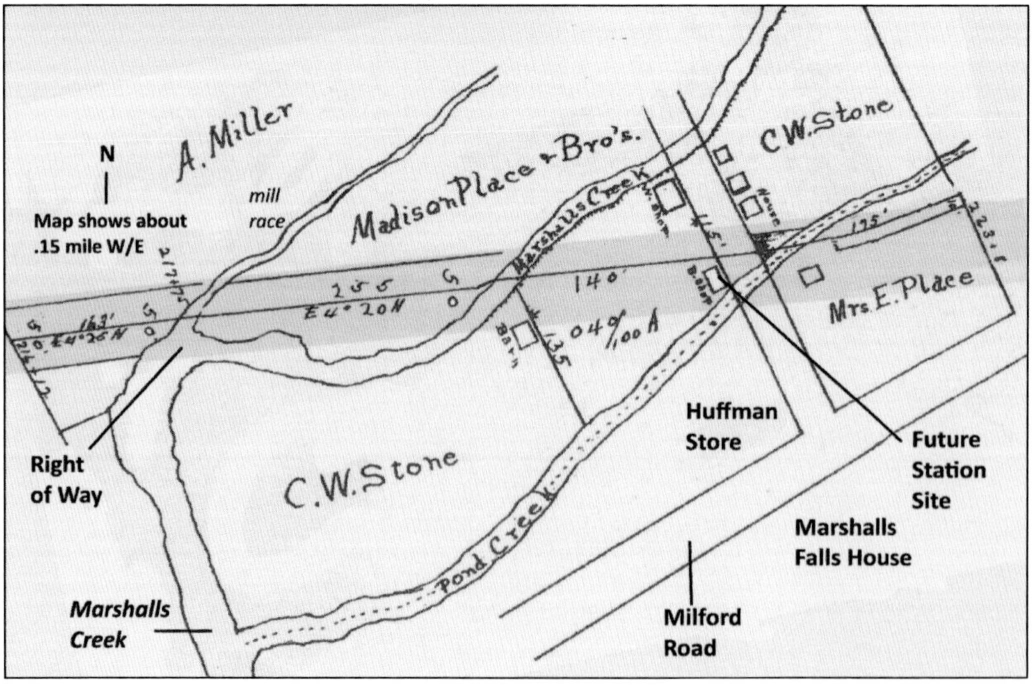

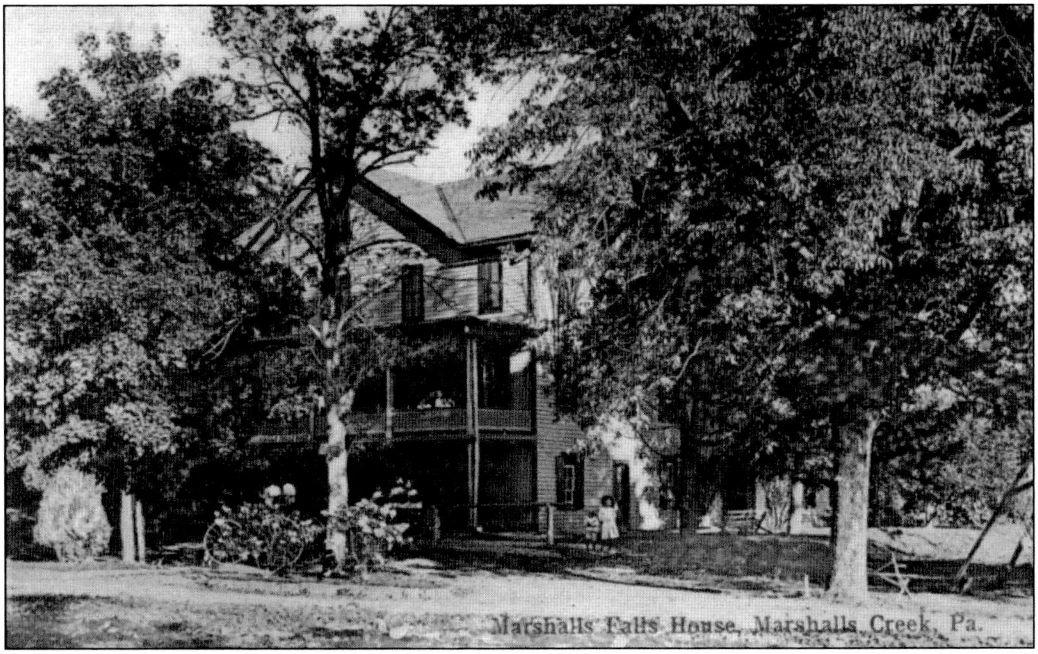

The 1870s Marshalls Falls House, seen here in 1910, stood at the crossroads of Marshalls Creek for a century. The house expanded to accommodate 100 guests and had bungalows at the lake, all run by the Huffman family. Marshalls Falls House later became the Village Inn and was removed in the 1970s. (Authors' collection.)

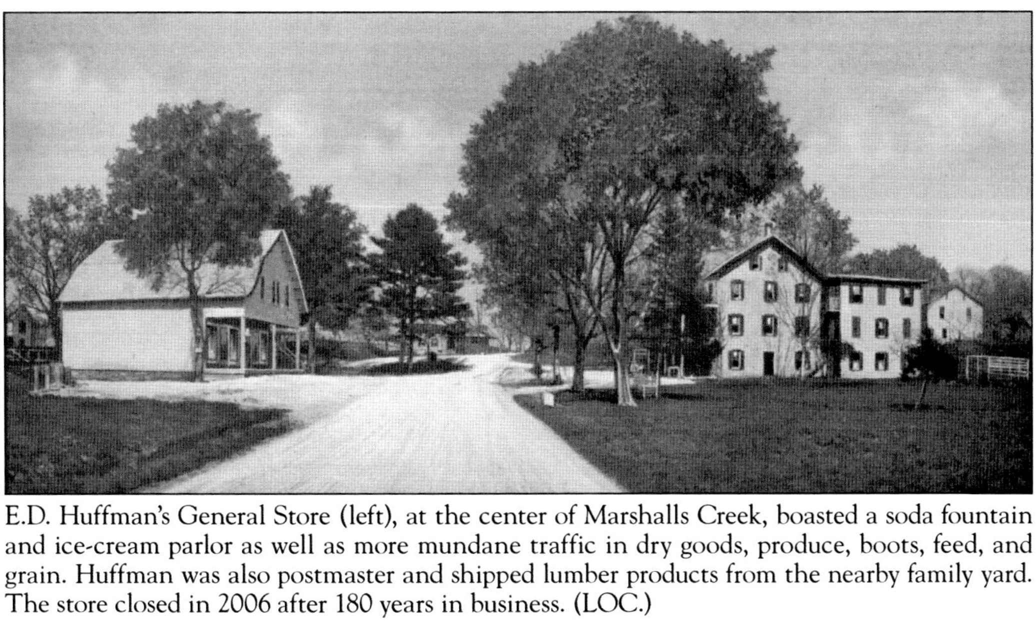

E.D. Huffman's General Store (left), at the center of Marshalls Creek, boasted a soda fountain and ice-cream parlor as well as more mundane traffic in dry goods, produce, boots, feed, and grain. Huffman was also postmaster and shipped lumber products from the nearby family yard. The store closed in 2006 after 180 years in business. (LOC.)

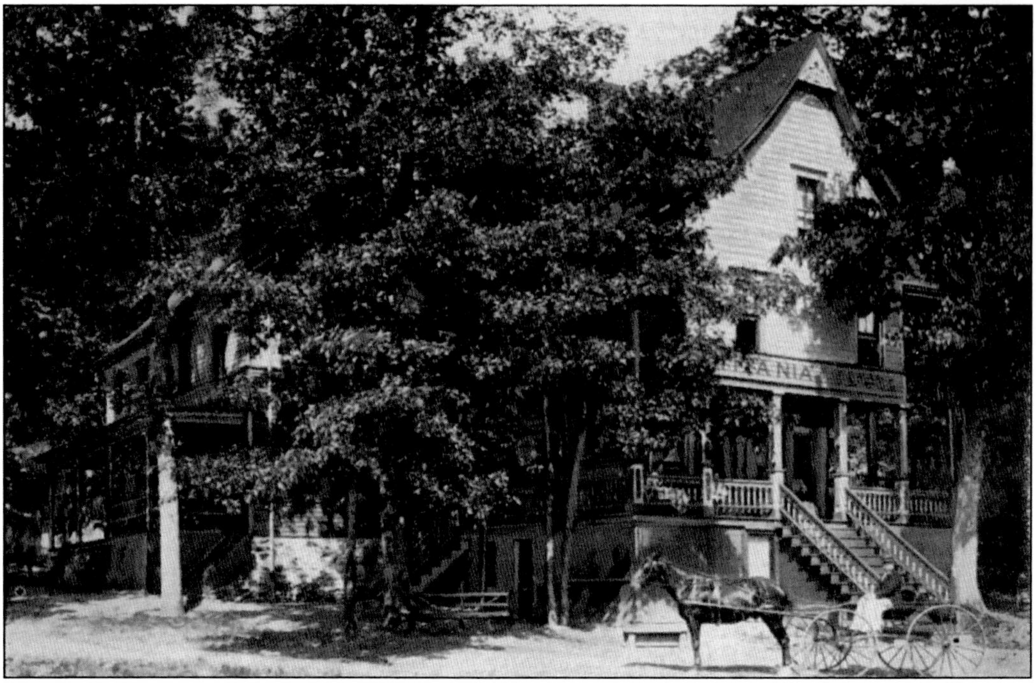

Titania House accommodated 30 guests on Marshalls Creek Road a half mile from the railway station. Its 17 acres included Marshalls Falls (free entry to house guests), Lake Sylva, trails, picnic grounds, a green, and trout ponds. The grounds are now planned as a township park. (EMPL.)

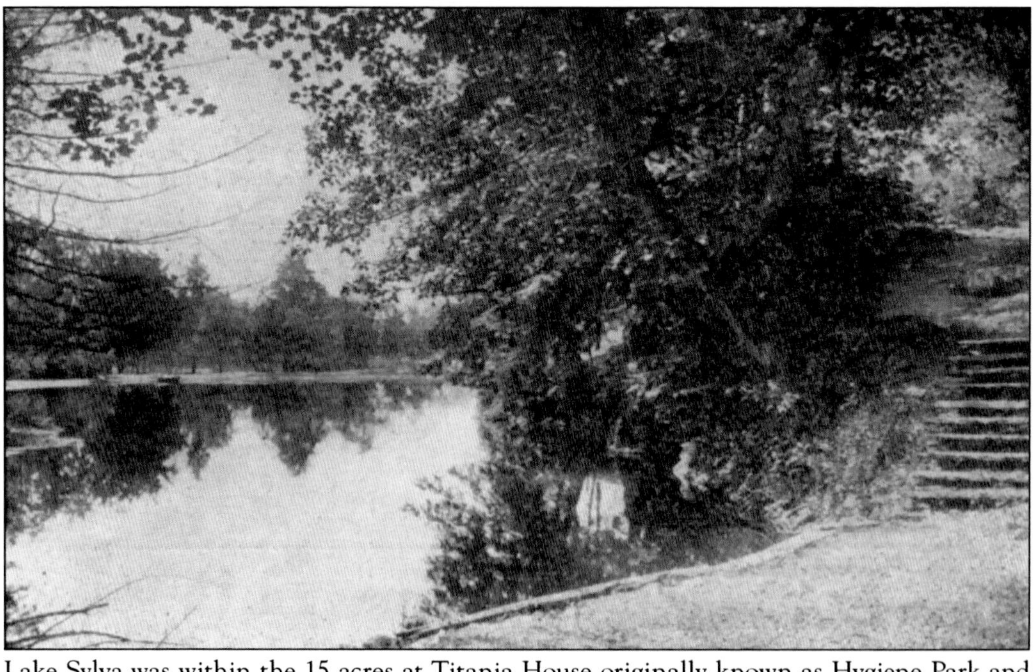

Lake Sylva was within the 15 acres at Titania House originally known as Hygiene Park and promoted as a place to benefit one's health. Sections of the park were named Gypsy Green, the Ramble, and the Pinery, evoking romantic or picturesque places where visitors could stroll and admire nature. (BLTHS.)

Rising in the Pocono Plateau and dropping 650 feet to the Delaware River with three waterfalls, Marshalls Creek provided scenic glens for vacationing visitors as well as power for nearly a dozen countryside and village mills. Pond Creek, arising from Coolbaugh and Echo Lakes, flows into Marshalls Creek in the village center. (LOC.)

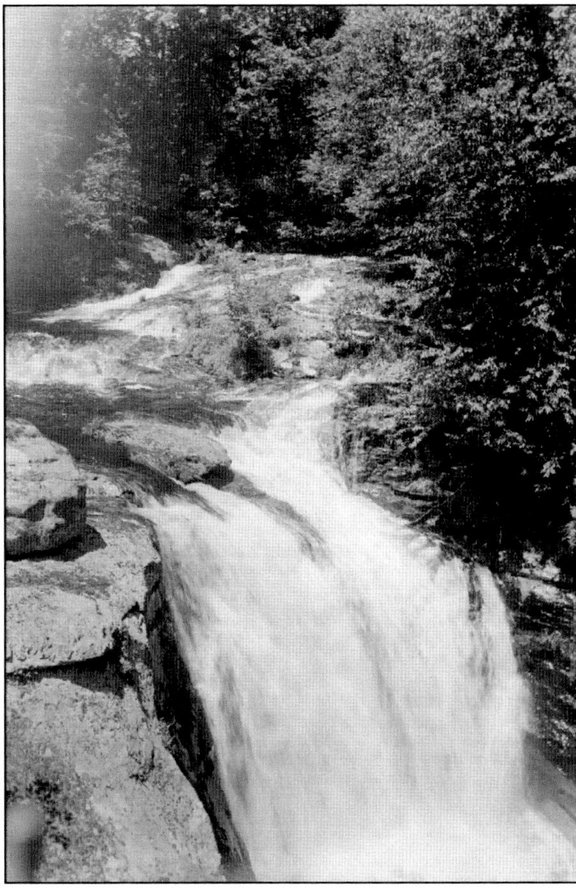

The modest Hotel Lake Marshall, seen here in 1911, transformed under the Huffman family's ownership into the grand Mountain Lake House overlooking Lake Marshall (or Mountain Lake) from the north. The resort closed in 2000. (Authors' collection.)

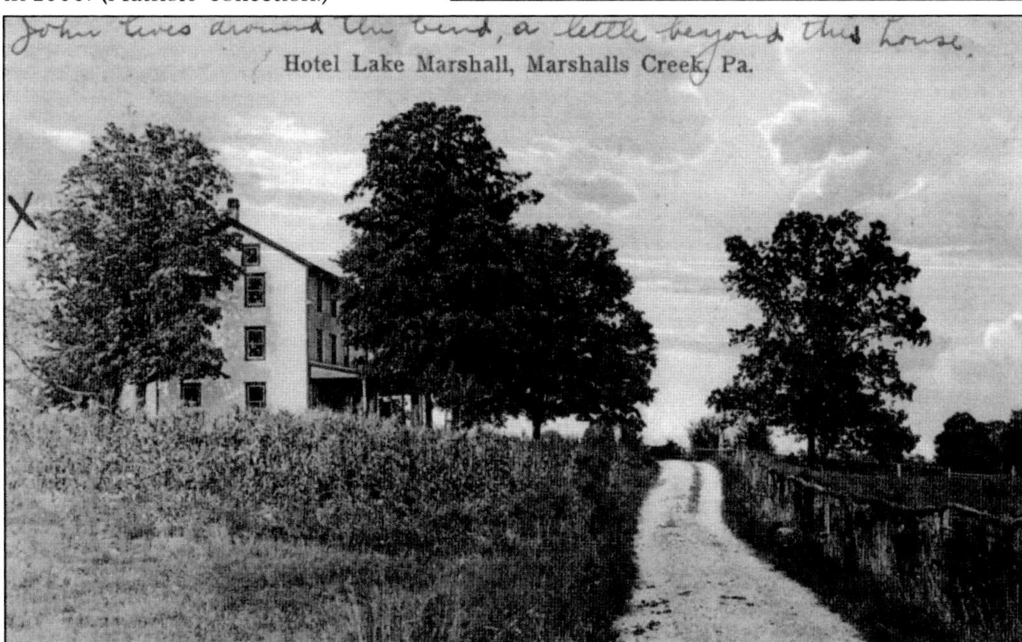

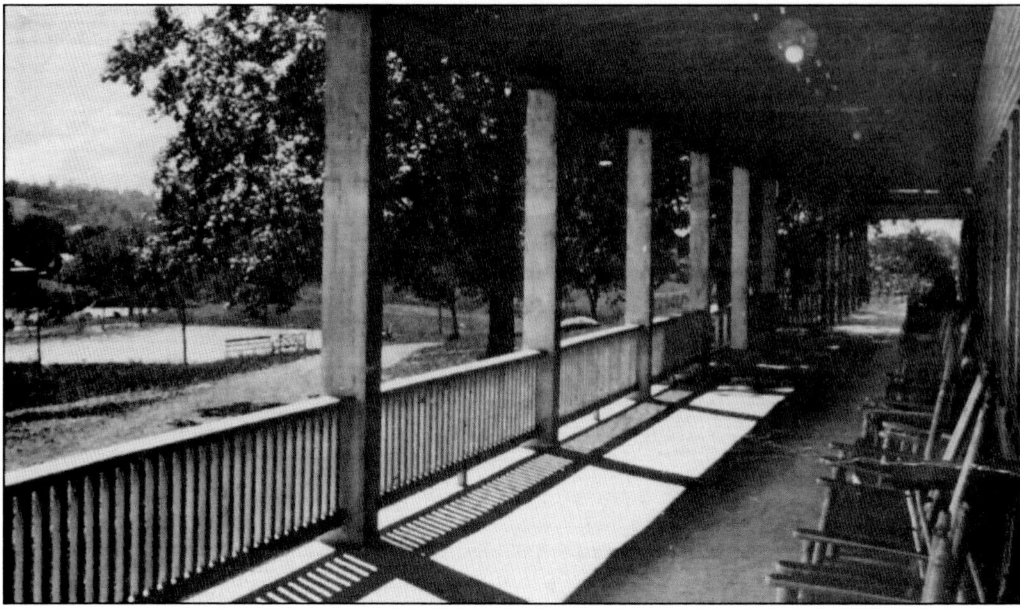

A wide veranda offered shady seating and the chance for conversation before the age of air-conditioning and television. Among the activities to be supervised from the rocking chairs were swimming, boating, tennis, and the passage of the dinkey along the far bank of Lake Marshall. (Authors' collection.)

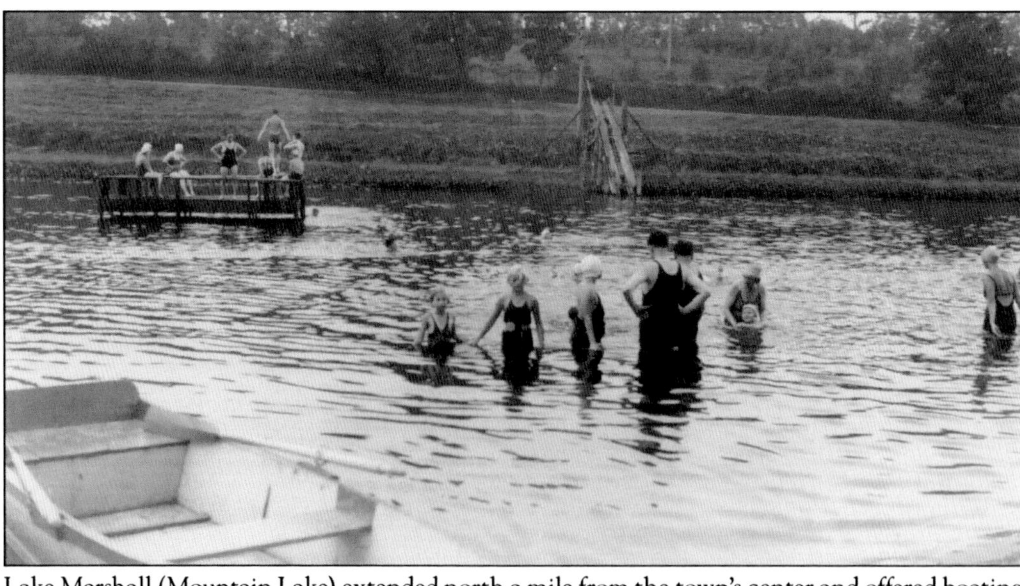

Lake Marshall (Mountain Lake) extended north a mile from the town's center and offered boating, fishing, bathing, and rustic cabins. The dinkey chugged along the southeast bank. The wood structure may be an old ice chute; the lake's ice harvest was drifted downstream to a storage barn by the dam. (Bob Huffman.)

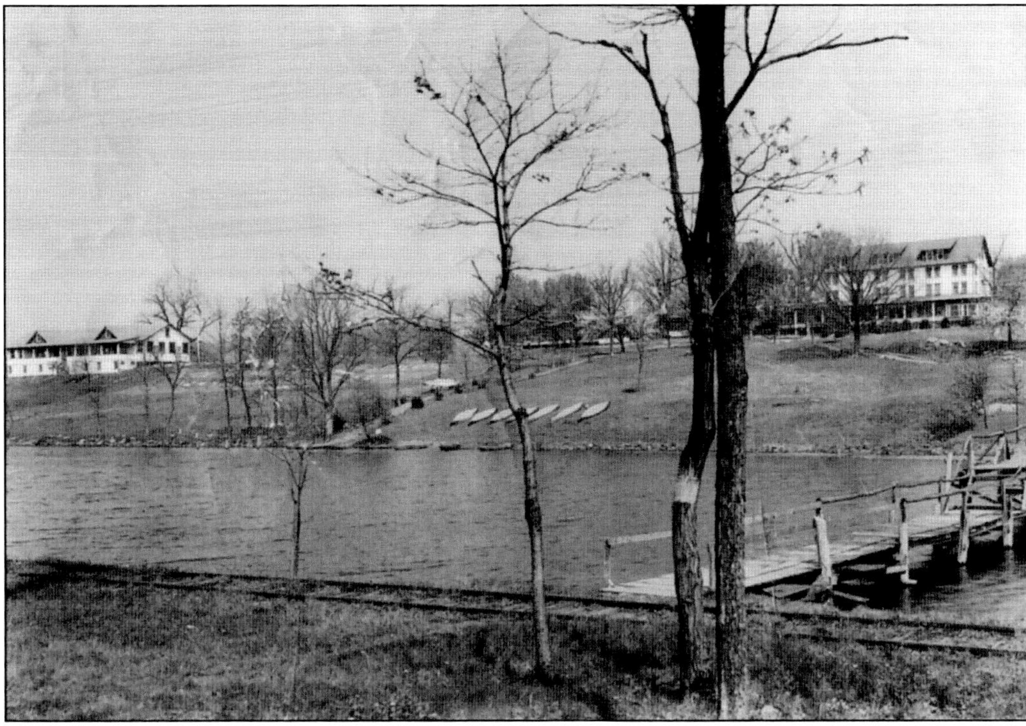

The railway track is still in use, though probably only for freight, in this view west over Lake Marshall to Mountain Lake House. The footbridge across the lake had a lift section to let boats through. Long after the railway era, digging holes in the abandoned railbed to set up fireworks for the hotel brought up old rail spikes. (Bob Huffman.)

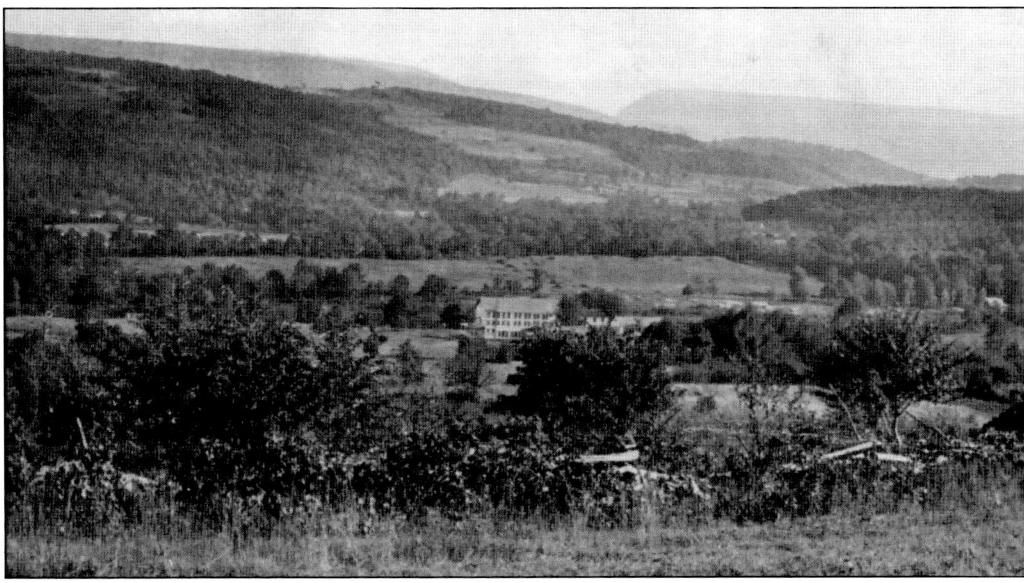

A view of the valley at Marshalls Creek looks east past Mountain Lake House. Lake Marshall is just visible to the right of the hotel, with Milford Road beyond it in the trees. The railway ran along the far bank of Lake Marshall. The Delaware Water Gap, less than five miles away, is in the center distance. (Authors' collection.)

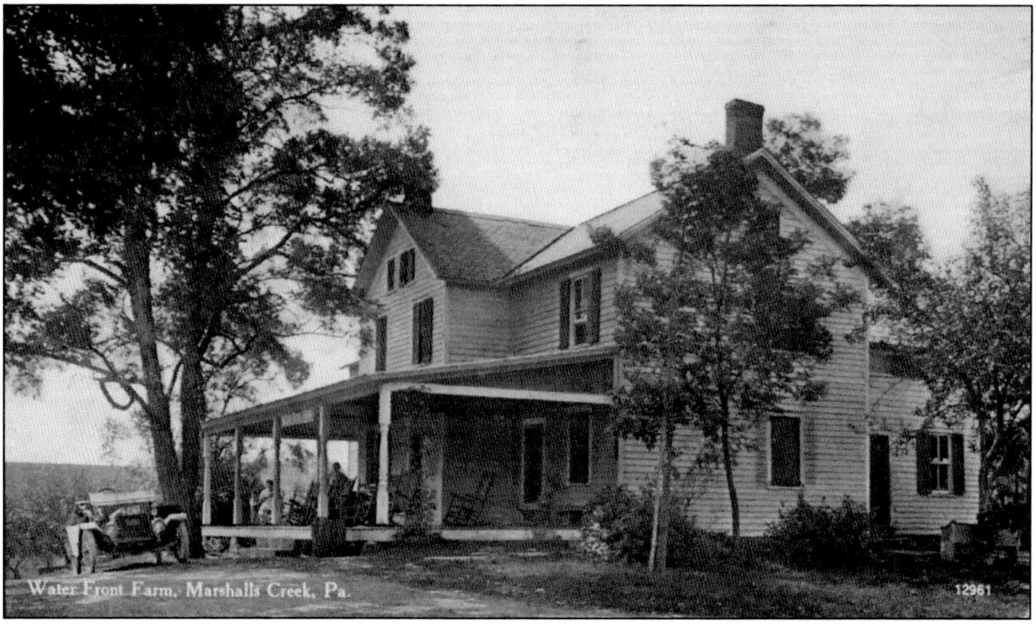

Marshalls Creek was only four miles from Delaware Water Gap via Seven Bridge Road, and farm guesthouses within easy distance of Marshalls Creek and Craigs Corners dotted the route. Twin Falls Farm and Water Front Farm (pictured) along Marshalls Creek both took in guests. Water Front Farm and House are now Water Front Park. (Authors' collection.)

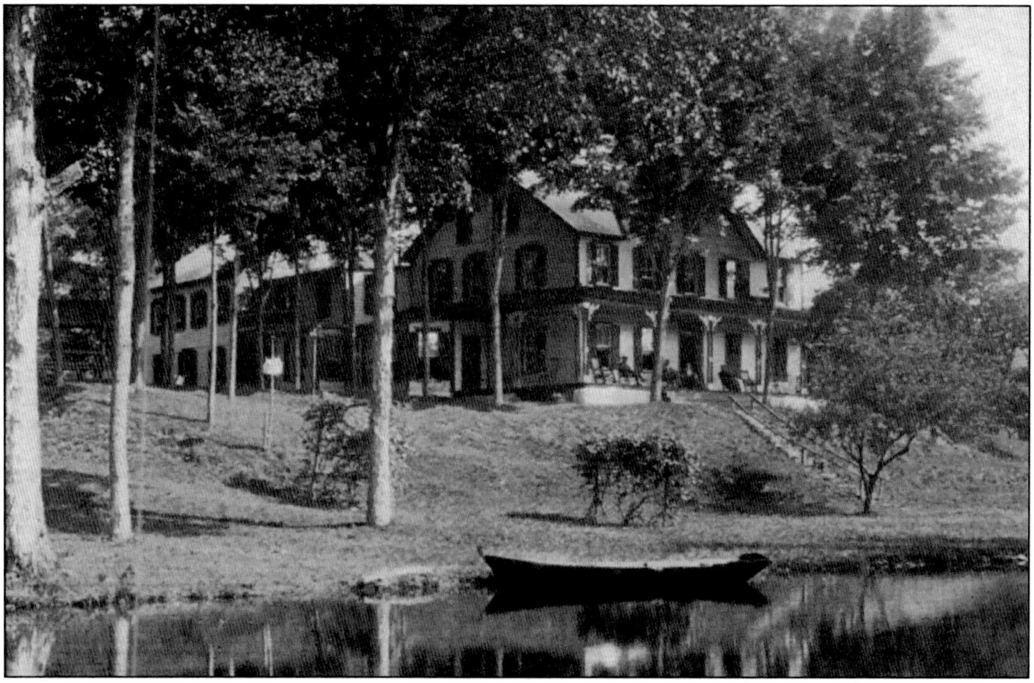

Starting as a cottage cooled by the shade of oak trees and overlooking the pooled waters of Pond Creek, Oak Grove had grown by the railway era into a full-scale resort styled New Oak Grove House. Through the years it added a pool, tennis courts, and a patio with dancing for the singles set. It closed in 1968. (EMPL.)

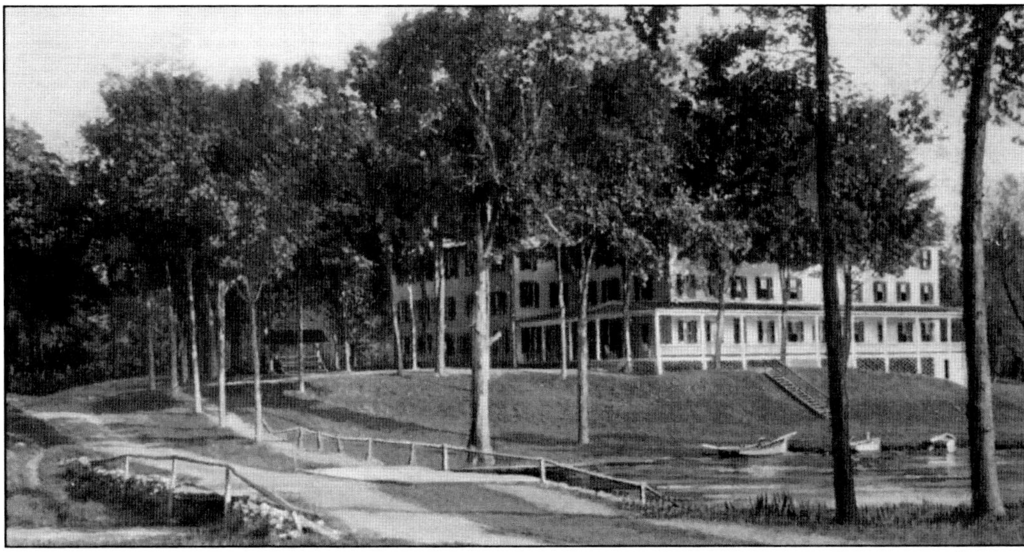

The railway established a station on the hotel's property at the road into Oak Grove. The stop was a minute's walk from the hotel's door via this bridge over Pond Creek. Traffic has since been rerouted around the north of the complex, removing the bridge and making the road to the remaining buildings a dead end. (Authors' collection.)

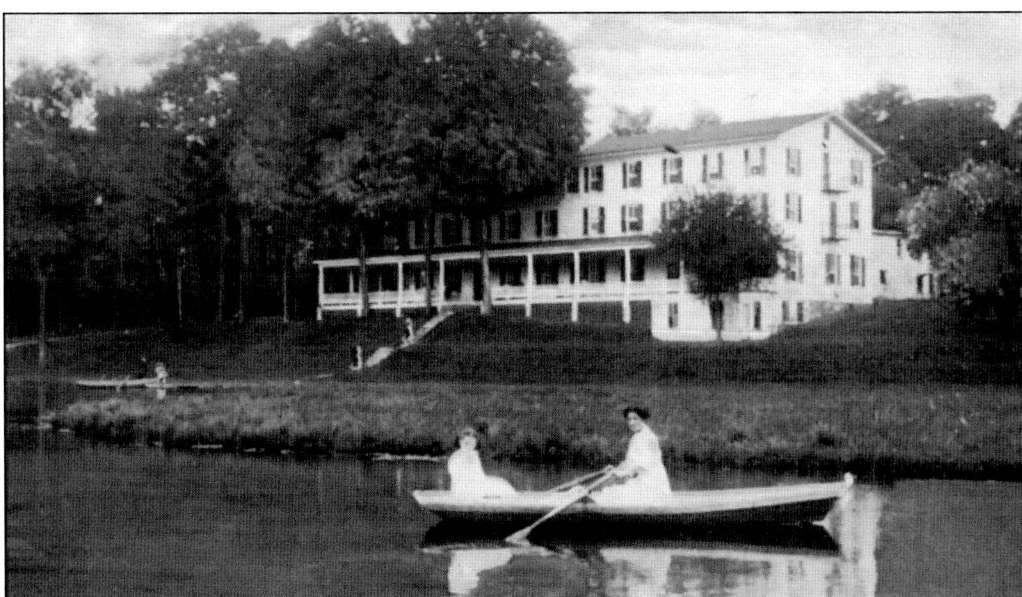

Slow-moving Pond Creek, backed up by Lake Marshall and the dam at the center of Marshalls Creek, provided easy boating for Oak Grove guests. From Coolbaugh Lake, the creek descends barely 20 feet in the three miles to Oak Grove. In later years, some Mountain Lake House guests would row upstream to Oak Grove for a drink. (Authors' collection.)

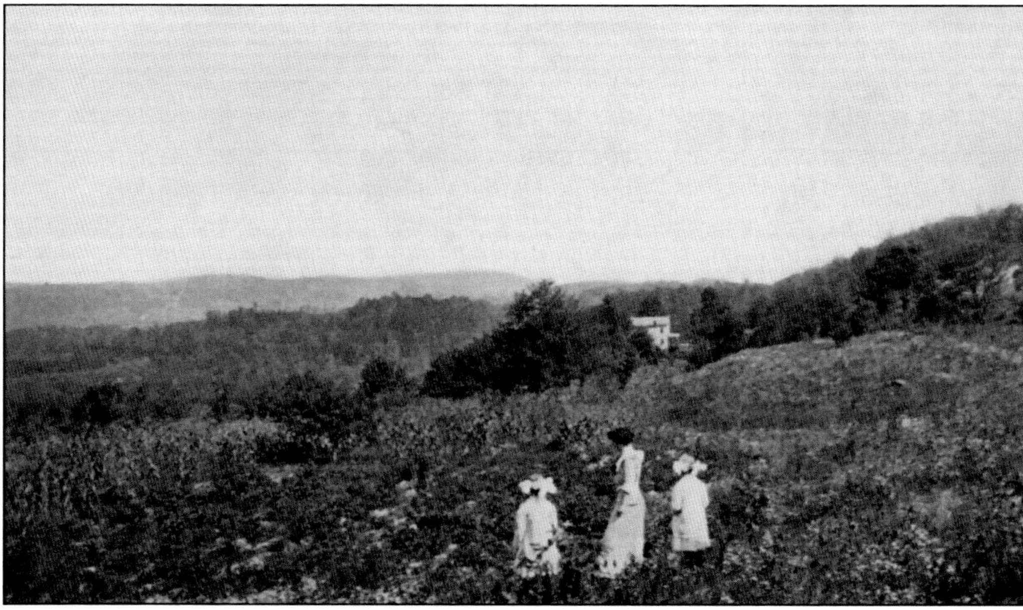

A 1912 hiking guide suggested taking the railway to Oak Grove for an outing to Mount Nebo. "A most extensive and magnificent prospect. High Point 30 miles away to your right, Mount Pocono 20 miles away on the left . . . all the intervening landscape between the two points, a stretch of more than 50 miles, in full view." (Authors' collection.)

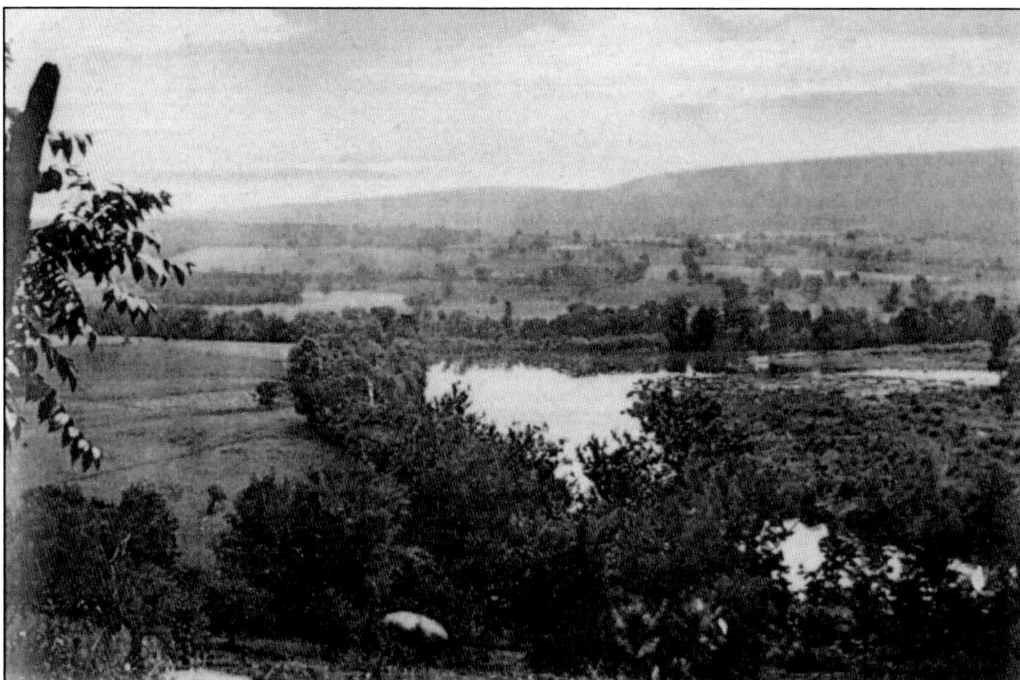

Mount Nebo was once known as Scantling Hill for the lumbering operations there. This view looking southwest from the mountain, taking in the north end of Lake Marshall, is no longer possible due to forest regrowth. Also lost to the regrowth is the view from the east side of Mount Nebo over the Delaware Valley. (MCHA.)

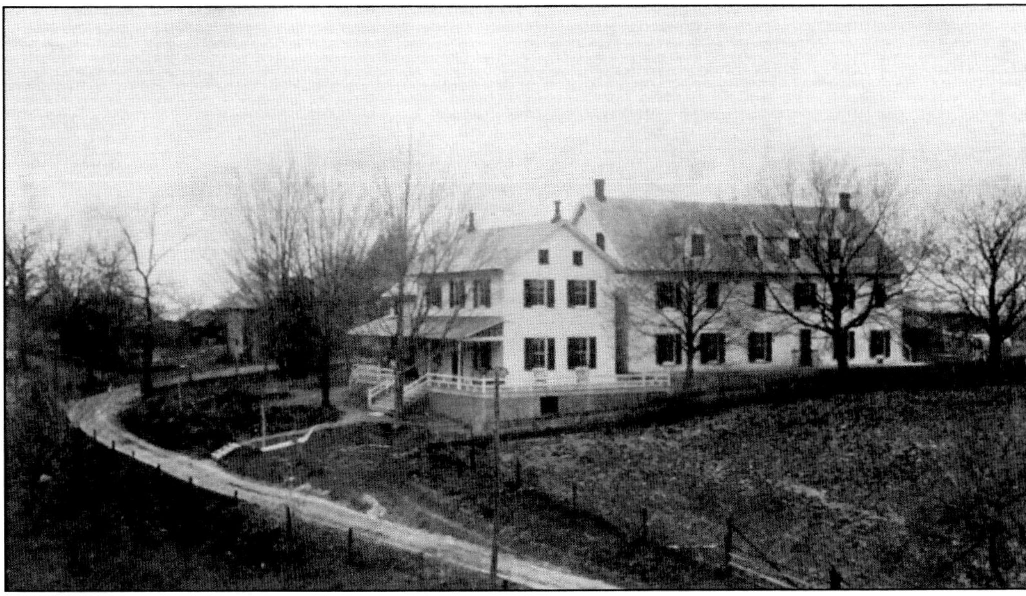

Sunset House, on Mount Nebo Road, was a mile from the Oak Grove station. It offered rooms for 50 and trails up the slope of Mount Nebo to impressive vistas. The view west is still seen from the restaurant of Rainbow Mountain Resort. (Authors' collection.)

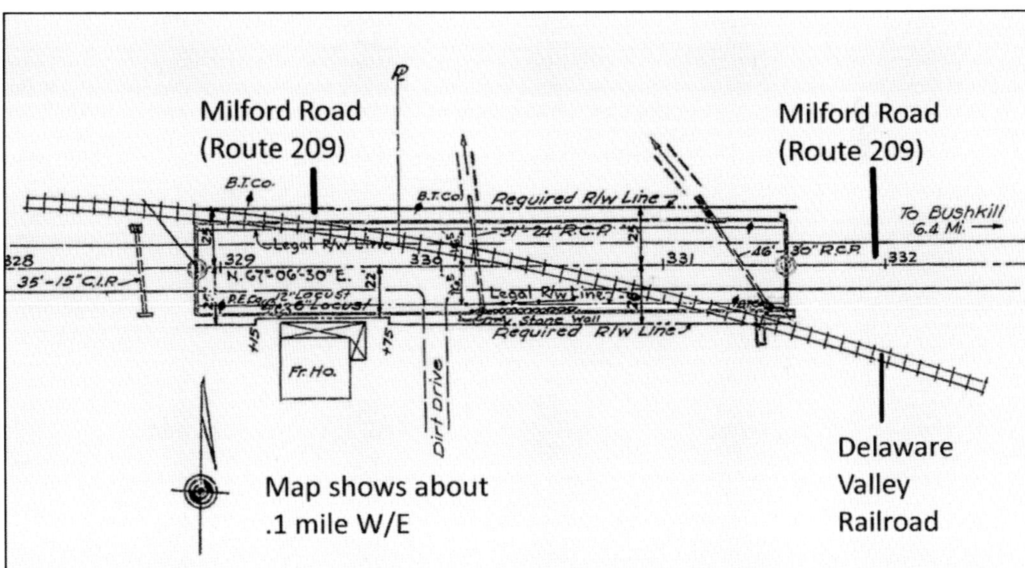

After leaving the Oak Grove stop, the railway sidled across Milford Road, taking about 250 feet to make the crossing. This 1936 paving plan is about midway between Oak Grove and Mount Nebo Road (not shown). The lake at Pardee's Loop did not yet exist, and the track ran through fields to Frutcheys. (PennDOT.)

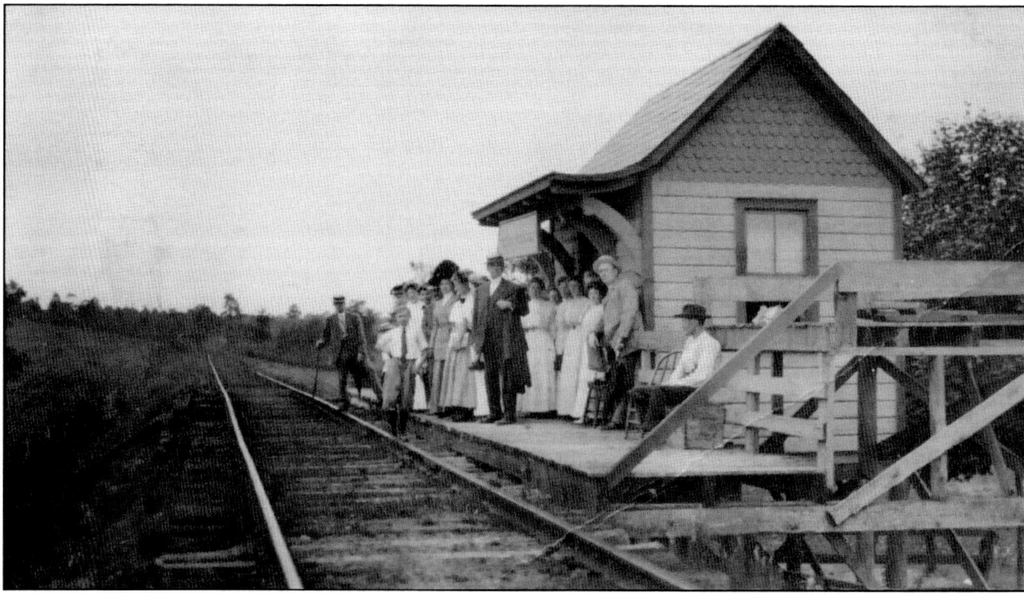

Cameras and walking sticks at the ready, intrepid sightseers await the dinkey at the Turn Villa station in 1910. They may be planning a day's outing in town. A valley resident perched on a pear crate perhaps hopes to ship some produce to a hotel down the valley. The embankment, now much overgrown, still threads through the woods today. (Depot Square Publishing Collection.)

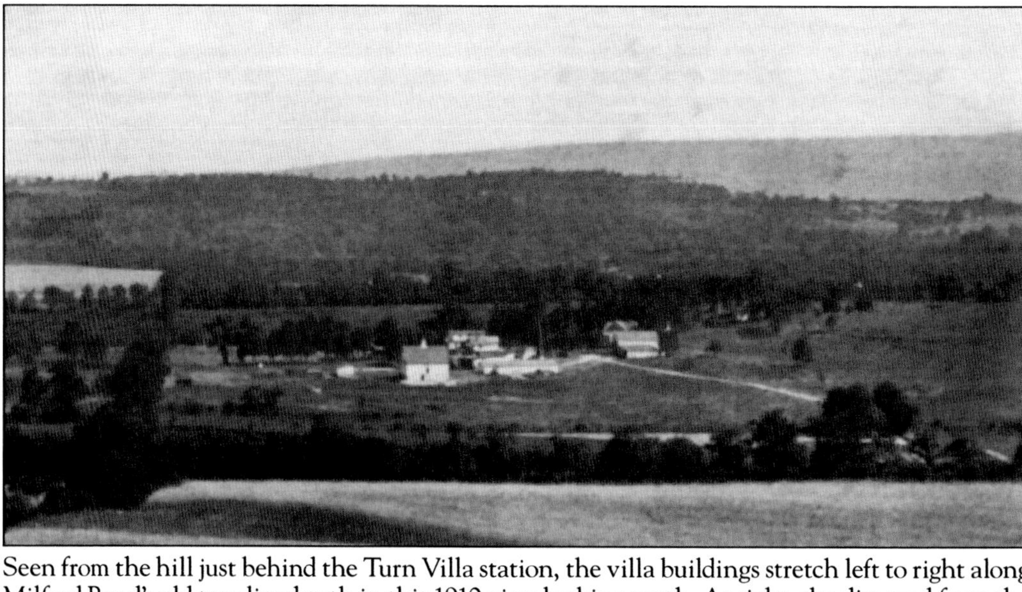

Seen from the hill just behind the Turn Villa station, the villa buildings stretch left to right along Milford Road's old tree-lined path in this 1910 view looking south. At right, the dirt road from the station leads up to the villa. The railway's 11-foot-high embankment runs across the foreground beyond the tree row. In the distance is New Jersey's Kittatinny Ridge. (Authors' collection.)

Five

Middle Smithfield Township

Prominent citizens at "the northern end of the county" were interested in a railroad from the 1880s, even proposing in 1897 to turn the idled electric railway bed into a bike path and turnpike. The list of grantors of the right-of-way include many well-known valley names, such as Angle, Hanna, Michael, Overfield, Place, Van Allen, Van Gorden, and Van Why.

With half the railway's stops either in the township or just at its border, Middle Smithfield was the center of gravity of the railway route. Yet the local population alone would not have been enough to sustain the railway. It was the scenic valley and its growing hotel and guesthouse business that attracted investment, and nowhere along the line was there more scenery than in Middle Smithfield and in Bushkill, just across the county line.

Middle Smithfield is well watered and the grand resorts all had lake access—Oak Grove on Pond Creek, Turn Villa near Echo Lake, and Sunnybrook on Werry Lake. Roughing it in camps, bungalows, and lakeside cabins in the valley was all the vogue, and a number of smaller accommodations appealed to ethnic and cultural clienteles as well. By 1910, the Lackawanna Railroad could advertise nearly 1,200 hotel rooms from the East Stroudsburg line through Bushkill—two-thirds that of the Stroudsburgs and half that of the village of Delaware Water Gap.

The guests were promised more than a place in the country. They needed hot water, which meant hauling in coal even in summer; fresh dairy and produce, which meant shipments from farms close by, and plenty of ice; and services such as daily mail—all available from the railway. As a bonus, the railway could carry away surplus milk and produce from local farms and lumber products from the logs that rumbled in by wagon from the north and west. The identity and economy of the township, from dairying for the hotels to building new hotels, over time became increasingly linked to the resort industry.

A few more recent establishments still continue the tradition of hospitality in Middle Smithfield, most notably Pocono Palace, the successor of various Echo Lake enterprises.

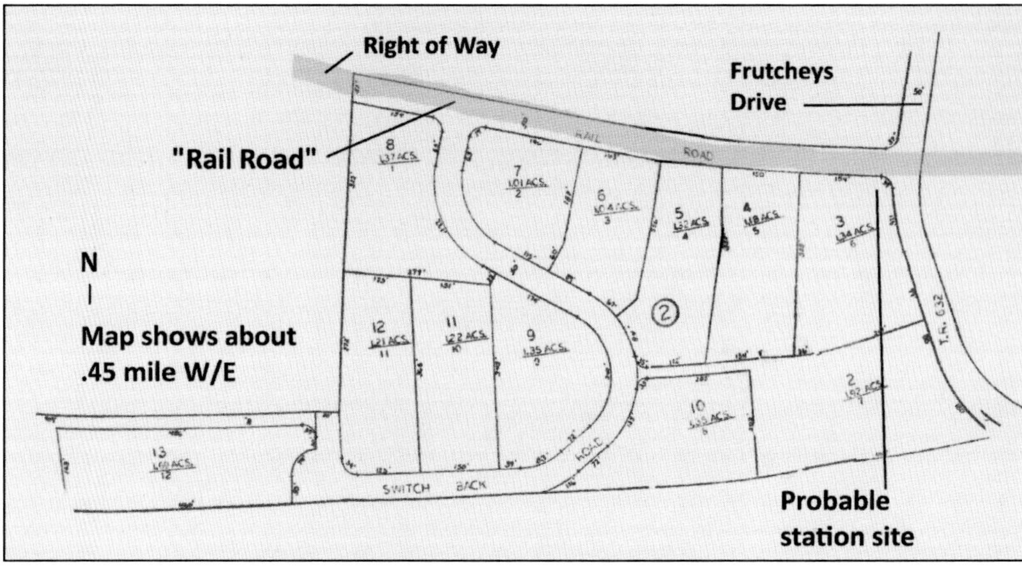

The railway headed east along a creek that has since been dammed to form the lake between Milford Road and Pardee's Loop. From here to Frutcheys, the right-of-way is on private property and overgrown, but county tax maps show this stretch as Rail Road, with divided plots along it. There are no definite remains of the station. (MCRD.)

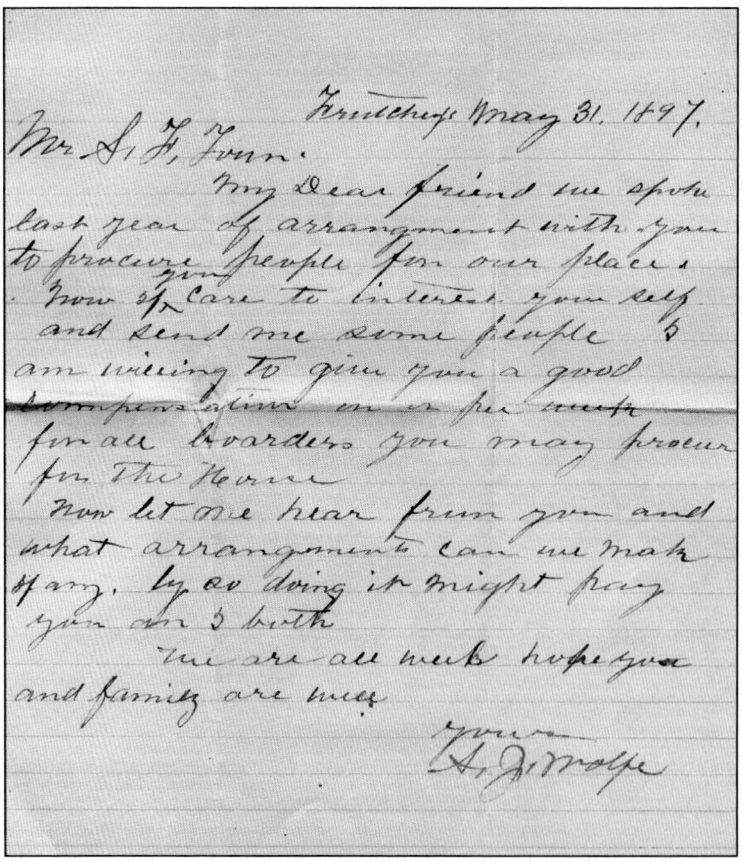

Frutcheys May 31. 1897.
Mr S. F. Turn.
My Dear friend we spoke last year of arrangment with you to procure people for our place. Now if you care to interest your self and send me some people I am willing to give you a good compensation on a per week for all boarders you may procure for the Home
Now let me hear from you and what arrangments can we make if any. by so doing it might pay you and I both
We are all well hope you and family are well
yours
S. J. Wolfe

"Now if you care to interest your self and send me some people, I am willing to give you a good compensation." In May 1897, S.J. Wolfe posted a letter from Frutcheys asking a friend in Philadelphia to find some summer boarders for him. The writer was probably Stogdell Wolfe, grantor of the right-of-way at Frutcheys; the recipient was perhaps a member of the local Turn family. (Authors' collection.)

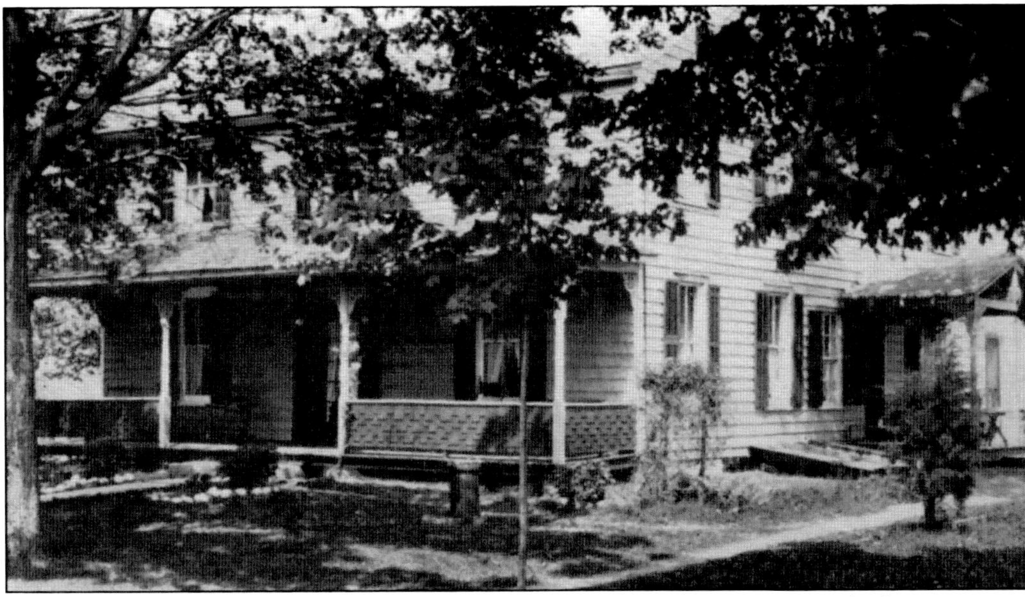

Frutcheys, also referred to by railway crew as Kintner's after its stationmaster, had a station and freight depot 250 yards south of Milford Road at a low point on Frutcheys Drive. The message written on the back of this 1920s card of the Bon-Aire Inn on Milford Pike in Frutcheys exclaims, "Nice R.R. stations in Pennsylvania!" (Authors' collection.)

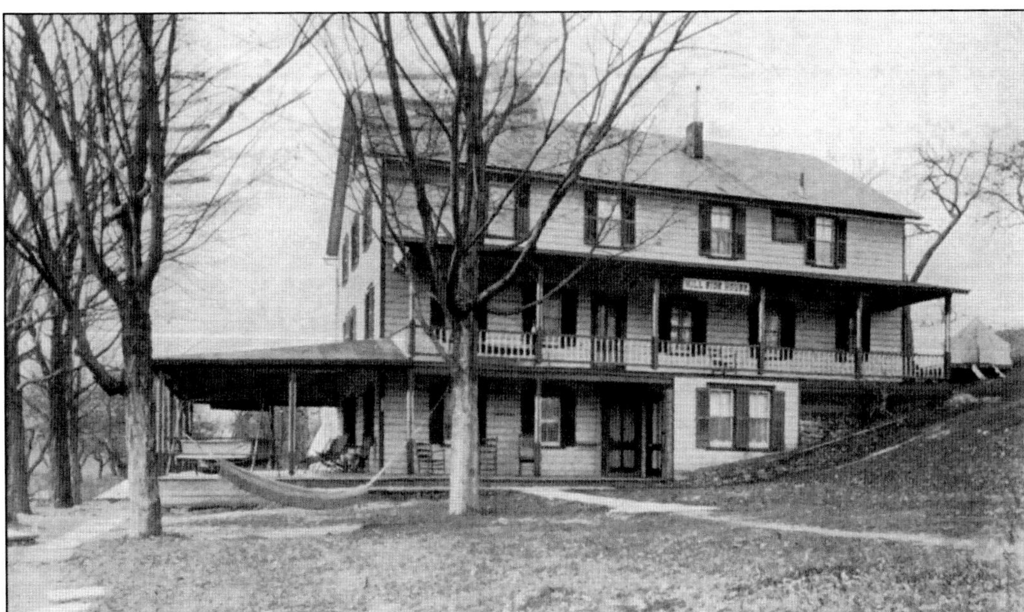

Hillside Hotel was a guesthouse on Frutcheys Drive two minutes' walk from the station. In 1955, ownership devolved to Judge A. Murray, making it one of the few Pocono resorts owned by African Americans. In the 1980s, it expanded to 80 rooms, and it is now an inpatient center. This building is no longer standing. (Authors' collection.)

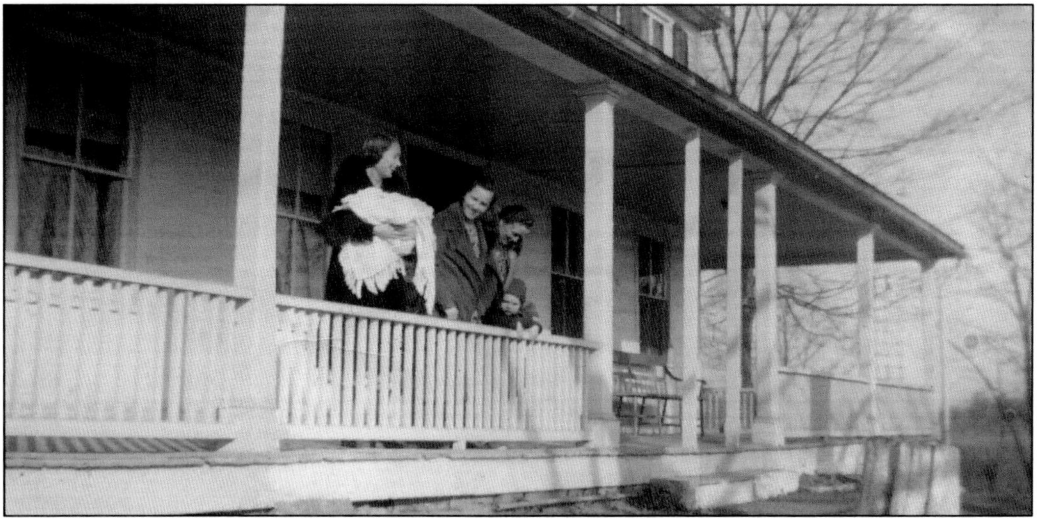

Delaware Valley station was across Milford Road from Delaware Valley Inn. In 1913, the Regina family bought the property and gave their royal name to the inn. The inn's porch faced south across Milford Road (today's Hollow Road) toward the station. The inn's sign is now across the present alignment of Milford Road and inside Regina Farms Garden Center. (Ed Regina.)

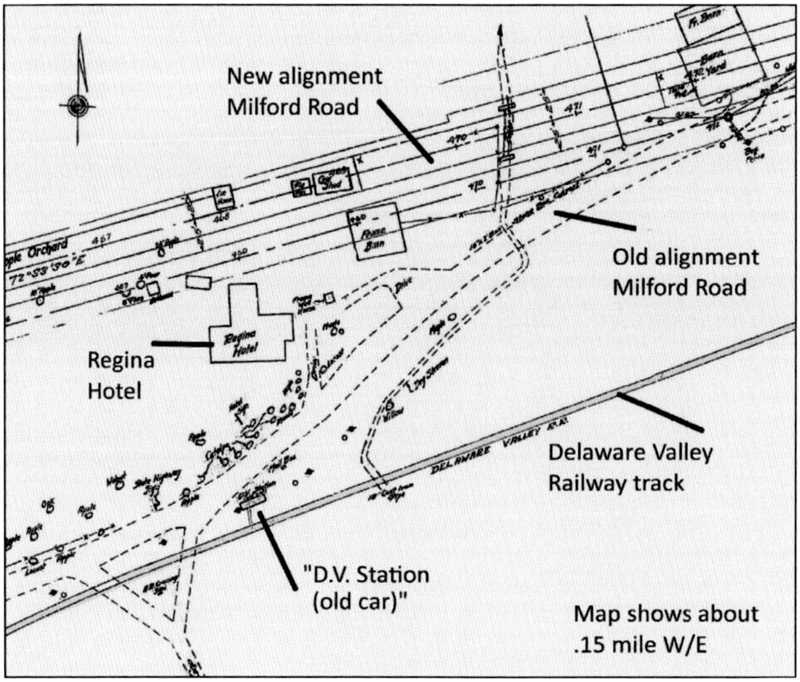

The realignment of Milford Road later moved traffic north of the hotel. The Regina itself was destroyed in an explosion on Route 209 in 1964. (PennDOT.)

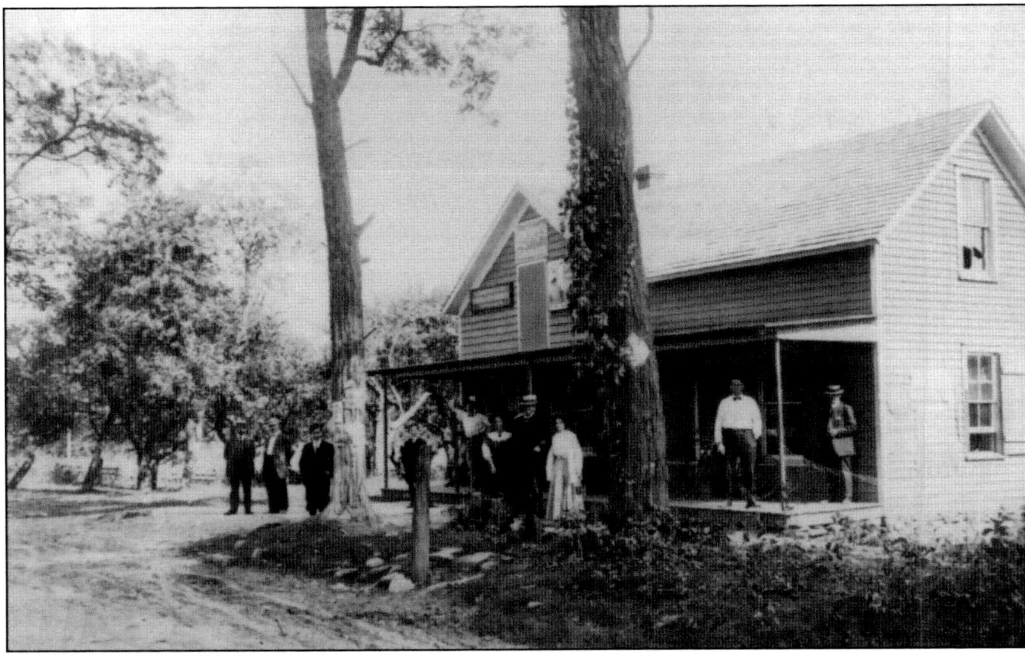

"E.R. McCole & Co. General Merchandise, Coolbaugh PA" may have been located on the McCole property at McCole Road across from the entrance to Werry's Sunnybrook (now the Lake of the Pines community). Goods for stores and food for hotels provided steady northbound freight business for the railway. (MCHA.)

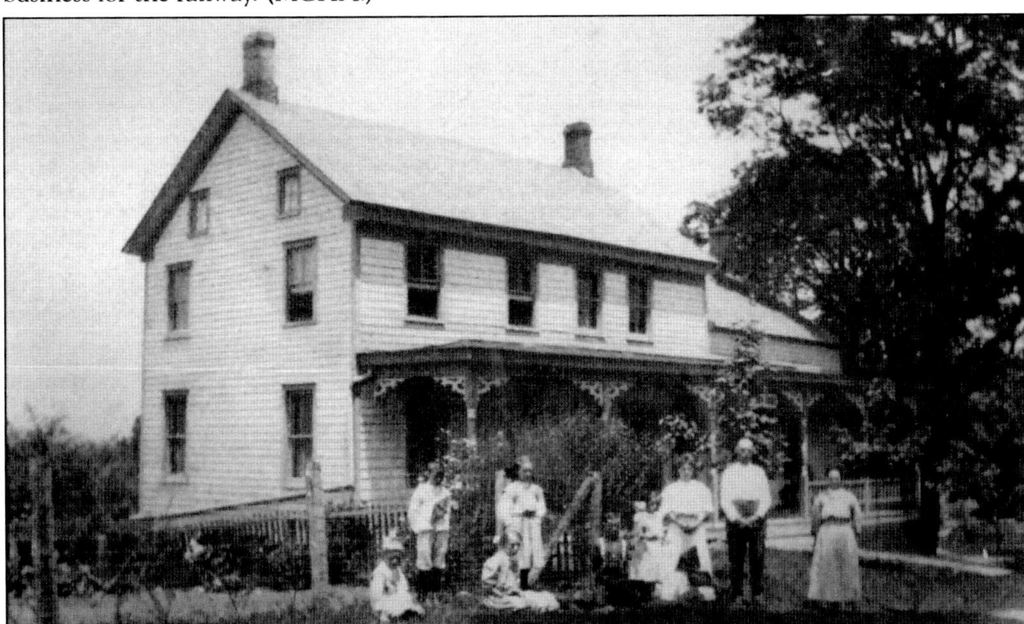

Locust Farm was home to four generations of the Colabaugh family. Southwest of Hidden Lake and about a mile from the railway, it was also a 70-acre dairy farm with a milk route and a guesthouse for 15 visitors. Colabaugh children rode the dinkey to high school in East Stroudsburg. (Kim Williams.)

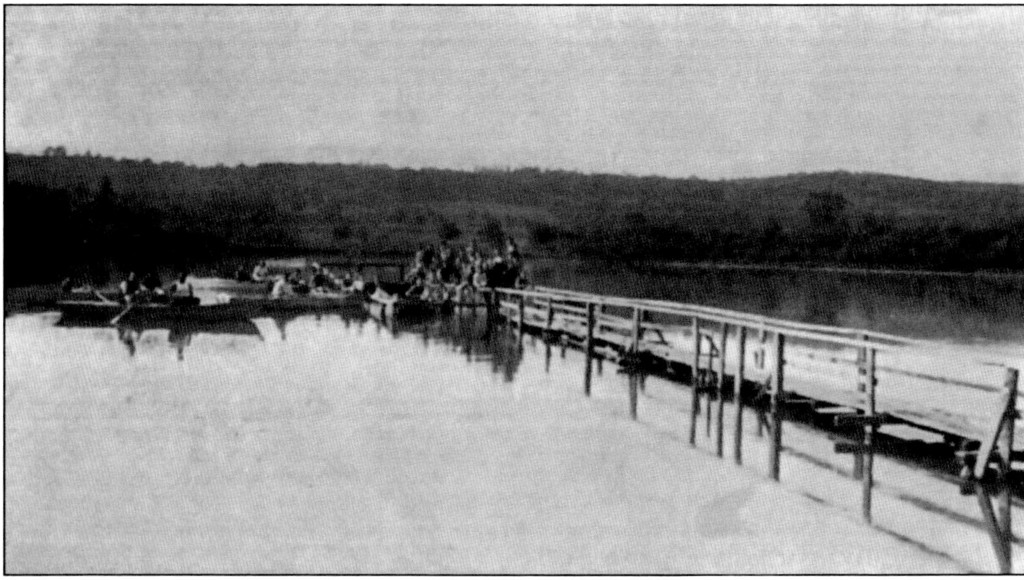

From about 1900, Rabbi David Davidson directed a summer school and camp for Jewish boys in Coolbaugh. The camp advertised in Jewish newspapers such as Brooklyn's *Messenger.* Camp property included a dairy and produce farm, the railway's Coolbaugh station near today's Keystone Road, access to Coolbaugh Lake (pictured), and the Coolbaugh College Inn for visitors. (LOC.)

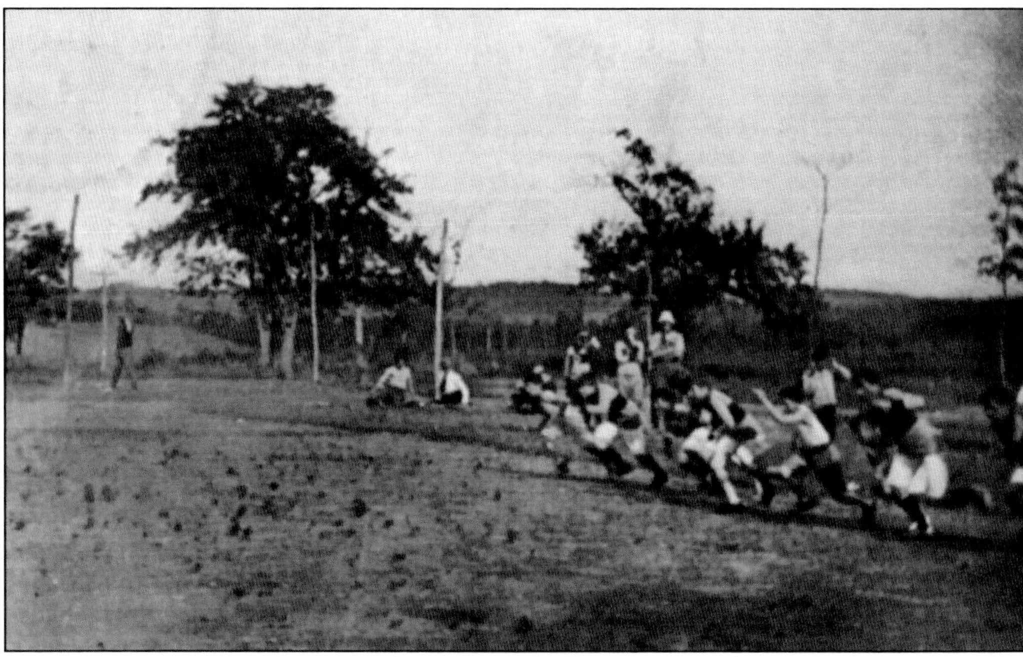

Davidson's camp believed in exercise, like the 100-yard dash (pictured). In 1904, the campers challenged Echo Lake House to baseball but lost 36-10, both teams providing both good and "ludicrous" plays according to local coverage. The property sold in 1939, after Davidson's death. The motel at Blue Ridge Inn later stood alongside the right-of-way. (MCHA.)

This advertisement for "The Cardinal Points" appears in the railway's 1902 promotional brochure, *The Colonial Route.* Edith Levin, proprietor, was also manager of Lakeview Summer Art School, which listed in the premier arts journal *International Studio* around the same time and featured artist scholars such as American impressionist Robert Bruce Crane (1857–1937). (BLTHS.)

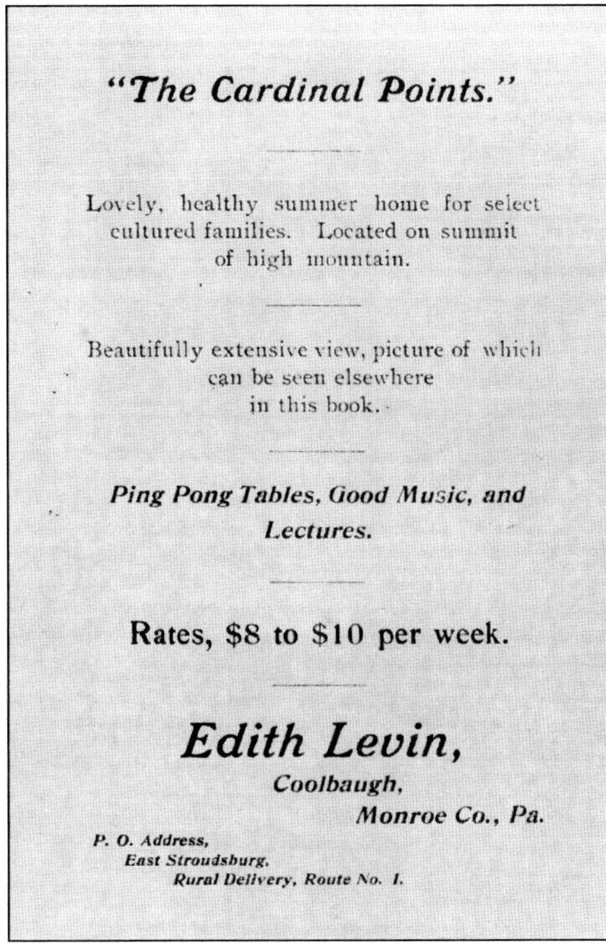

This "view of valley at Coolbaugh from Cardinal Points House" from *The Colonial Route* appears to be taken from McCole Road with a view looking north over Milford Road to Echo Lake. If so, the railway would have run through the wooded area across the middle ground. (BLTHS.)

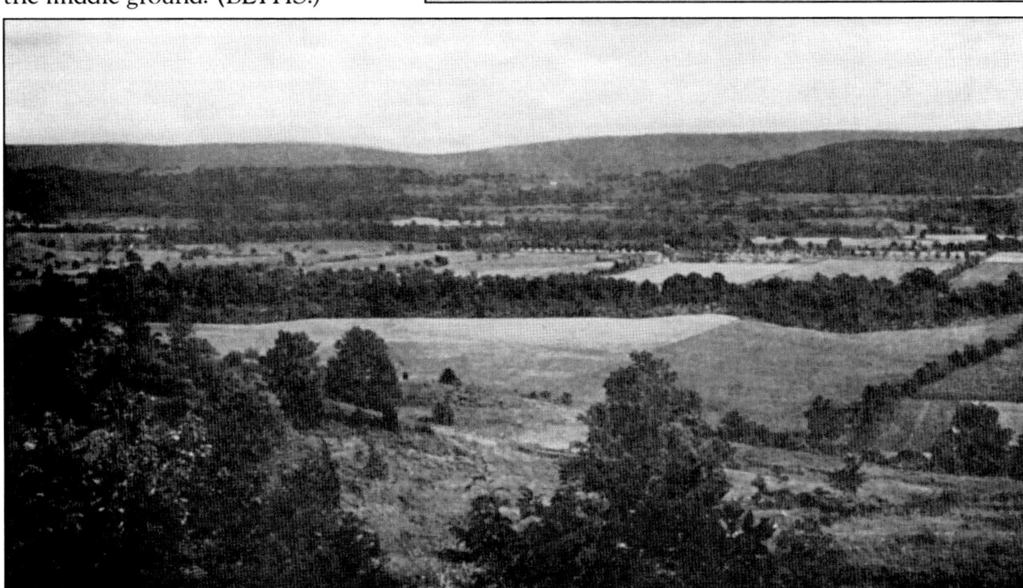

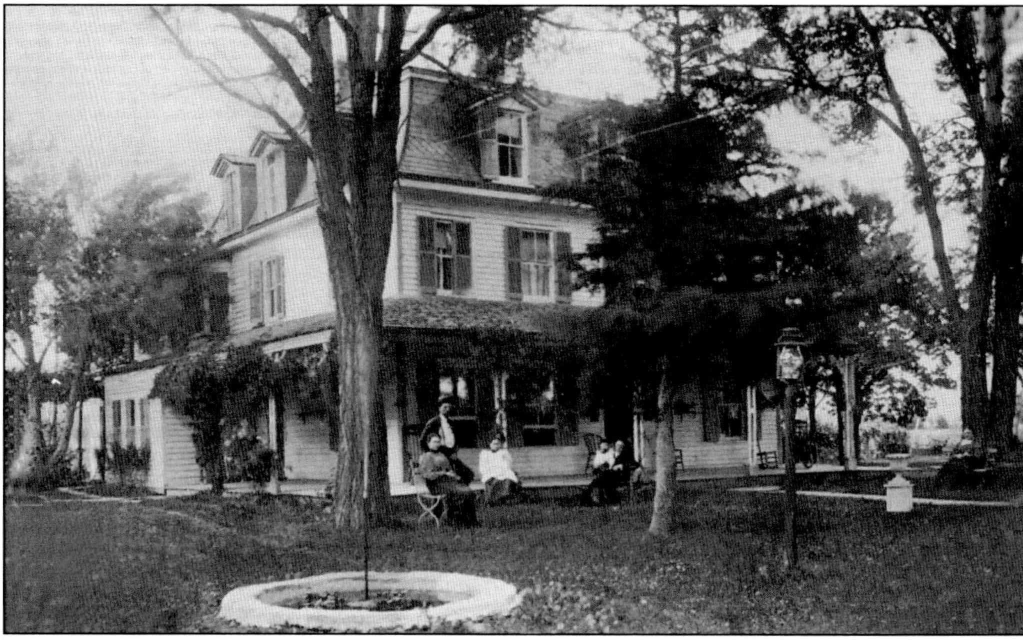

Rev. Dr. Charles E. Van Allen established Echo Lake House around 1865, and by the railway era, the expanded hotel accommodated 75 guests. The railway ran through the middle of his property, parallel to and southeast of Milford Road. Van Allen had a flag station built just a few minutes' walk from the hotel. (EMPL.)

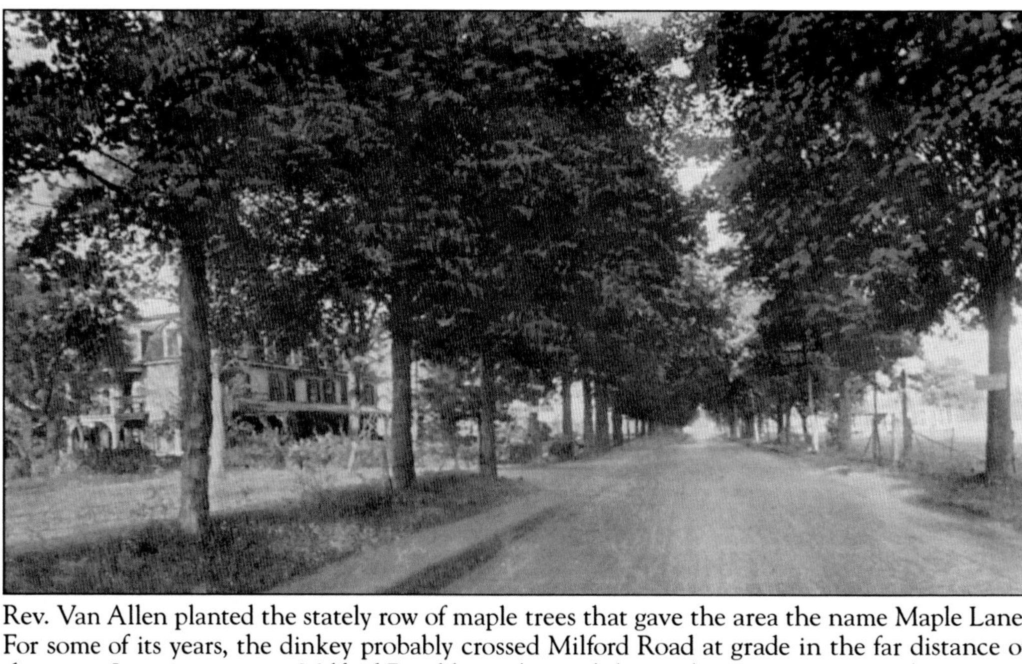

Rev. Van Allen planted the stately row of maple trees that gave the area the name Maple Lane. For some of its years, the dinkey probably crossed Milford Road at grade in the far distance of this view. Improvements to Milford Road later changed the grade crossing to an underpass and eliminated the maple trees. (Authors' collection.)

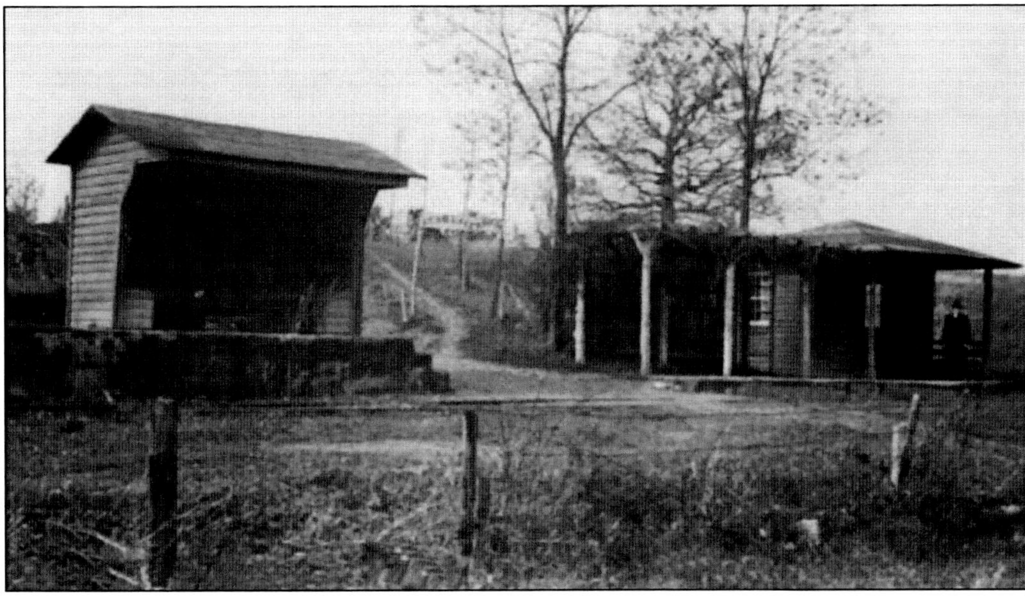

Rev. Van Allen and Arthur J. Shinn, proprietor of Echo Lake Bungalows, had a station built for Echo Lake in 1910. Guests reached Echo Lake House (probably the structure in the distance) by going up the slope and across the field to Milford Road. Nothing remains of the station. The site is on private land; do not trespass. (Kim Williams.)

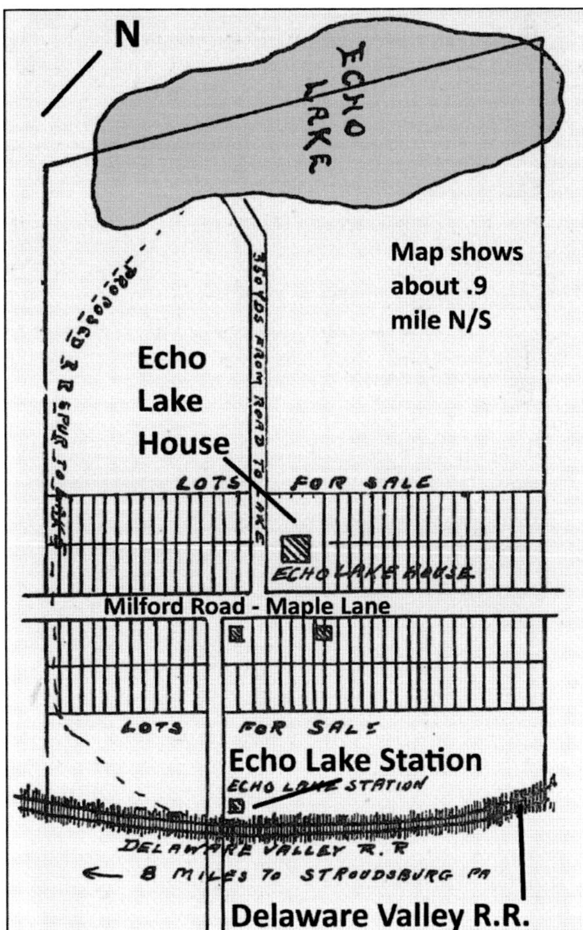

In 1915, Rev. Van Allen advertised lots for sale at his Echo Lake House along both sides of Maple Lane (Milford Road). The proposed spur to the south end of Echo Lake sketched in at the left is not mentioned elsewhere and was perhaps Van Allen's own dream rather than a railway plan. (LOC.)

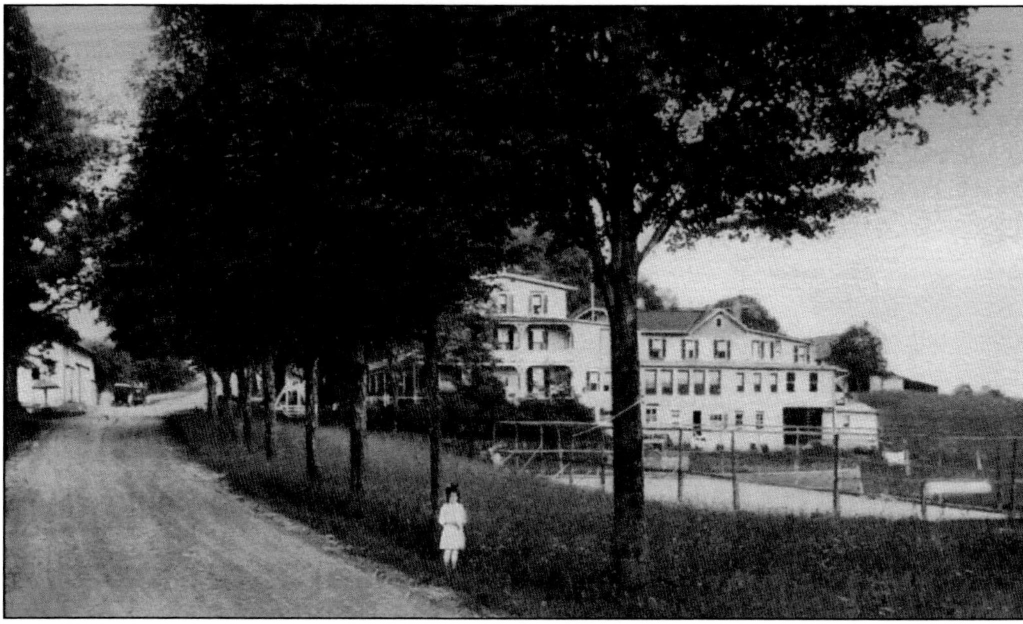

This view looks south at Turn Villa, with the little girl standing on the northwest of the original unpaved alignment of Milford Road. Once the home of M. Depue Turn and called Ridge View, the house has expanded northward to accommodate guests. The railway ran in the distance, beyond the hill at the far right. (Authors' collection.)

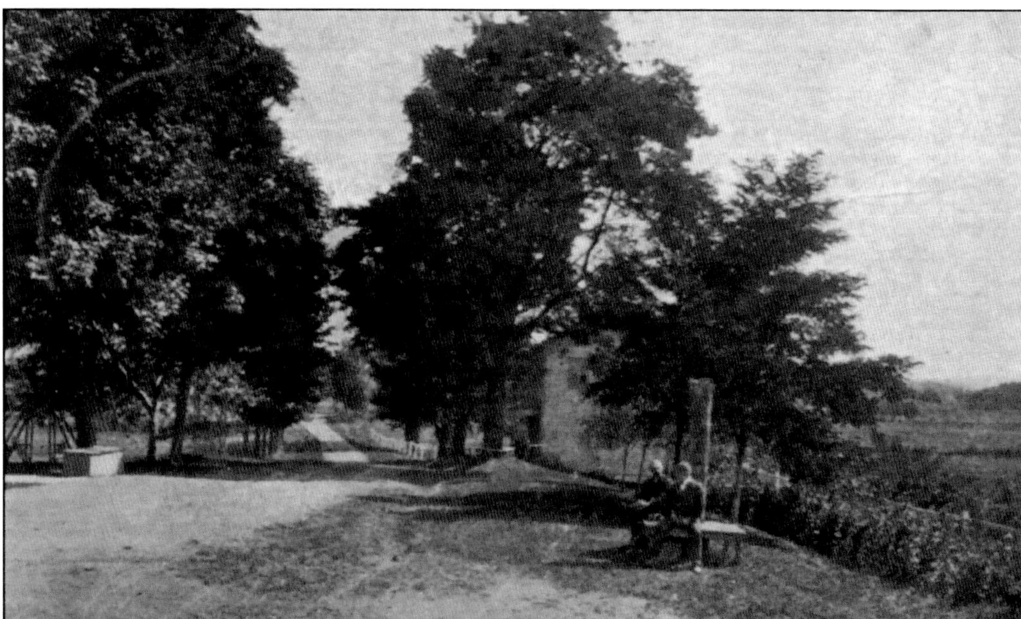

This view looks north from in front of Turn Villa around 1905, with the two young men sitting along the southeast side of the original unpaved alignment of Milford Road. The fields at the right are now filled with the new alignment of Milford Road (Route 209) and with businesses near the Lake of the Pines community. (Authors' collection.)

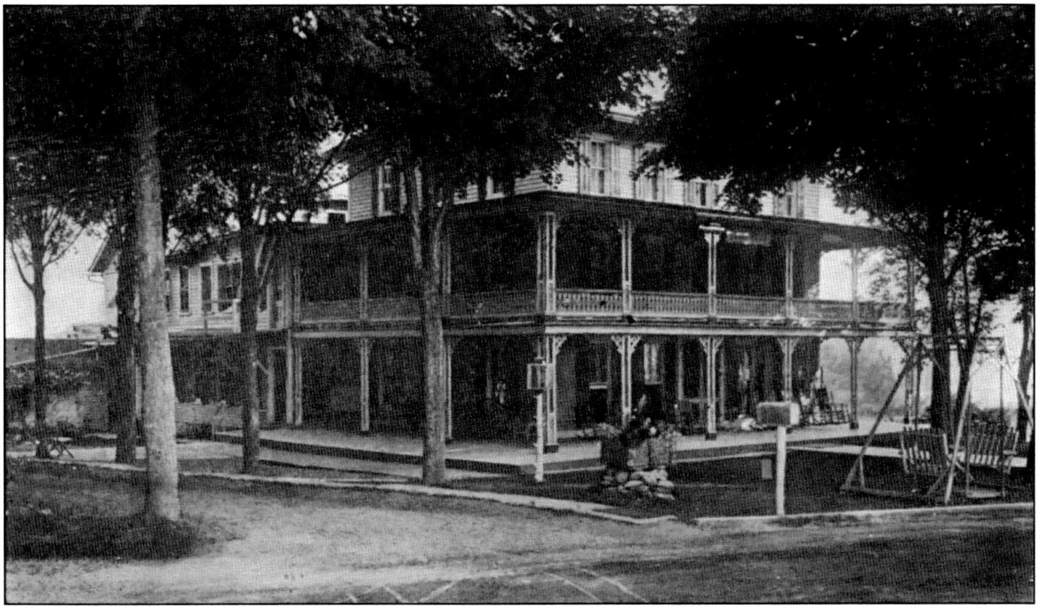

Turn Villa station was a half mile from the villa itself via the dirt road at the left in this 1914 view. Across the foreground is the original alignment of Milford Road, later shifted away from the building. As Echo Lake Farms, the property had an entrance driveway bordered with stone walls and a fountain. (Authors' collection.)

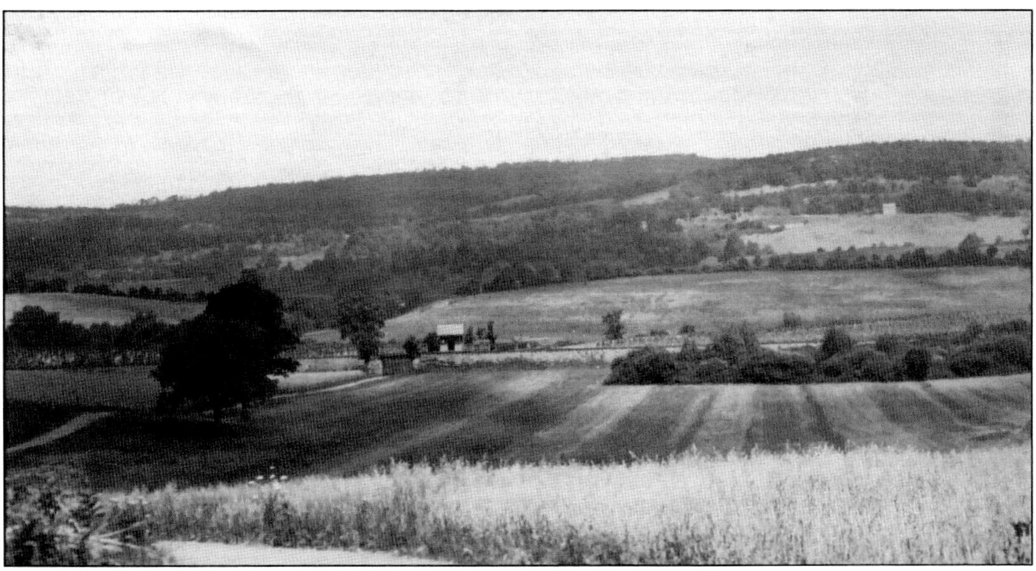

The railway ran across the middle of this view looking north from Turn Villa around 1910. The dirt road to Echo Lake (left) runs under the railway's embankment with the small white station house atop. Today, houses at the south end of the Lake of the Pines community stand in the distance. (Depot Square Publishing Collection.)

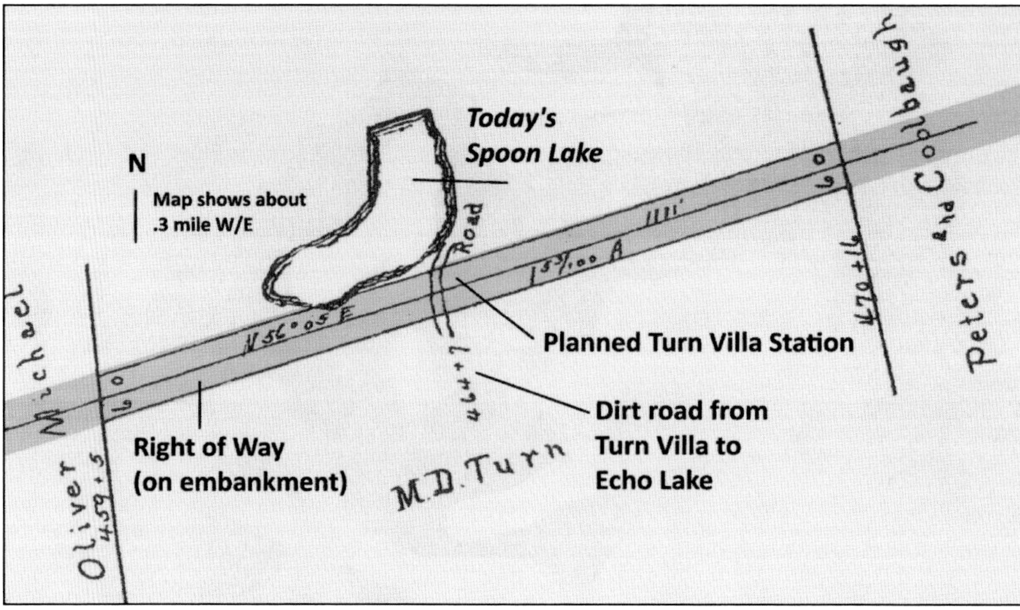

As the railway reached the Turn Villa station, it was on an 11-foot-high embankment that passed over the dirt road to Echo Lake. The 1901 right-of-way deed also protected the fishing pond (today's Spoon Lake), with requirements for drainage, fencing, and cattle paths. Today, the pond is filling in. (MCRD.)

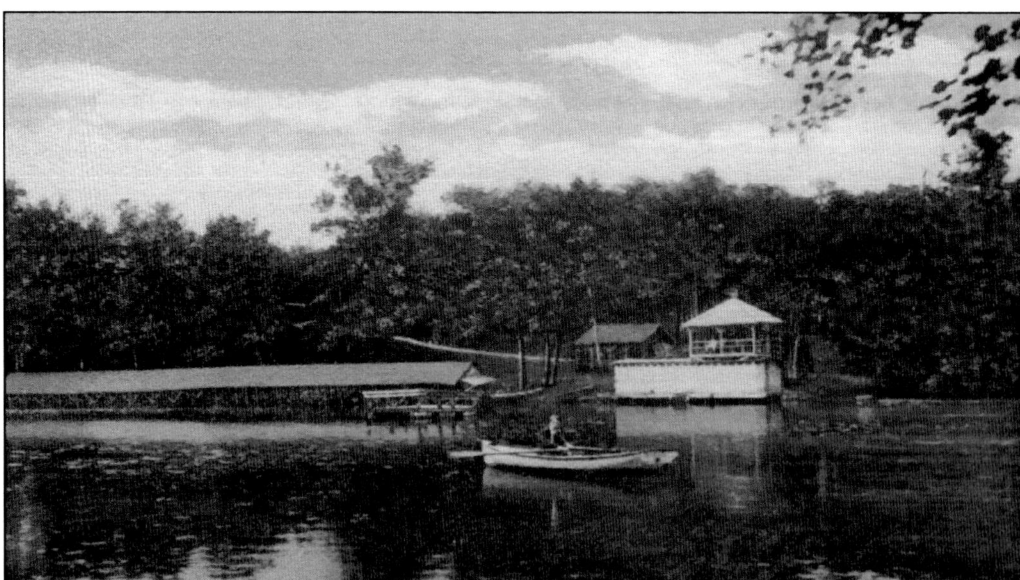

A century after guests of Echo Lake House and Turn Villa rowed across it, beautiful Echo Lake is still the centerpiece of resort activity. Echo Lake Farms, a family resort, flourished from the 1940s, and Vacation Valley, a singles resort, lined the north side of the lake in the 1960s. Vacation Valley became today's Pocono Palace. (Authors' collection.)

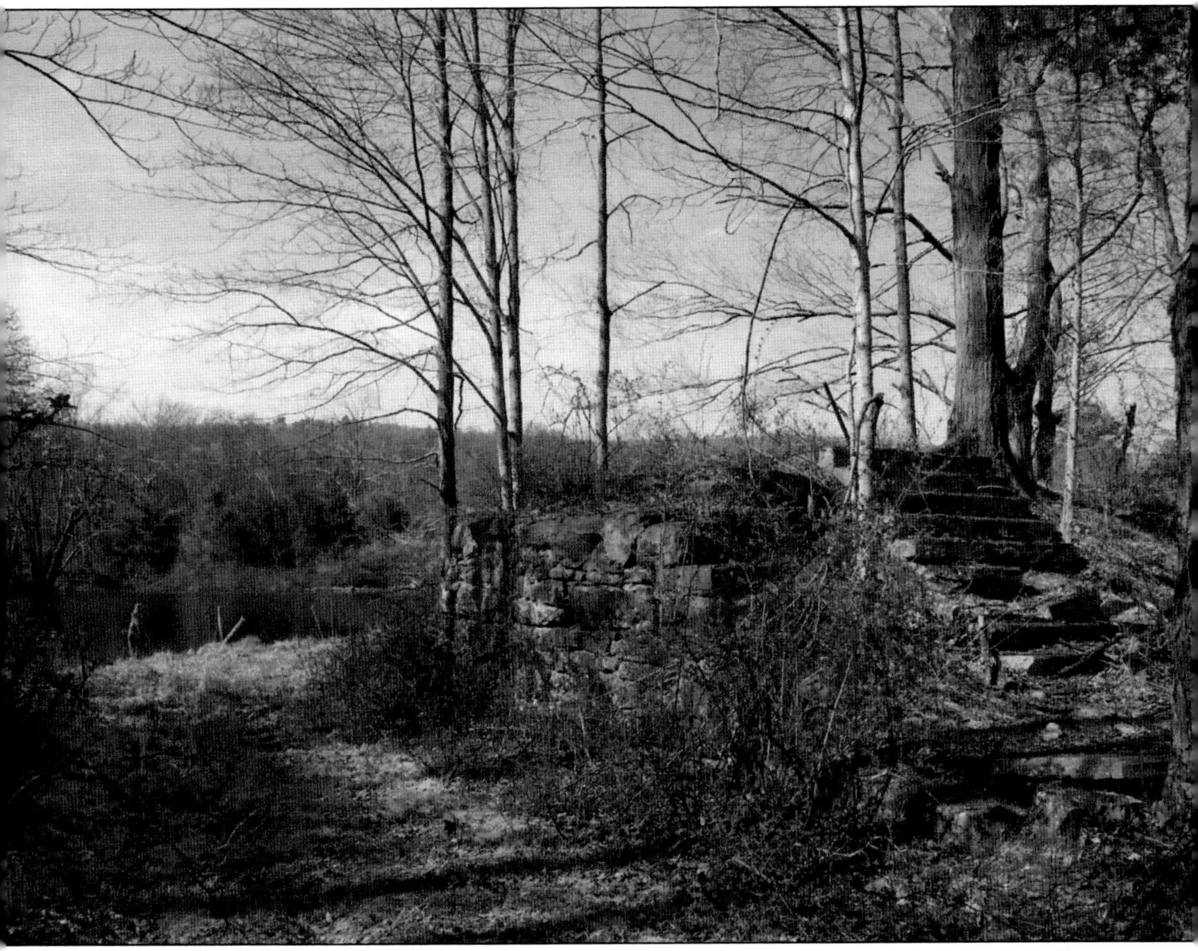

The railway agreed—among other concessions—to build an unenclosed station for Turn Villa with steps not less than four feet wide. The exact location of such steps is not cited, but these concrete steps at the Turn Villa station site certainly date from sometime in the dinkey's day. On the far side of the embankment is a wall and atop the embankment is a concrete strip, likely the base for the station platform. The dirt road to Echo Lake passed between the stone walls of the embankment's cut and curled to the right around Spoon Lake. It was passable until overgrown in the 1990s. Today, this station site is on private property and not visible from any public road. Please respect the landowner's rights and "visit" this station site through images only. (Kim Williams.)

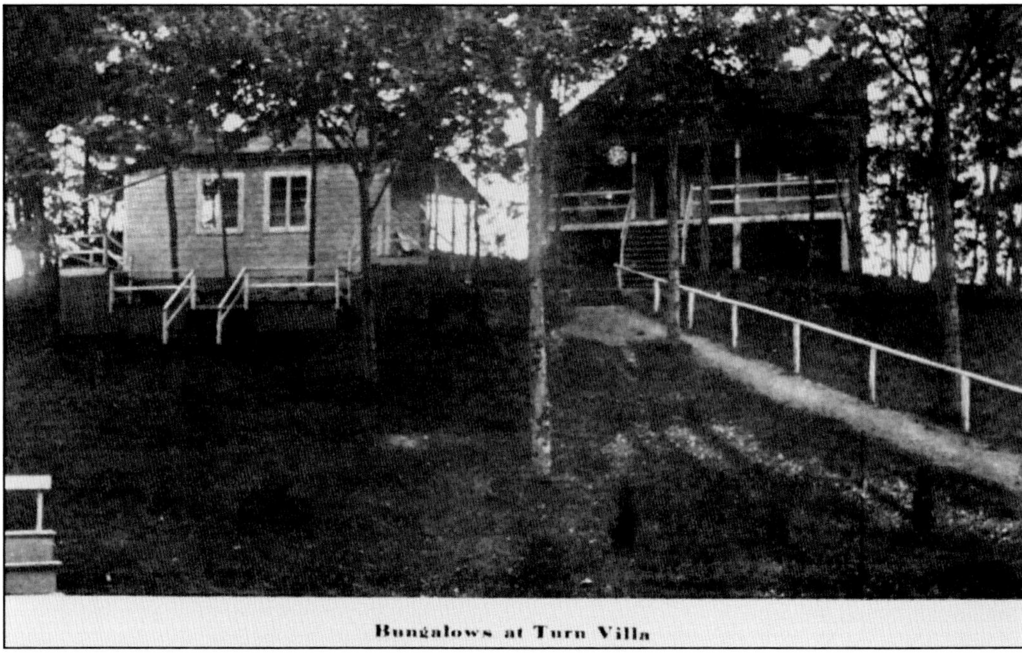

Bungalow living could vary. Marshalls Falls House styled its cabins at Lake Marshall as "dainty little summer homes," where residents enjoyed seclusion but still could take meals at the hotel. Bungalows at Echo Lake (pictured) could fit a family or group. Cabins at Forest Park and Tamiment's Sandyville were deliberately rustic. (Authors' collection.)

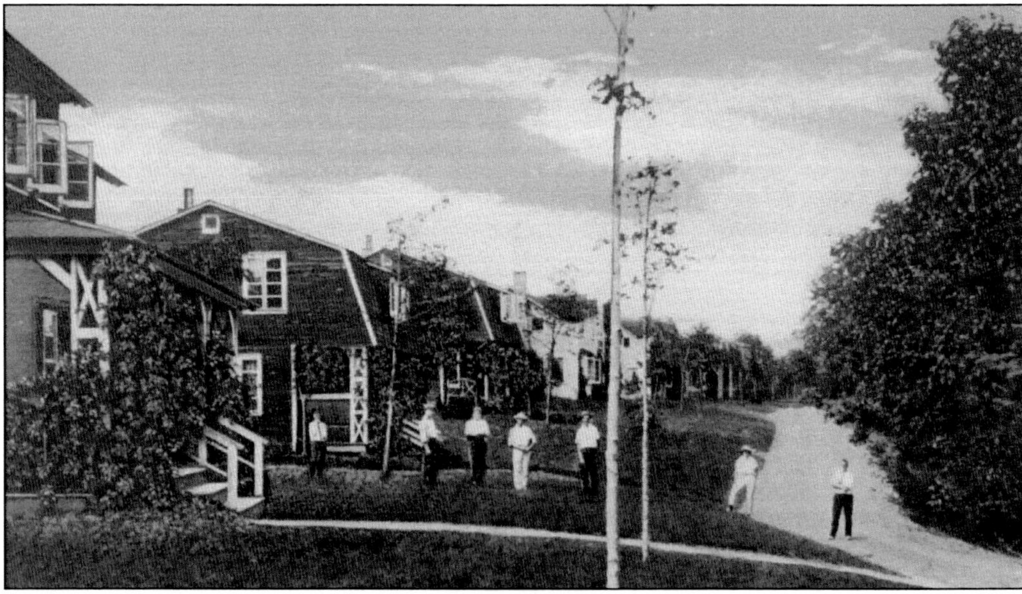

Arthur J. Shinn's Echo Lake Bungalows operated from 1909 to World War II on the edge of Echo Lake. One way to reach them was by rowboat from Echo Lake House. This card was stamped on the back by a World War I women's auxiliary in Times Square, New York, perhaps for servicemen seeking recreation accessible by rail. Shinn's property became Vacation Valley after World War II. (Authors' collection.)

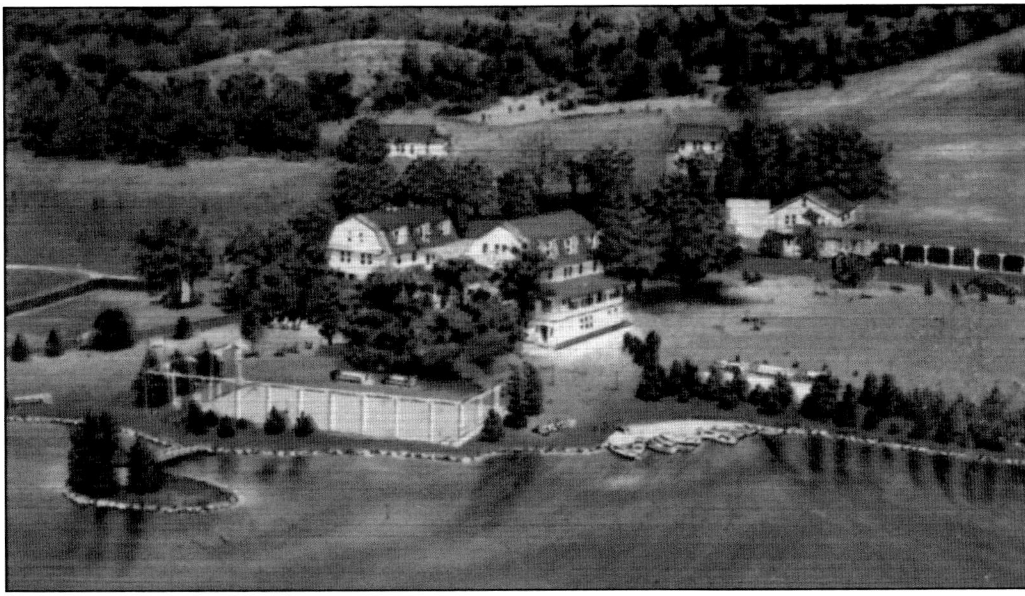

The railway ran past the bridge over Werry Lake to Sunnybrook without a stop. The resort expanded from the large original house (left) to a new duplicate wing (right) with connecting lower floors as well as outbuildings. The property became a Baptist camp in the 1960s, then part of the Lake of the Pines community. (Authors' collection.)

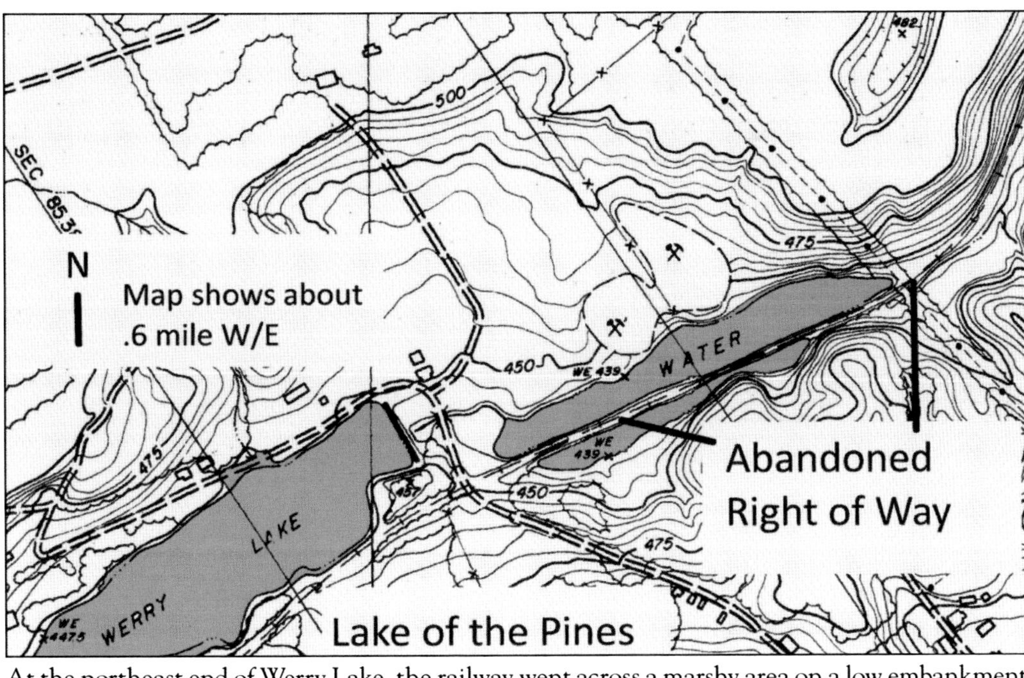

At the northeast end of Werry Lake, the railway went across a marshy area on a low embankment. By the time of this 1967 map, that area had become a body of water (see chapter 8). The railway then followed a creek to the village of Shoemakers, where the station was an old rail shed at today's Winona Falls Road. (DEWA.)

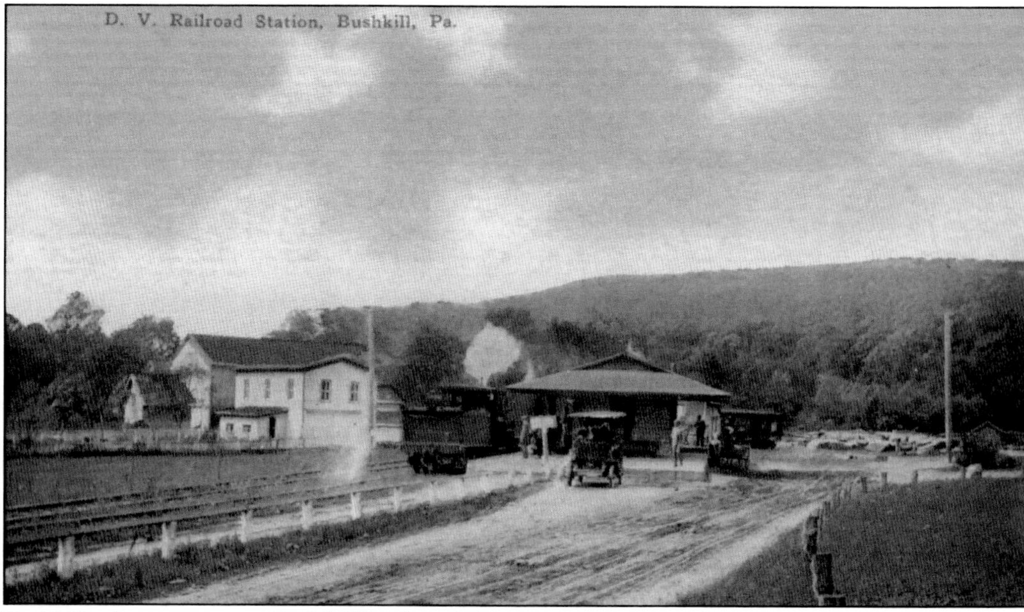

By 1908, the terminus at Bushkill had a solid new station. Here, the train has arrived, met by an auto-taxi, but the engine has not yet been shifted for the return run. At right are piles of lumber in the lumberyard; at left are farm buildings. (Authors' collection.)

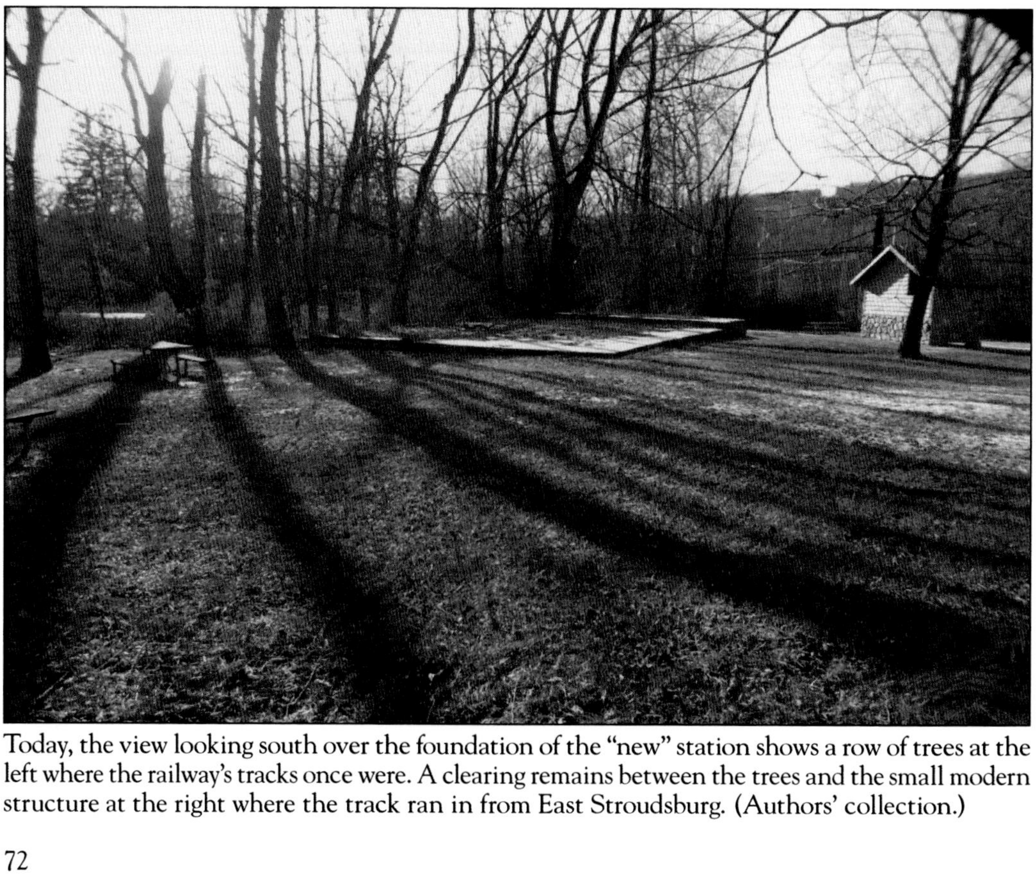

Today, the view looking south over the foundation of the "new" station shows a row of trees at the left where the railway's tracks once were. A clearing remains between the trees and the small modern structure at the right where the track ran in from East Stroudsburg. (Authors' collection.)

Six

Shoemakers and Bushkill

On Saturday, January 18, 1902, the *Stroudsburg Times* announced on page 1 the arrival of the first Delaware Valley Railway train in Bushkill that day. The bridge over Bush Kill had been completed only that morning. Regular service began in June.

The railway had come to a halt in the northwest corner of the intersection of Milford Road (Bushkill's Main Street) and the Road to Forest Park (today's Bushkill Falls Road). A wooden station would be in place that year; the terminus would also have a standpipe and a small enginehouse for a time. Main Street was only steps away.

This was a thriving village in the railway era. Peters Hotel produced its own electric power and shared it with other locations in town. Goods—lumber, produce, and milk—rolled into Bushkill from its hinterland of Pike and western Monroe Counties, all needing shipment south. Arriving for the village by rail were coal and ice, goods for the general store, an occasional four-footed passenger, and at least a carload a day of food for the resorts. There were 500 hotel rooms in and near the village and space for 300 more people at Forest Park. Horse-drawn carriages, auto-taxis, and, in time, buses shuttled arriving passengers to their hotels and farther north to Dingmans Ferry and Milford. Bushkill could even lay claim to the railway's first train-auto fender bender (no one was hurt) in the middle of the Main Street crossing.

For those staying right in town, there was the "Wanamaker's of Bushkill," Nyce Brothers General Store (later Turn & Cook). "Renew the days of your youth," advertising invited in 1902. "Come in and talk politics with us just as you did before you moved to the city."

Today, more than any other stop on the railway line, Bushkill retains a sprinkling of structures from those busy times. What would a railway traveler recognize today? The home of the Peters family (later a gift shop and then a craft guild store); the Dutch Reformed church (now Bushkill Outreach), behind which are the coal bins; perhaps the old Bushkill Post Office (now vacant); and the Turn & Cook Store (now a lunch spot and market called the Roost).

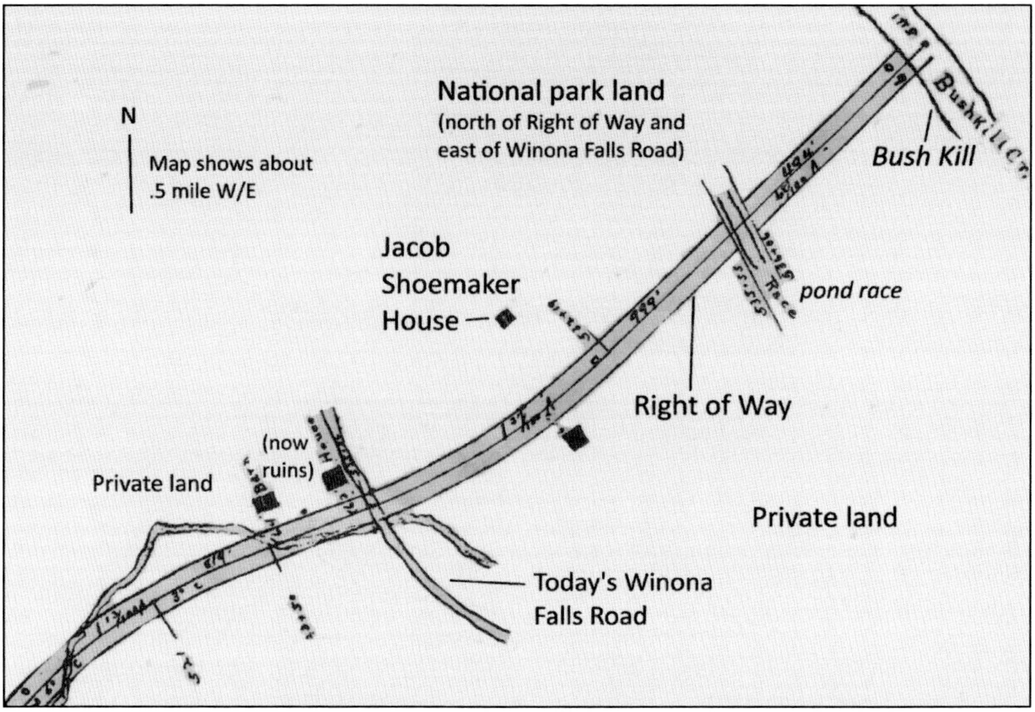

Emerging from forest, the railway reached the village of Shoemakers near Jacob Shoemaker's stone house (see chapter 9) on today's Winona Falls Road about a quarter mile north of the village center on Milford Road. The Bushkill-bound train then rode northeast on an embankment to Bush Kill. (MCRD.)

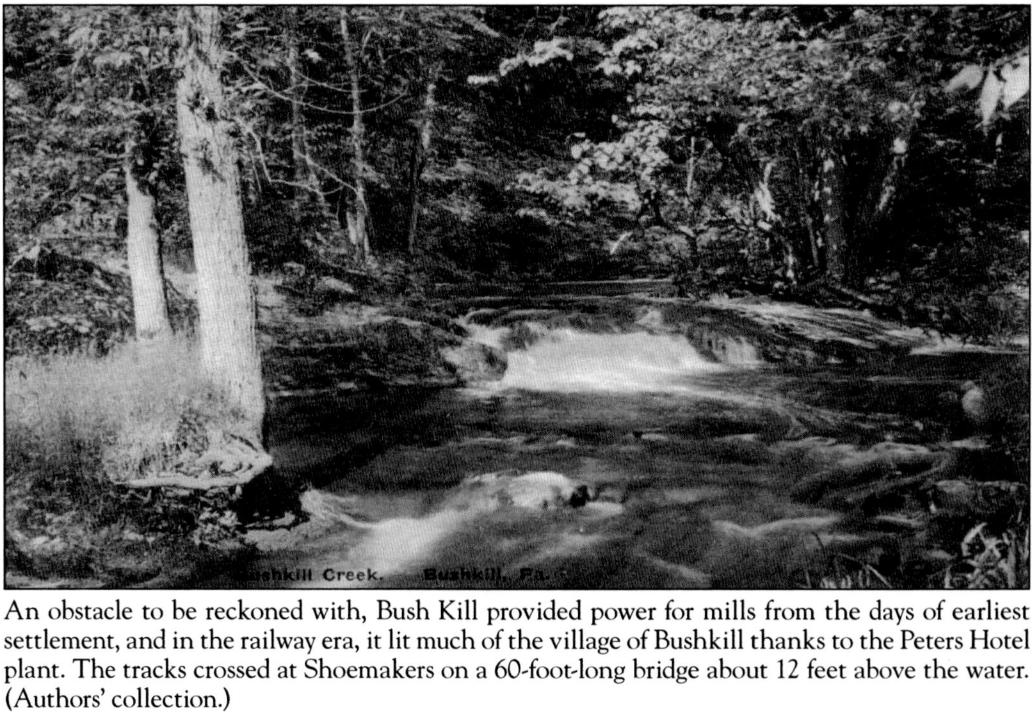

An obstacle to be reckoned with, Bush Kill provided power for mills from the days of earliest settlement, and in the railway era, it lit much of the village of Bushkill thanks to the Peters Hotel plant. The tracks crossed at Shoemakers on a 60-foot-long bridge about 12 feet above the water. (Authors' collection.)

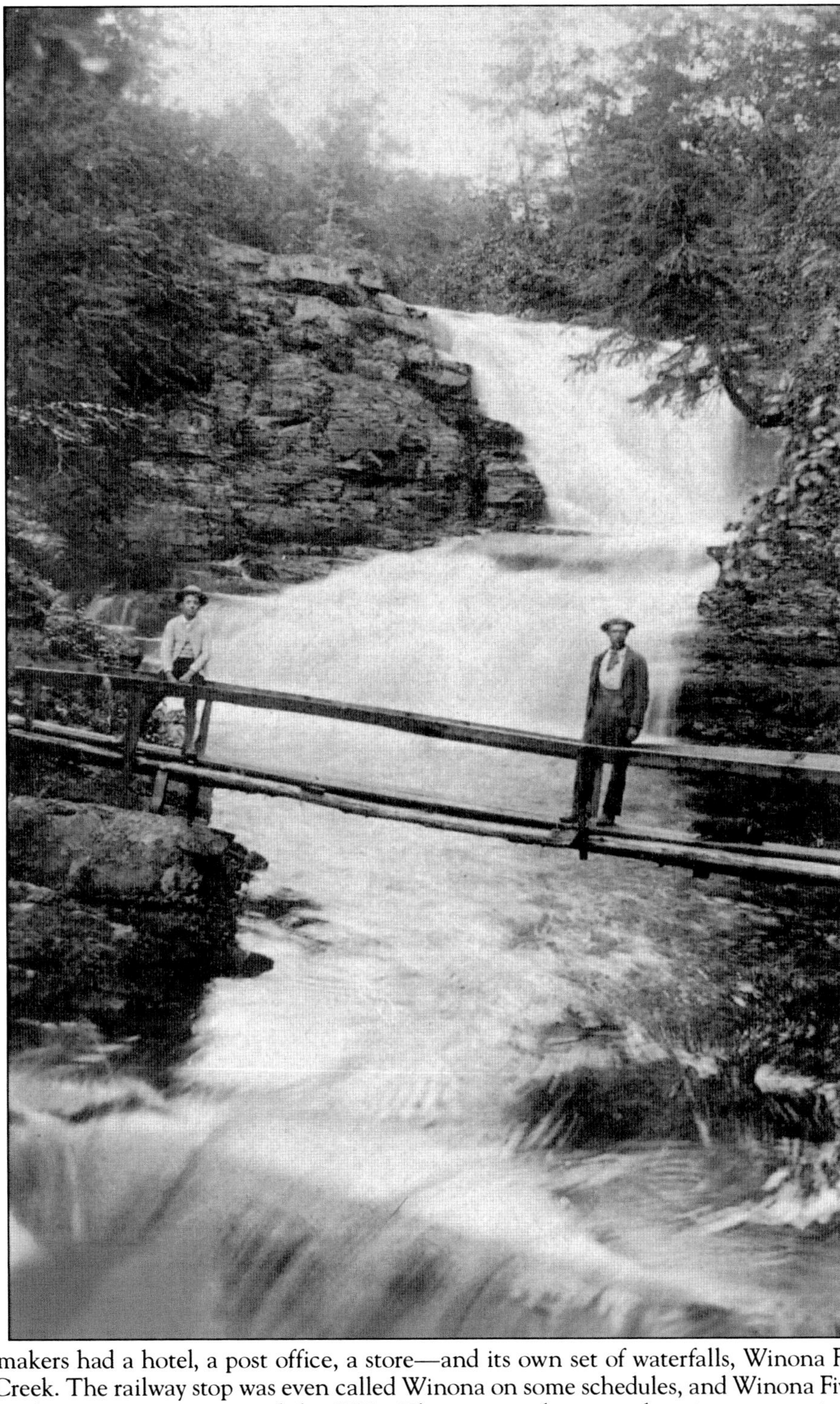

Shoemakers had a hotel, a post office, a store—and its own set of waterfalls, Winona Falls on Saw Creek. The railway stop was even called Winona on some schedules, and Winona Five Falls remained an area attraction until the 1970s. The property became a housing community in the 1980s. (BLTHS.)

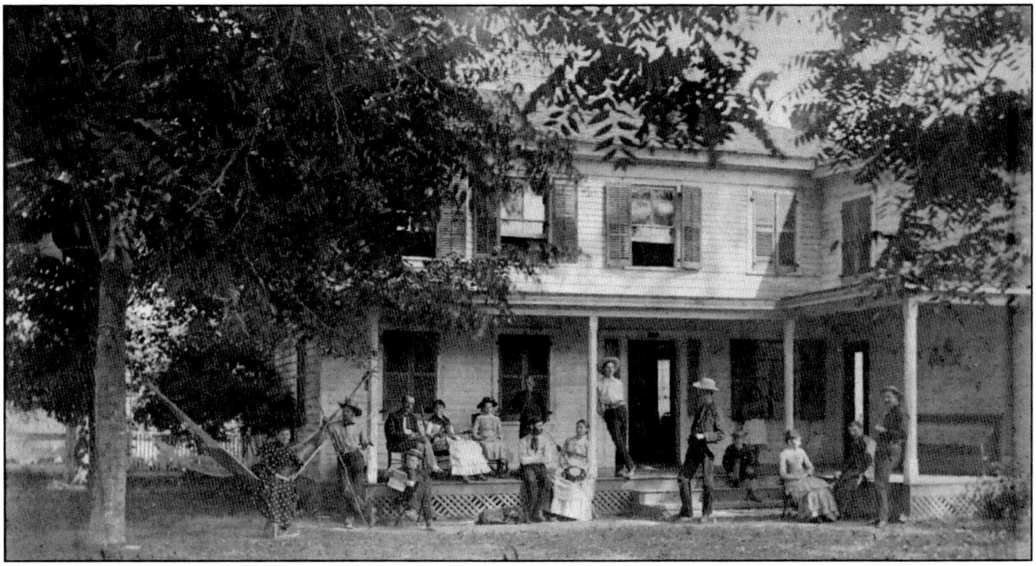

The Maples on Creek Road opened its doors to guests in 1900 and was managed by the Cook family until the 1970s. It served 25 guests, many returning every year. Its five acres included a garden and campsites and a cabin along Bush Kill. (BLTHS.)

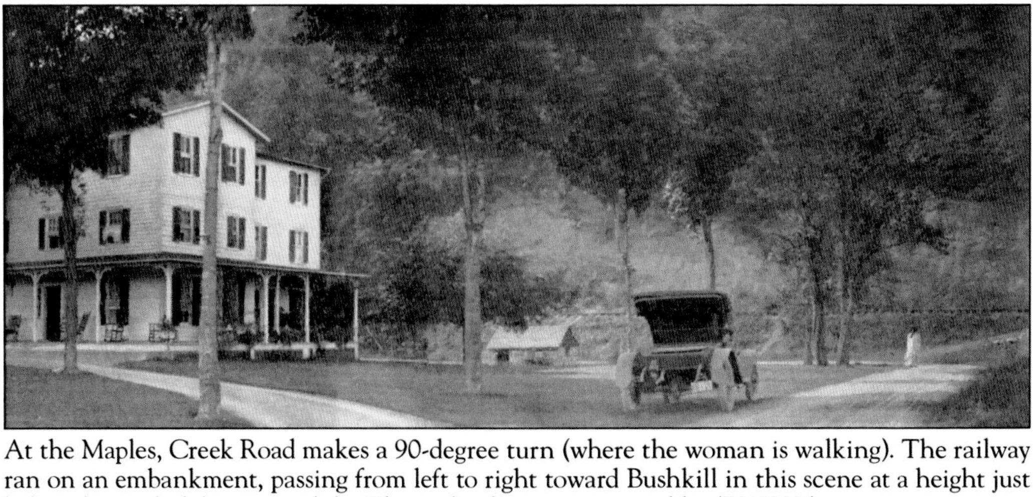

At the Maples, Creek Road makes a 90-degree turn (where the woman is walking). The railway ran on an embankment, passing from left to right toward Bushkill in this scene at a height just below the roof of the automobile. The ends of ties are just visible. (BLTHS.)

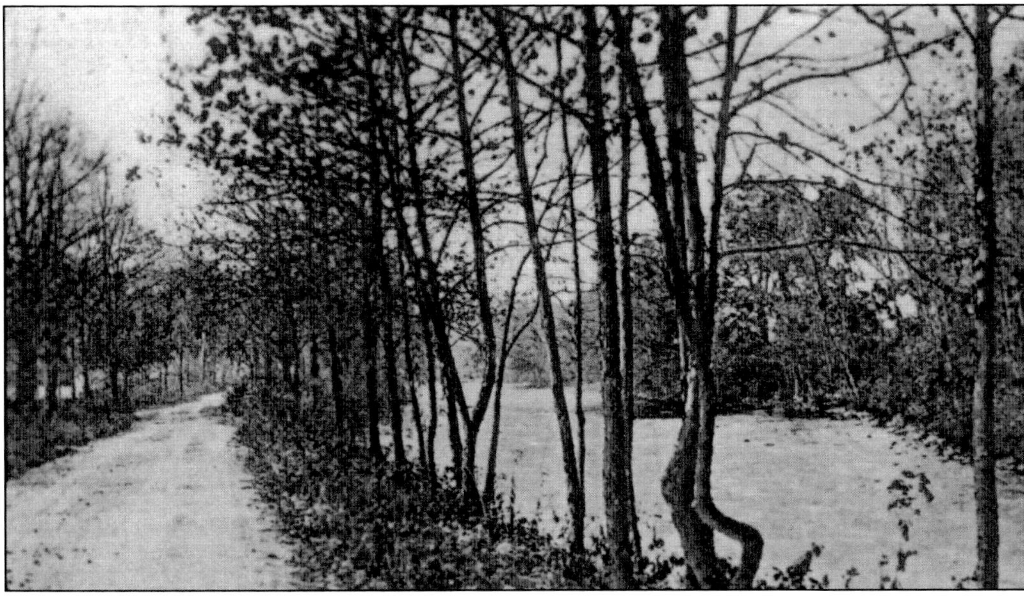

The Maples property extended southward to the edge of Bush Kill, where camping sites and a cabin were offered for guests. There was a swinging bridge from Creek Road to the Maple Grove part of Bushkill. The less daring could walk down the road a half mile or so to the center of town. (Authors' collection.)

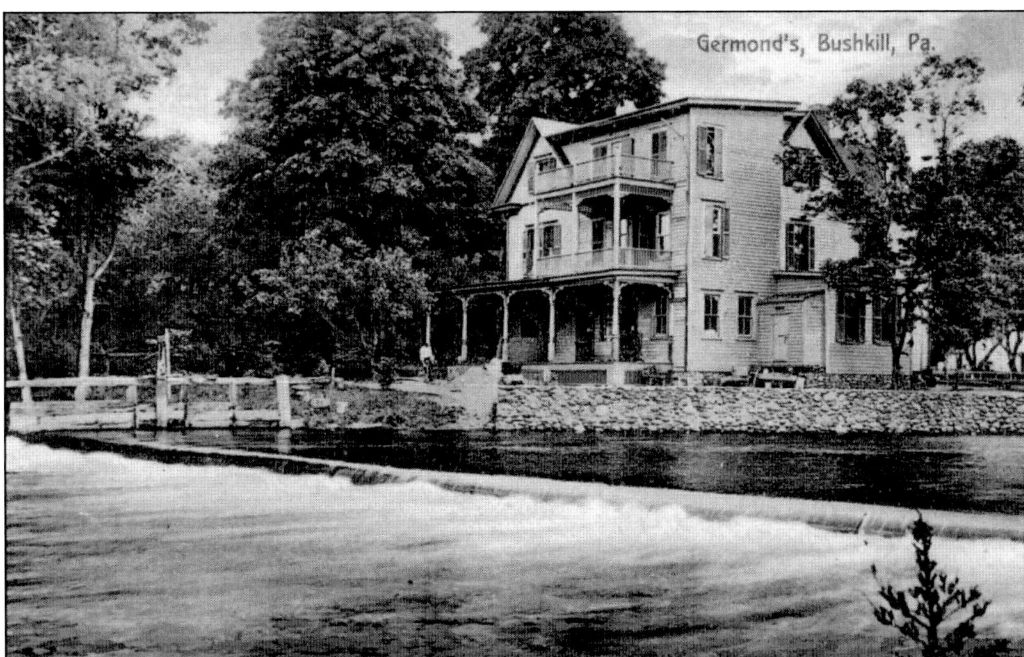

Germond's stood between Bush Kill and Milford Road at the dam that channeled water to the Peters electric plant. Renowned from 1915 for its French cuisine, over time Germond's also offered hotel rooms, cabins, a solarium, a playground, and swimming and fishing in the stream. Reputedly, some customers would arrive just for dinner and an overnight stay. (Kathleen Sandt.)

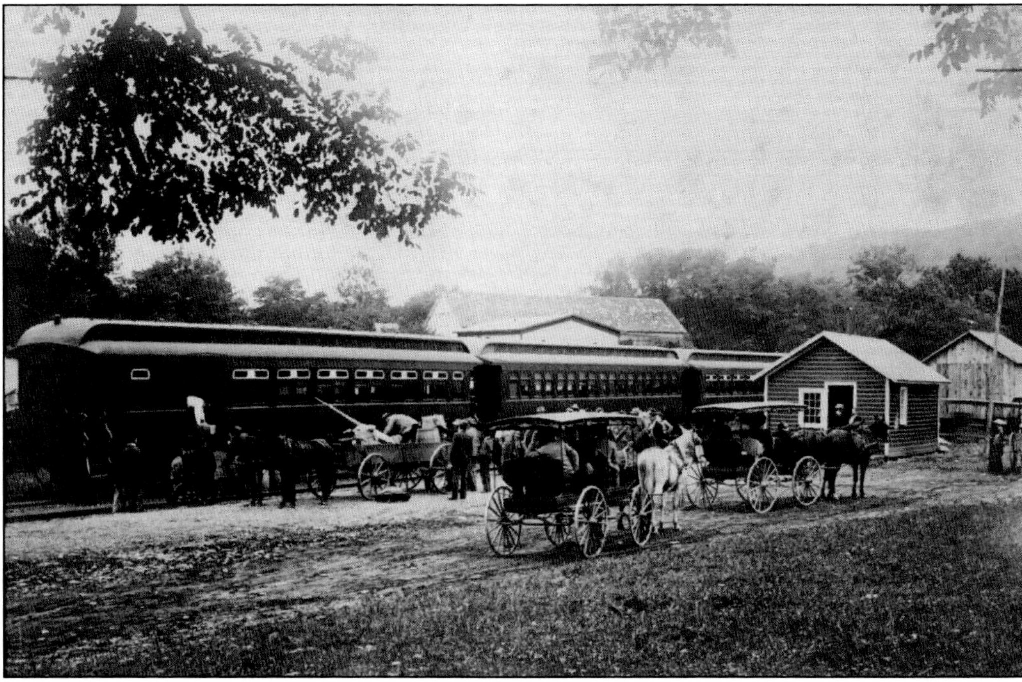

Bushkill's first railway station was a wooden structure and detached depot with a platform also of wood, in use from about 1902 to 1908. In this early view, auto-taxis are notably absent. The engine may be delivering or picking up coal at the Peters yard on the other side of Milford Road or repositioning itself on the runaround track. (PCHist.)

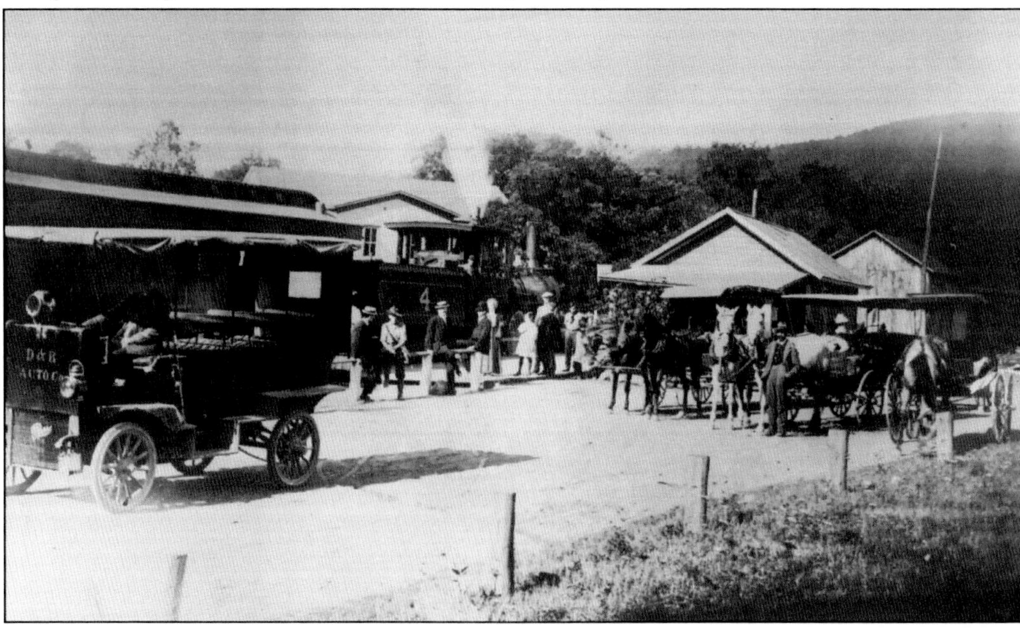

Milton Yetter's D&B (Dingmans and Bushkill) Auto Company, at left, has joined horse-drawn liveries to bring passengers to this departing run from the first station. The young man in uniform just to the left of the tender's "4" may have dropped off Scouts from a brotherhood camp such as St. John's in Bushkill. (PHMC/RRMPa.)

Running year-round, the railway braved the storms and wintry mix of the Poconos. Engines occasionally became snowbound, and at least twice the resourceful railway deployed sleighs to get its passengers to their destinations. (PCHist.)

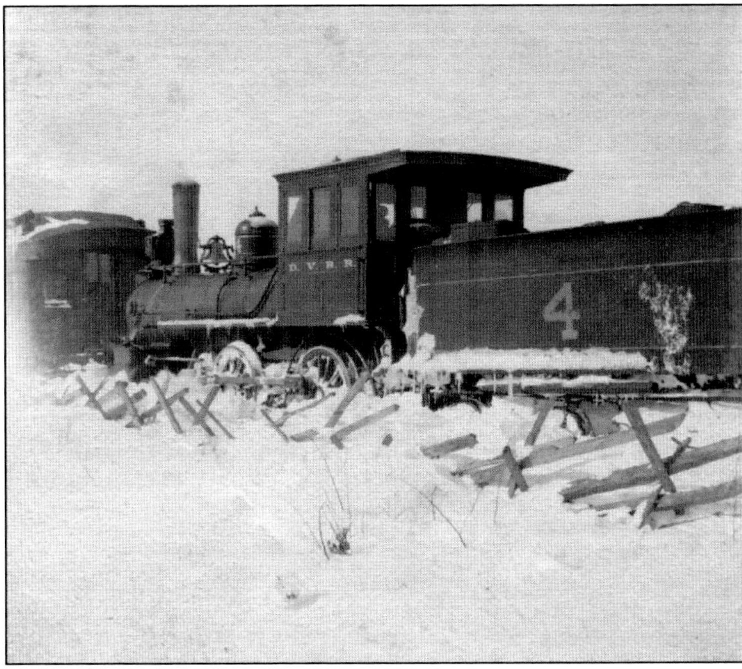

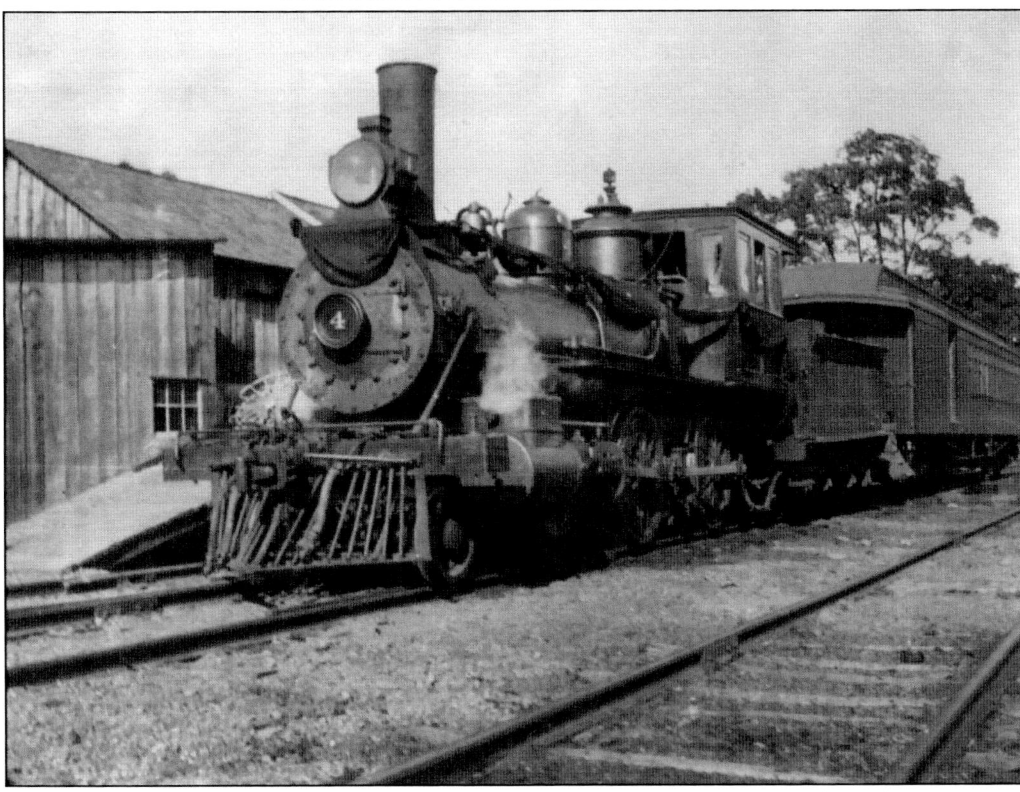

Engine No. 4 at Bushkill wears mourning in August or September 1911. The sad occasion was probably the death of Milton Yetter, who presided over the heyday of the railway from 1904 until his death on August 28, 1911. (MCHA.)

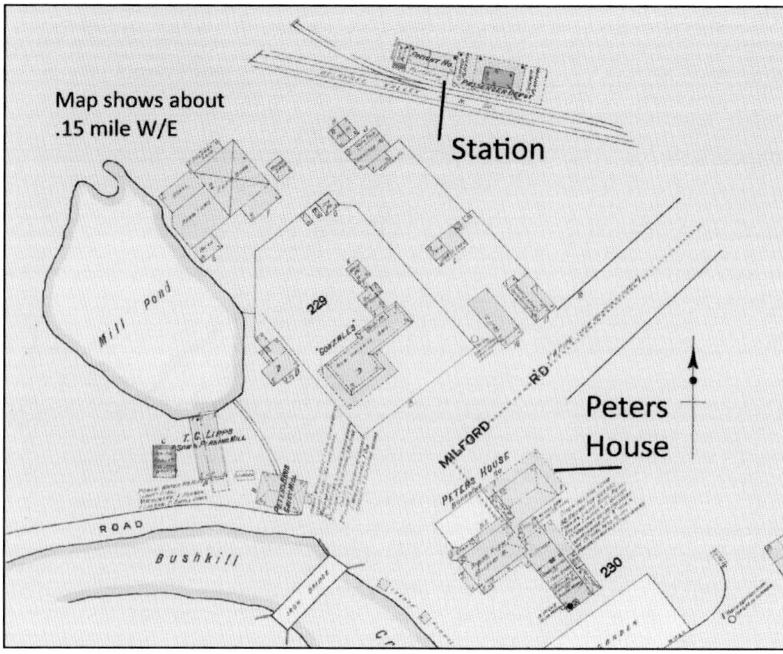

This Sanborn Insurance map of 1912 shows the village center and insured buildings, many belonging to the Peters family. The new station, its freight depot, and its main and runaround tracks show at the top. The curved spur is probably to the lumberyard. (PSU.)

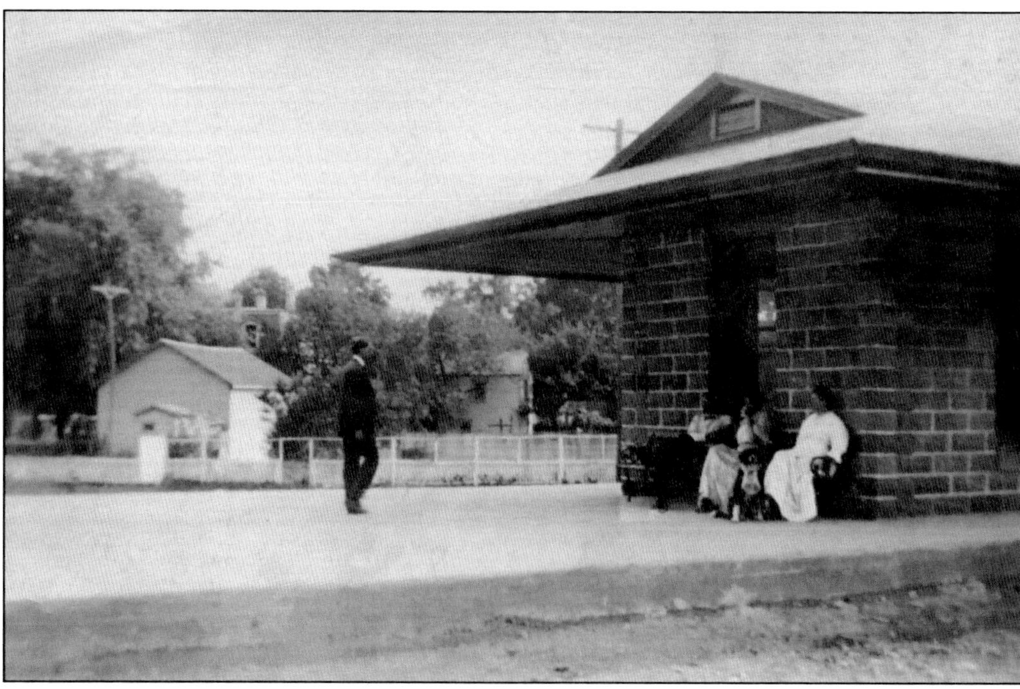

The new Bushkill station was built of concrete block on a 28-by-85-foot concrete platform more than 30 inches thick. The platform remains today. This view looks south to Main Street. (PCHist.)

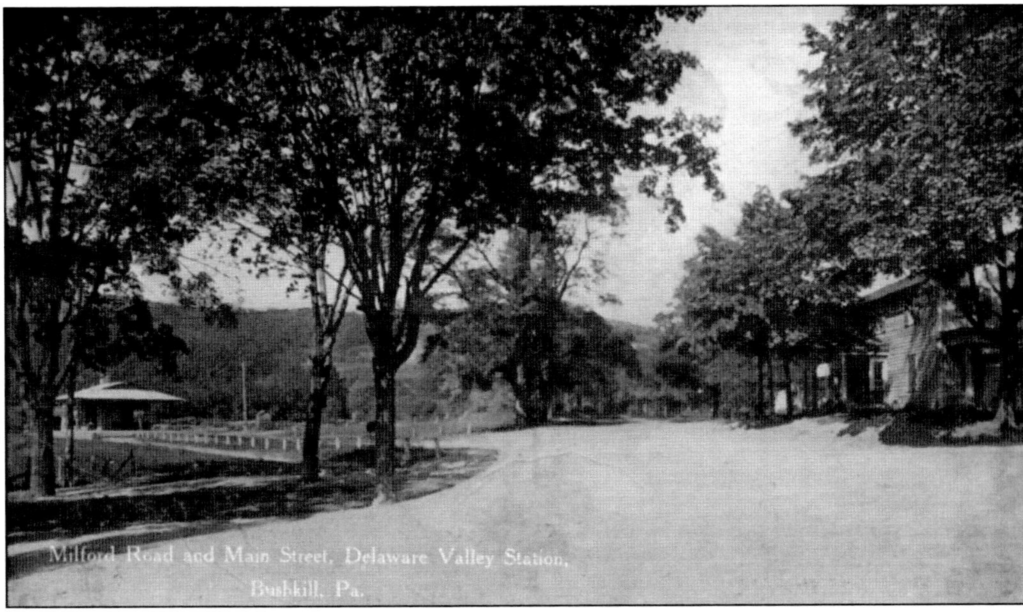

In this view looking north up the Road to Forest Park (now Bushkill Falls Road), the railway station is at left, and Main Street runs across the foreground. The Peter family home is at right. It was used by the family until 1918 and then became a teahouse and more recently a gift shop and a craft guild store. It still stands today. (BLTHS.)

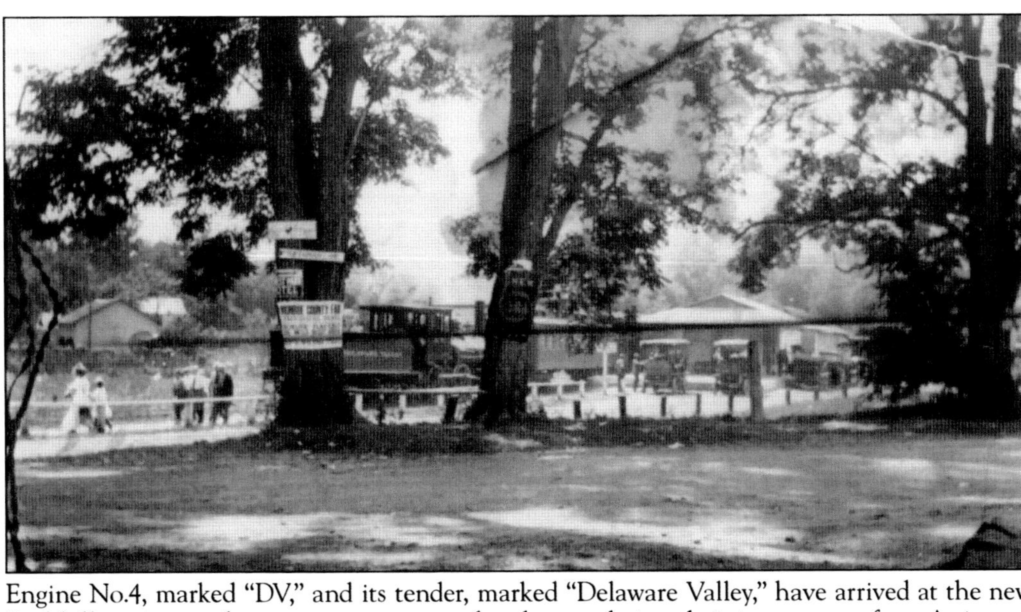

Engine No.4, marked "DV," and its tender, marked "Delaware Valley," have arrived at the new Bushkill station, and some passengers are already completing their journeys on foot. A sign on the tree promotes the 1911 Monroe County Fair in Stroudsburg. (BLTHS.)

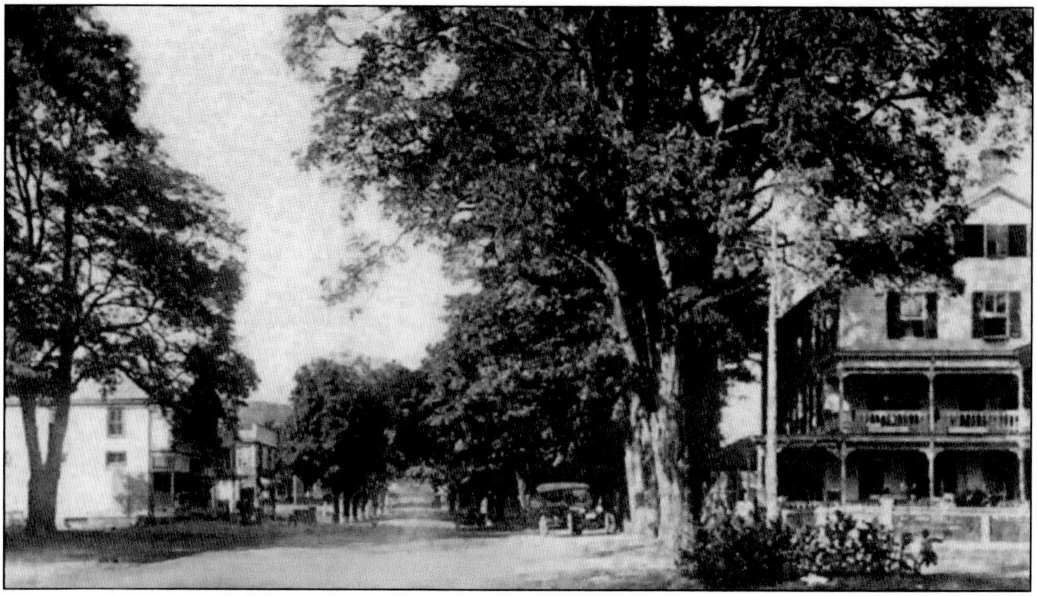

In a view looking northeast up Main Street (Milford Road) from Peters Hotel (right), the crossbuck sign is just visible on the right side of the road where the railway crossed Milford Road as it ran to the bins at the Peters coalyard. (BLTHS.)

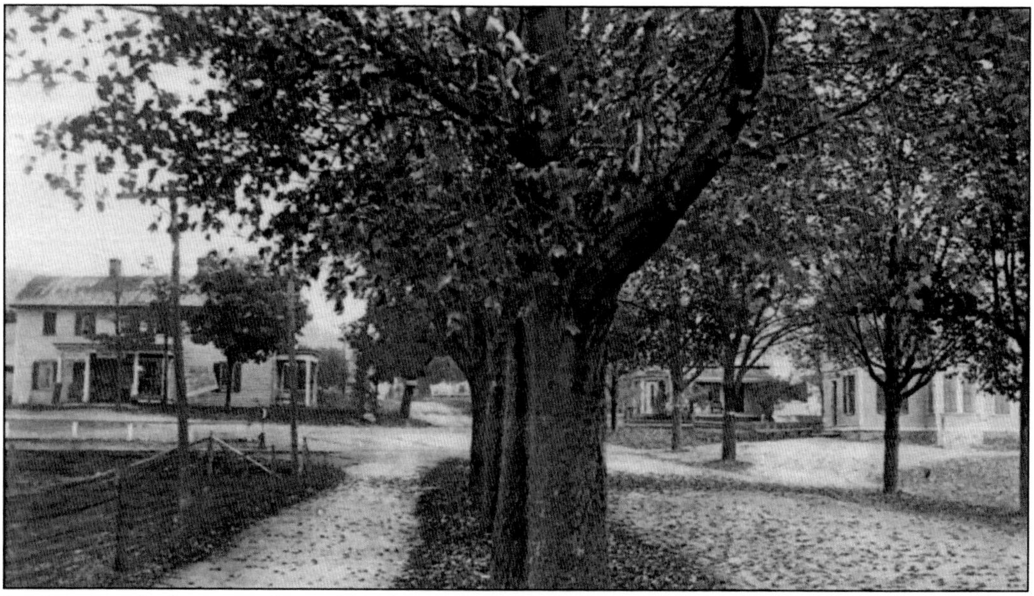

In this view looking northeast from a point on Main Street that is closer to the crossing, a few posts of the railway station's white fencing are visible at left, and on the far side of today's Bushkill Falls Road stands the Peter family home. The track to the coalyard ran between the houses on the right (southeast) side of Main Street. (Authors' collection.)

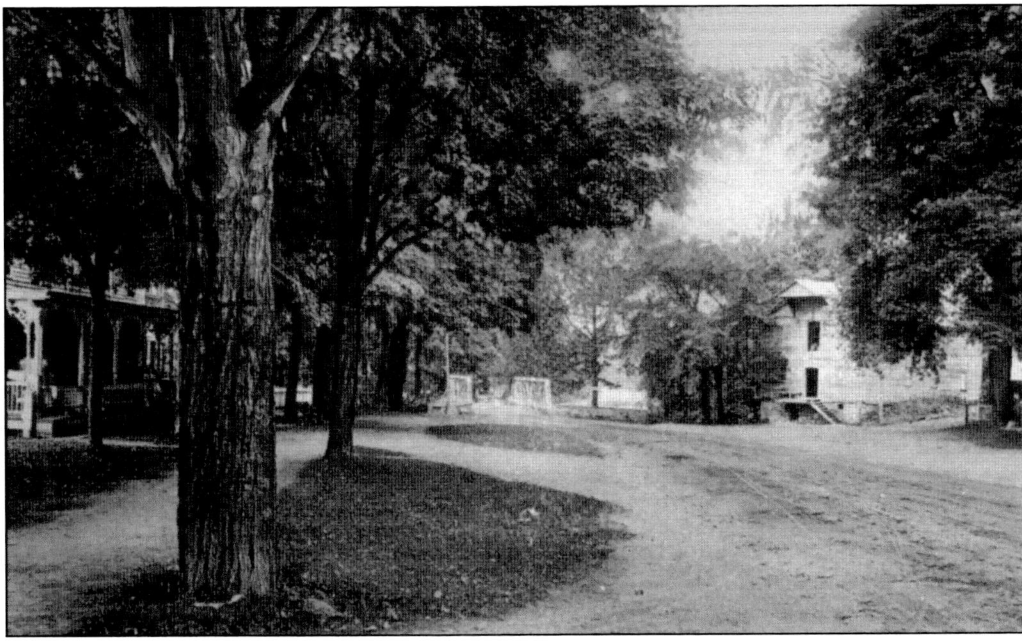

This view looks southwest down Main Street from Peters Hotel (left). In the center distance is the bridge over Bush Kill, and at the right of the bridge is the mill. Peters Hotel built many facilities in the area on the right. Perhaps best remembered is the annex building that eventually housed the A&P market. (Authors' collection.)

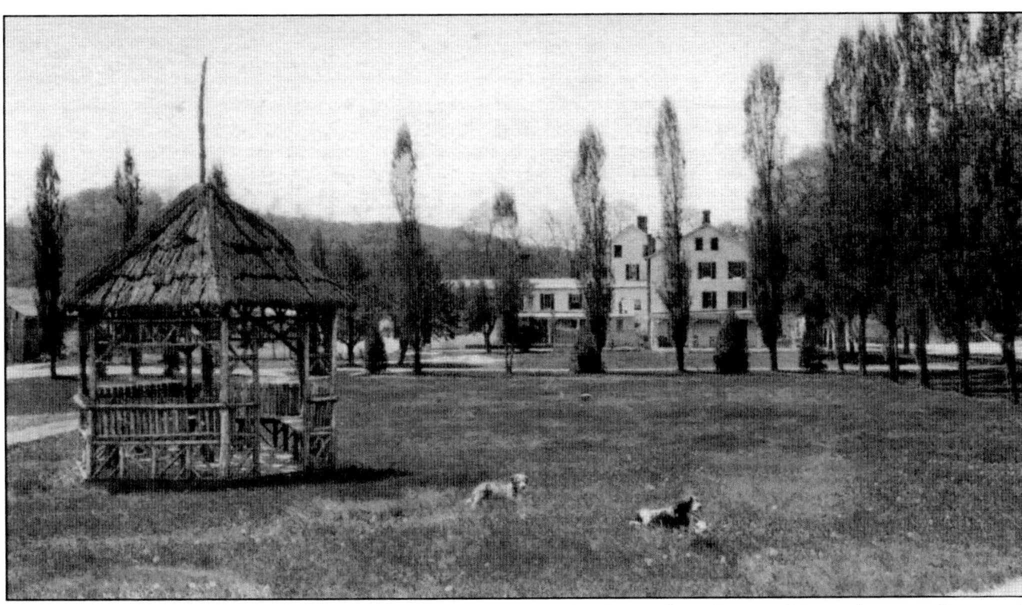

If the engineer looked to the south as he crossed Milford Road to the coal bins, he saw the north side of the Peters Hotel complex, which extended along Bush Kill to the Delaware River. Dating from about 1750, the hotel was remodeled in 1900 to offer 75 rooms and expanded again around 1917 with an annex. (Authors' collection.)

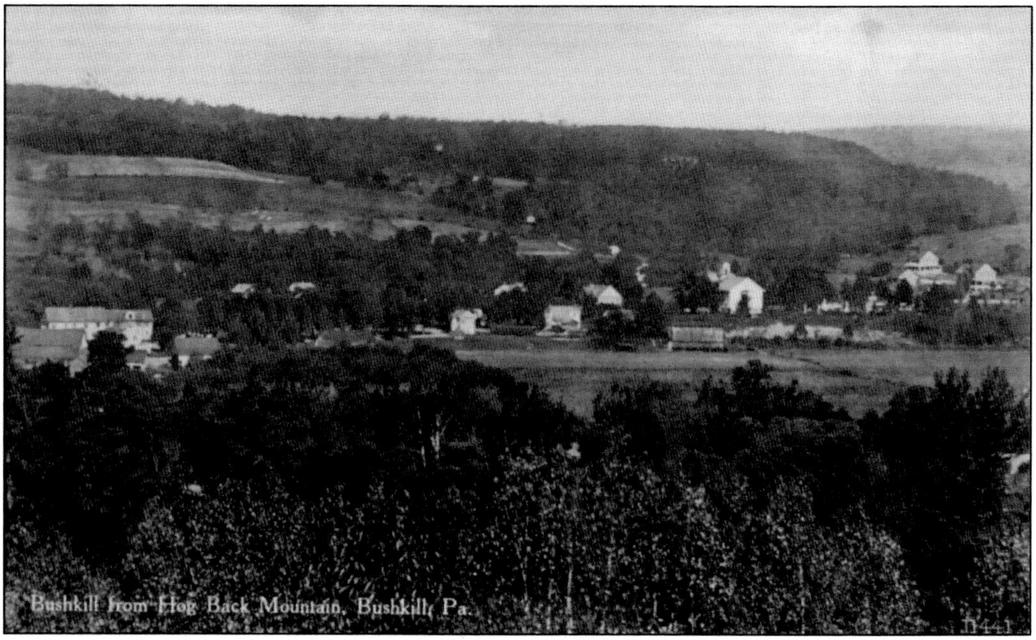

Seen from Hog Back Mountain, the Bushkill Dutch Reformed Church faces away towards Milford Road. On the near side of the church is the natural shelf where the dinkey stopped to drop its shipments of coal. The bins, or "pockets," were at the base of the shelf behind the unpainted shed in the middle ground, perhaps part of the coalyard itself. (Kathleen Sandt.)

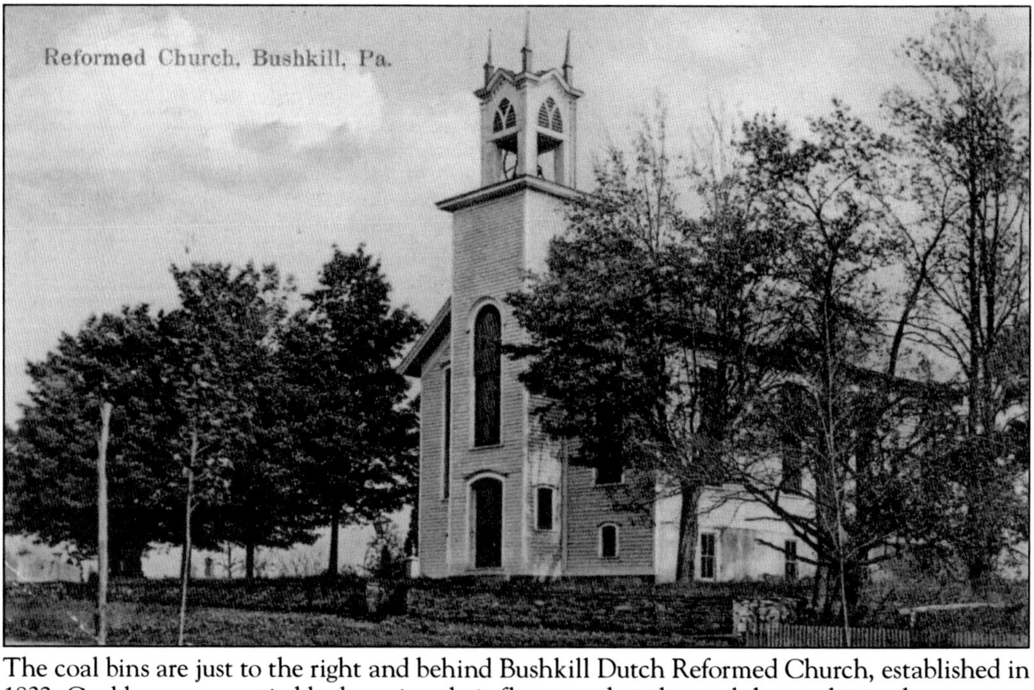

The coal bins are just to the right and behind Bushkill Dutch Reformed Church, established in 1832. Coal hoppers emptied by lowering their floors so that the coal dropped into the concrete bins, hopefully not during the sermon. The congregation has moved, and the buildings are now a community outreach center. (Authors' collection.)

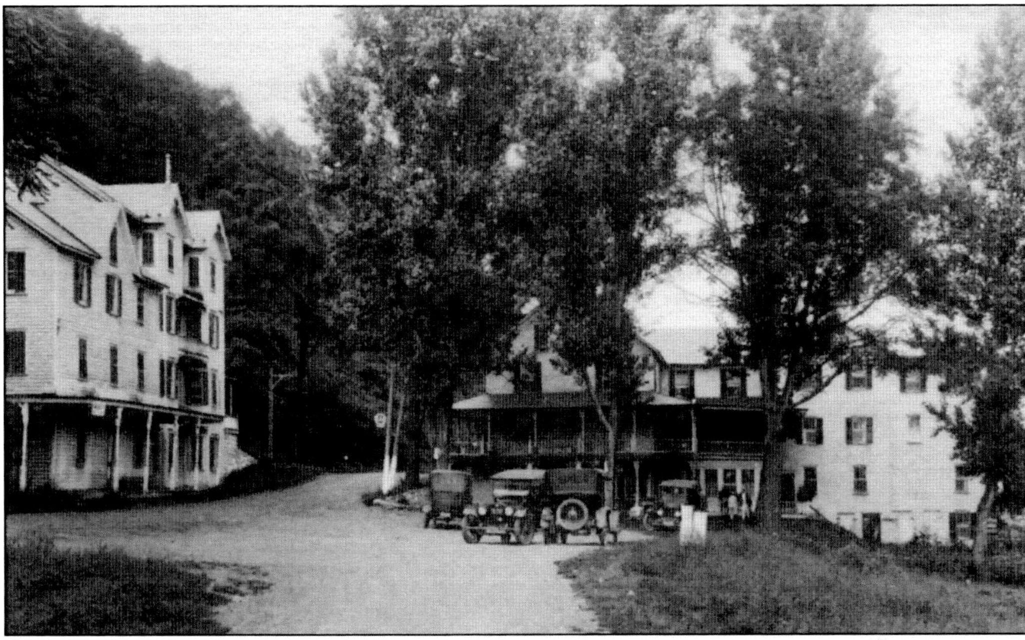

John H. Cook's Riverside Hotel (pictured) was on Milford Road two miles north of the railway station. It could serve 200 guests, rivalling Peters Hotel in capacity. On level land along the river, the tract yielded important American Indian artifacts in the 1970s. The buildings are gone; the property is an access point to the river. (Authors' collection.)

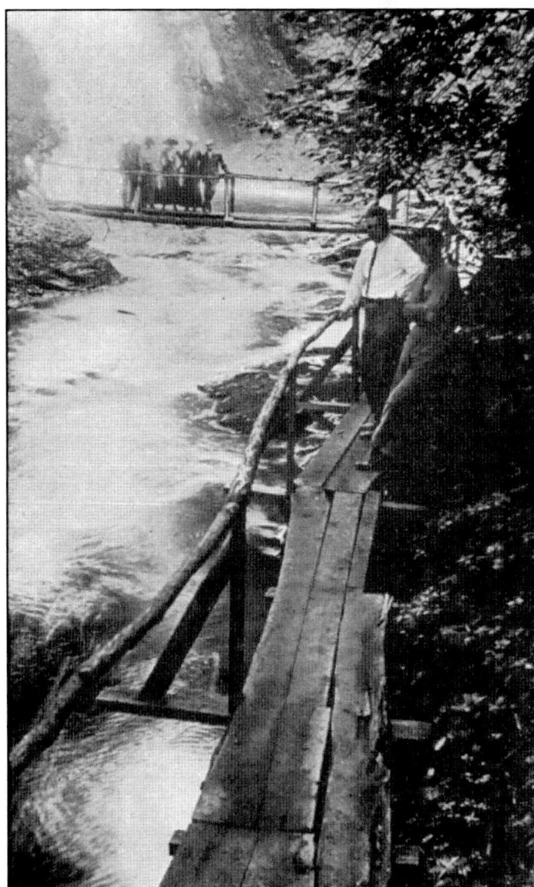

The most famous attraction of Bushkill in the railway era was Bushkill Falls, opened in 1904 by Charles Peters, who also established the Peters Hotel. The 300 acres offered a series of glens and waterfalls "in the spray," somewhat tamed for the visitor by bridges and walkways. Modern visitors can be assured that the paths meet quite different safety standards today. (Authors' collection.)

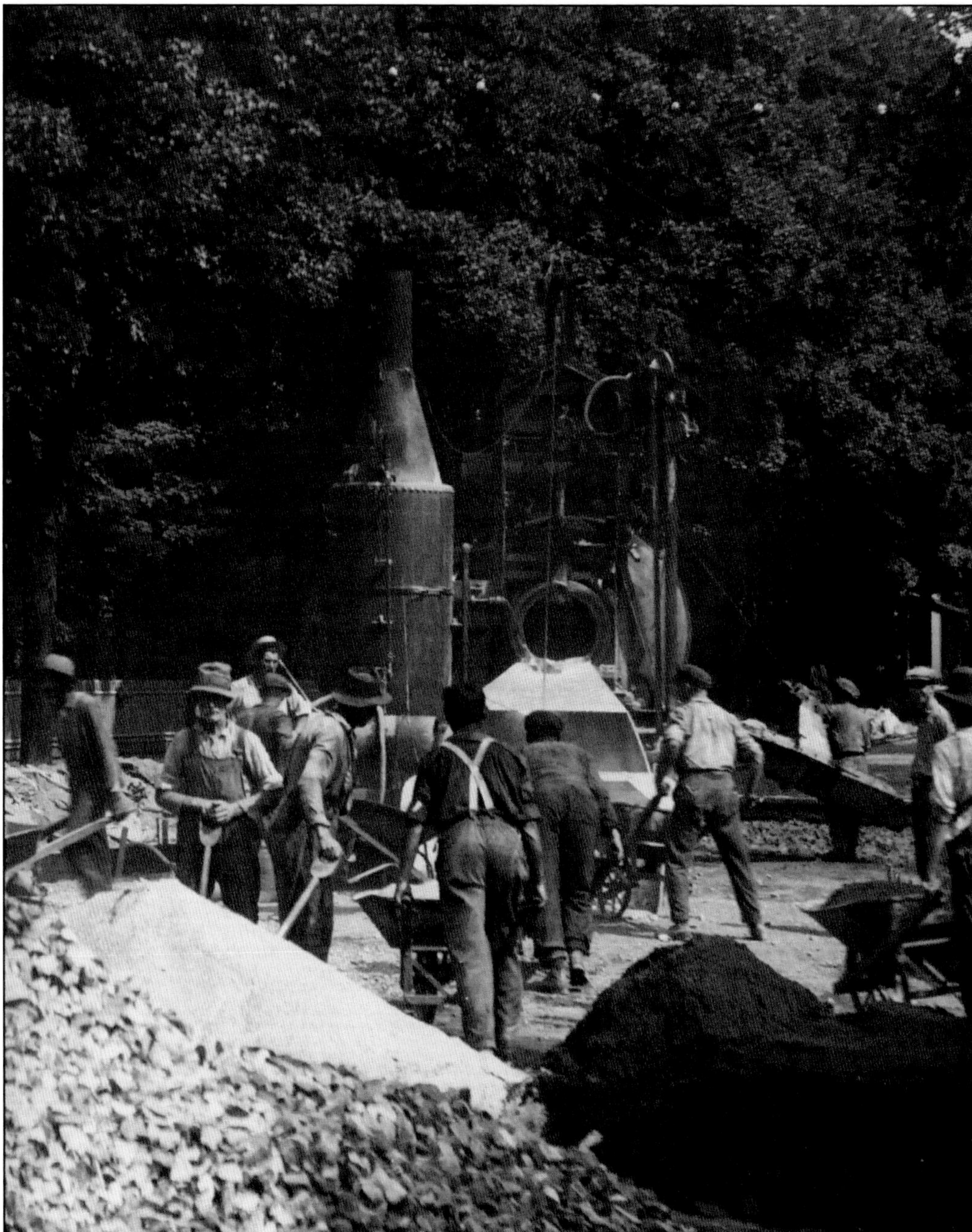

Milford photographer James Alfred Myer, working from 1880 onward, captured the beauty of Pike County as well as scenes of everyday life, such as these pavers at work. Paving projects along what is today Route 209 provided unskilled work for residents and, ironically, a brief boom in rail freight before the automobile took its toll. (PCHist.)

Seven

Dreams and Realities

As buses moved the vacationers and trucks picked up the freight, the "dinkey" remained what it was—in railroad parlance, a train of few cars and short route. It became an early victim of nationwide changes in transportation and travel. Mighty Pennsylvania Railroad, once the world's largest public corporation, was bankrupt by 1970 after merging with New York Central. Erie Lackawanna (a merger of Erie and DL&W), Central of New Jersey, and Lehigh Valley Railroads all filed for bankruptcy by 1973.

The railway was also late in getting started and never reached its hoped-for markets outside the valley. Perhaps it believed its prospectus that there was "no competition whatever" in the valley, yet in the early years of the century, resorts were already advertising facilities for "auto parties." There was no *rail* competition, as it turned out.

The era of the railway was fading into the age of asphalt and the automobile. The number of miles of paved roads in the country had doubled from 1914 to 1926. Paving projects on Milford Road in 1927, 1936, and 1961 improved 10 miles of the road outside of East Stroudsburg, and buses and trucks began to run along Milford Road (Route 209) parallel to the railway route.

Countering with its own bus line, the railway turned a profit, but paved highways soon allowed buses from New York City and Philadelphia to travel direct to the valley resorts, bypassing the local bus and rail systems entirely. The railway's bus ridership fell by 70 percent, and as freight traffic was already dwindling, this was a fatal blow. It was also a portent of a future in which planes would fly vacationers from big city airports completely over the Delaware Valley to resorts hundreds of miles distant. Americans, given a newer, faster, more convenient option, embraced it.

In May 1937, the railway filed to abandon the line; and on September 2, 1937, permission was granted. There was little notice in the press; the *Record* in Stroudsburg that Labor Day weekend was preoccupied with all roads leading into Monroe being "clogged with a continuous stream of cars." On September 22, the railway's assets were sold to the trustee acting for the shareholders, and a moderate article in the local paper noted the transaction. The following spring, the tracks were pulled up; it seems that only an amateur snapshot recorded the event. Today, only glimpses of the right-of-way reveal how two iron rails once connected these people and these places in the brief era of the railway.

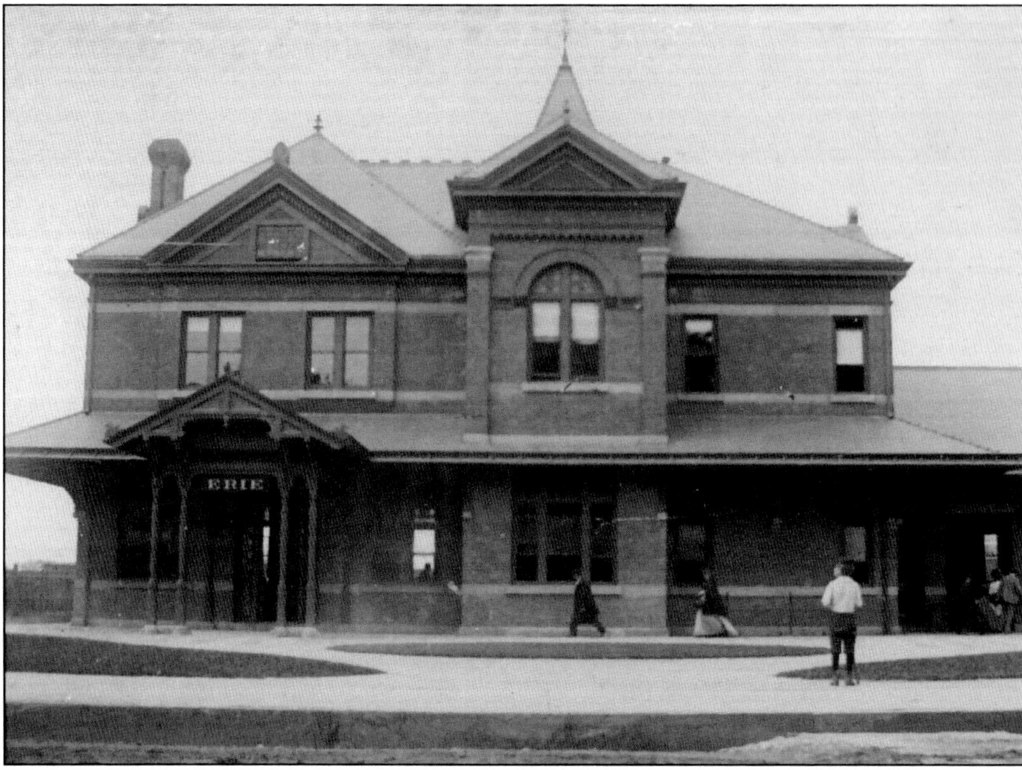

The railway was first envisioned as stretching from the slate and ice industries around Saylorsburg, 12 miles southwest of East Stroudsburg, to the Erie Terminal (pictured) in Port Jervis, New York. It was late to enter these markets: slate would decline with the manufacture of asbestos; the demand for ice, with electric refrigeration. (PCHist.)

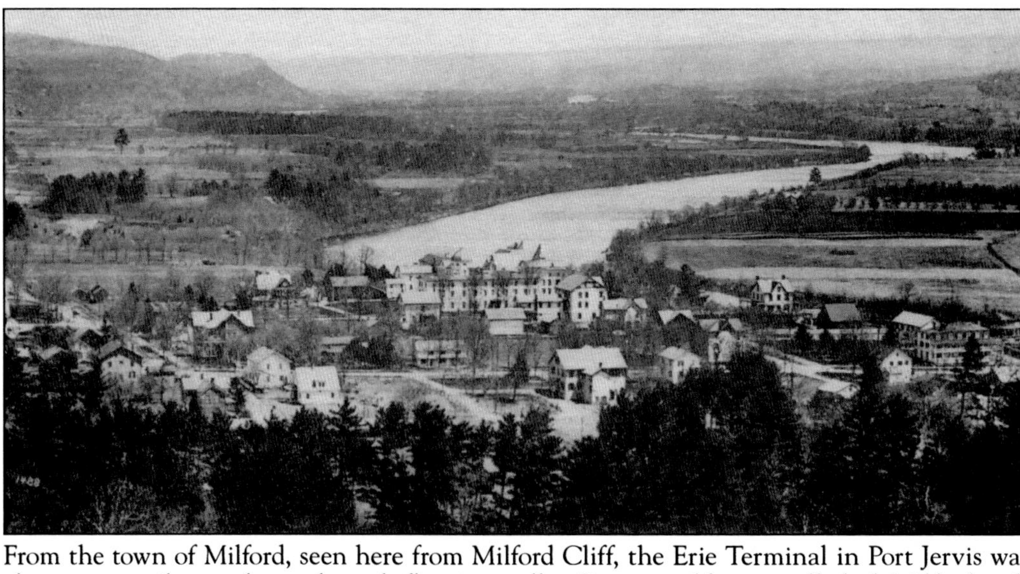

From the town of Milford, seen here from Milford Cliff, the Erie Terminal in Port Jervis was about seven miles northeast through flat river valley. Buses would eventually link Milford with Matamoras and Port Jervis and with Bushkill and East Stroudsburg to the southwest. Rail service still runs from Port Jervis to New York City. (Authors' collection.)

The Slate Belt is one of the country's richest slate deposits; its quarries once supplied half the nation's school slates and pencils. Track was laid from Wind Gap to Saylorsburg, but the route surveyed to East Stroudsburg was never built. Slate deposits explored near Shoemakers were not worth quarrying. (Slate Belt Heritage Center.)

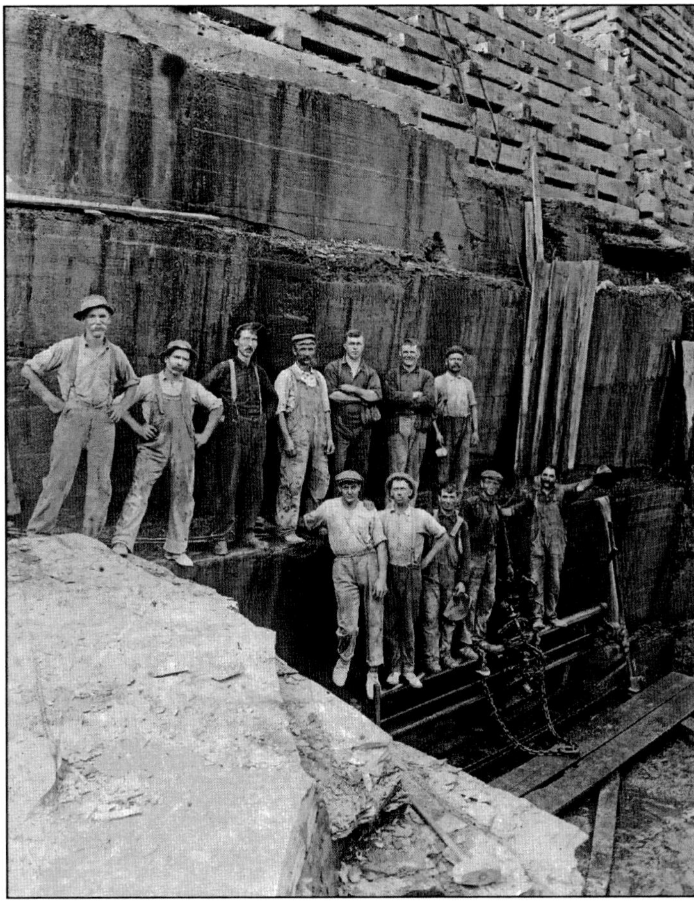

By 1915, businessmen were eyeing Echo, Coolbaugh, and Forest Lakes for ice export, but along the railway route, ice harvesting remained largely a local enterprise, as shown in this Appalachian village scene. In the 1930s, the dinkey was actually bringing ice northward to the resorts. (Anderson University and Church of God Archives.)

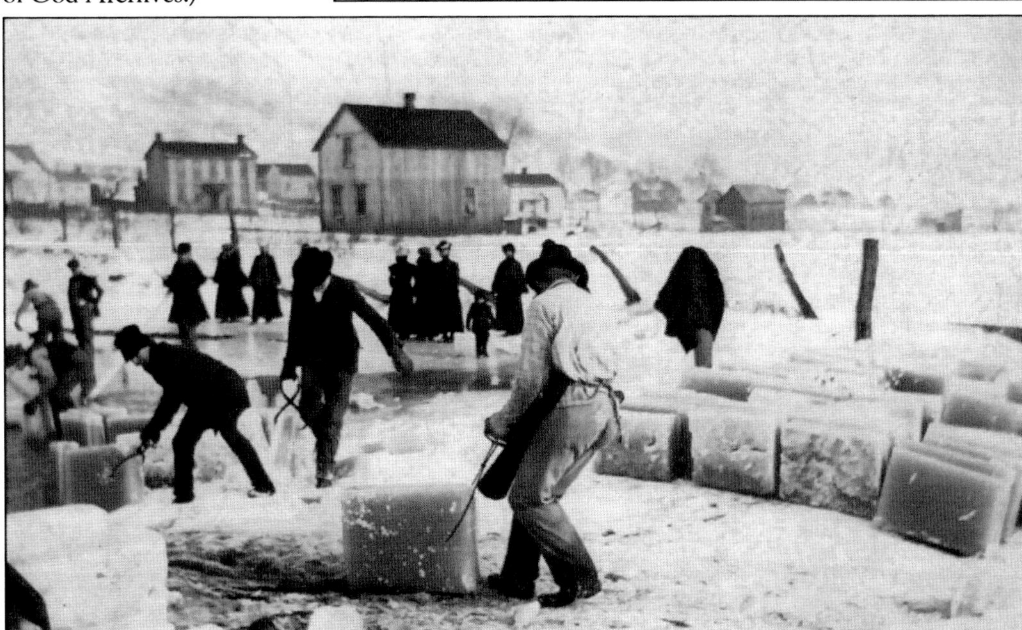

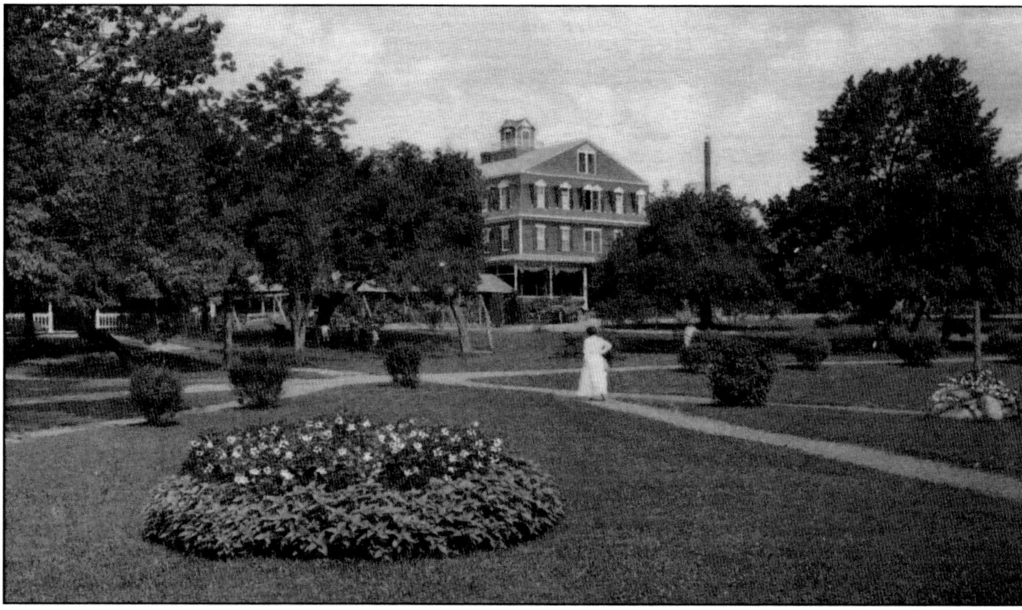

Successors to Forest Park, Unity House (pictured) and Tamiment both started with the aim of providing affordable relaxation and cultural education to city laborers. Both brought in customers for the railway and its bus division until direct buses bypassed the railroads completely. Unity House closed in 1990; Tamiment, in 2005. (Authors' collection.)

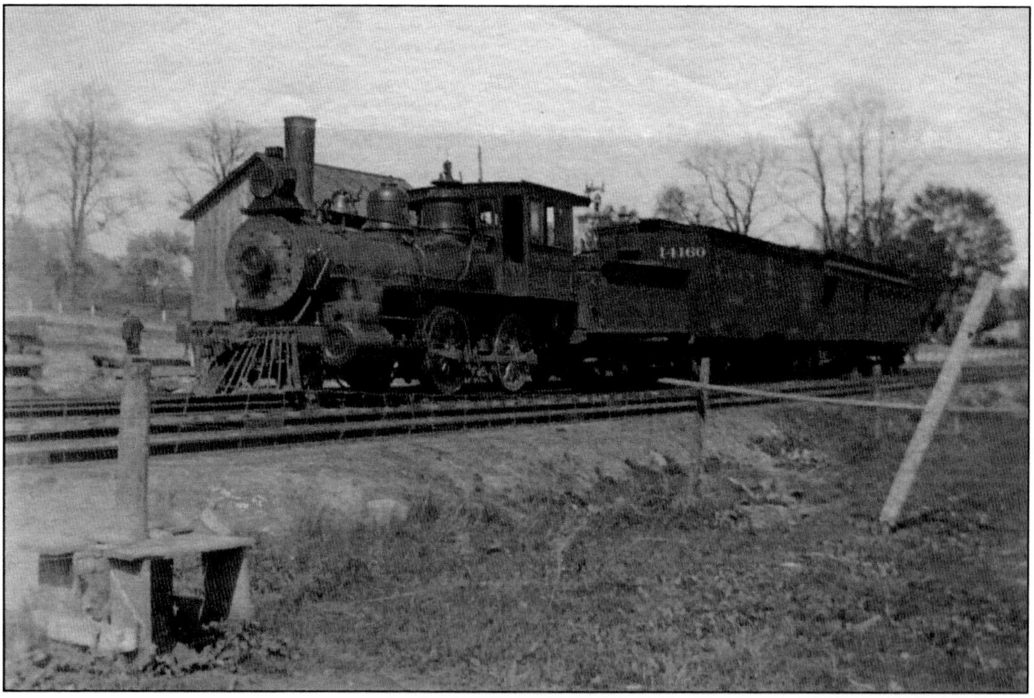

This run of engine, tender, boxcar, and combine is typical of the railway in action, even in its heyday. Behind the engine is the Bushkill freight depot. In the distance at the right is what is today Bushkill Falls Road. The foreground is now the backyard of the Turn & Cook Store on Main Street in Bushkill. (PCHist.)

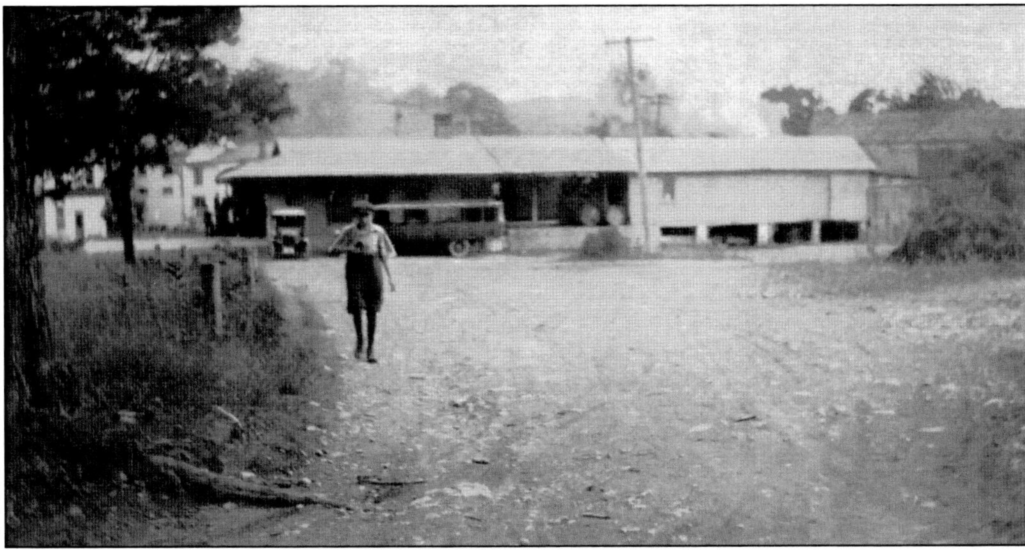

In 1924, the railway chartered its bus division, Delaware Valley Transportation Company (DVT). When auto-taxis and buses first appeared at the Bushkill station (above), they took railway travelers north to Milford. When the railway ended passenger service in 1928, DVT buses ran the entire route from East Stroudsburg to Port Jervis, also carrying the railway's small parcels for delivery. (BLTHS.)

Bus Schedule Camp Tamiment, Unity House, Bushkill, E. Stroudsburg

Read Down						Read Up		
8	6	2		3	1	9	5	7
*P. M.	A. M.	A. M.				*P. M.	*P.M.	‡P.M.
3.15	11.25	7.55	Camp Tamiment	7.35	10 15	1.30	6.05	7.40
3.20	11.30	8.00	Unity House	7.35	10.15	1.30	6.05	7.40
3.50	12.00	8.30	Bushkill	7.15	9.45	1.00	5.30	7.10
3.55	12.05	8.35	Shoemakers			12.50	5.25	7.05
4.00	12.10	8.40	Turn Villa			12.45	5.20	7.00
4.02	12.12	8.42	Echo Lake			12.43	5.18	6.57
4.04	12.14	8.44	Coolbaughs	7.05		12.41	5.16	6.55
4.07	12.17	8.47	Del. Valley Inn			12.38	5.13	6.52
4.10	12.20	8.50	Frutcheys			12.35	5.10	6.49
4.13	12.23	8.53	Oak Grove			12.32	5.07	6.46
4.18	12.28	8.58	Marshalls Creek	6.55		12.27	5.02	6.43
4.30	12.40	9.10	East Stroudsburg	6.45		12.15	4.50	6.30
	P. M.							

THIS SCHEDULE IS SUBJECT TO CHANGE WITHOUT NOTICE

* Daily ‡ Daily Except Sunday

Bus Schedule East Stroudsburg, Bushkill, Milford and Port Jervis

Read Down			Read Up	
P. M.	A. M.		A. M.	P. M.
12.15	7.30	East Stroudsburg	11.15	4.15
12.30	7.45	Marshalls Creek	11.00	4.00
12.50	8.05	Bushkill	10.40	3 40
1.10	8.25	Egypt Mills	10.20	3.20
1.25	8.40	Dingmans Ferry	10.05	3.05
1.40	8.55	Milford	9.50	2.50
1.55	9.10	Matamoras	.35	2.35
2.00	9.15	Port Jervis	9.30	2.30
P. M.	A. M.		A. M.	P. M.

THIS SCHEDULE IS SUBJECT TO CHANGE WITHOUT NOTICE

DELAWARE VALLEY TRANSPORTATION CO.

CALL TAXI AND SERVICE SPECIAL BUS PARTIES ARRANGED

PHONE BUSHKILL 162

The package and small freight business soon encountered competition from truckers, but the passenger service was a success. DVT lived on after the railway, transferred to another carrier and serving other routes. (Authors' collection.)

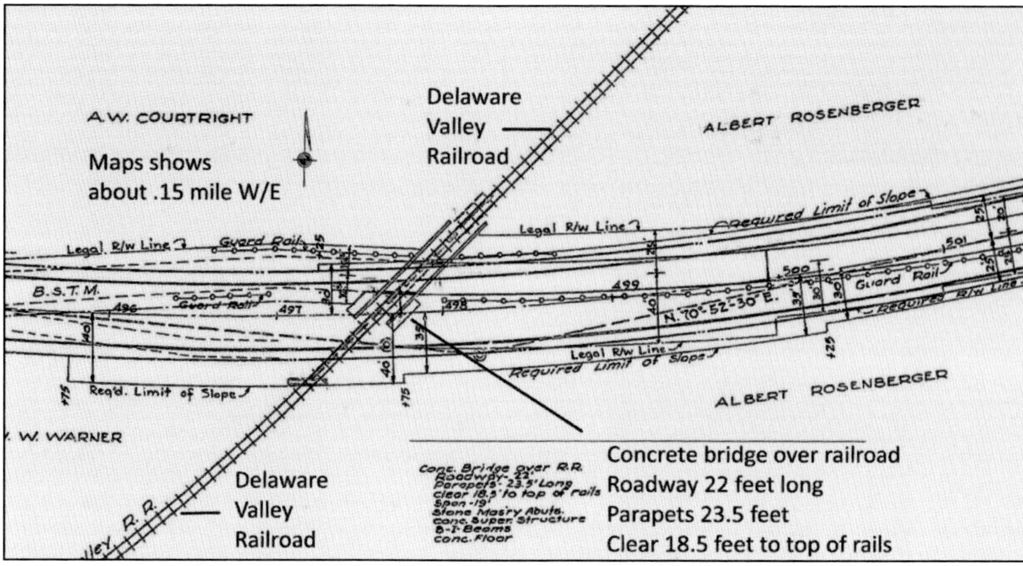

Paving plans for 1937 show that just south of today's Pub 570, the track was to be shifted to an underpass beneath a new concrete bridge (see chapter 8). The railway had already stopped running that spring, though, and the underpass was probably little used. It was later filled in. (PennDOT.)

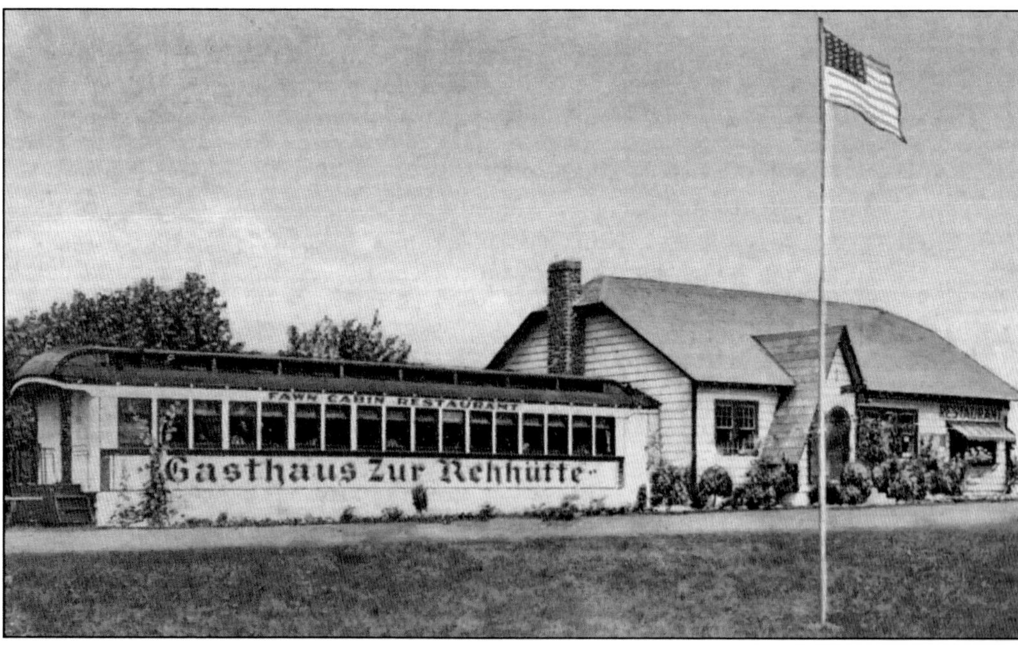

A survivor, for a time, was the "Honeymoon Express," a railway passenger car adapted as a dining area for Fawn Cabin Restaurant, just northeast of the railway crossing of Milford Road. A 1937 map refers to a lunch wagon at this site, but over time, Fawn Cabin evolved into Heddy's, then the Steak & Rib, then Pub 570. (Authors' collection.)

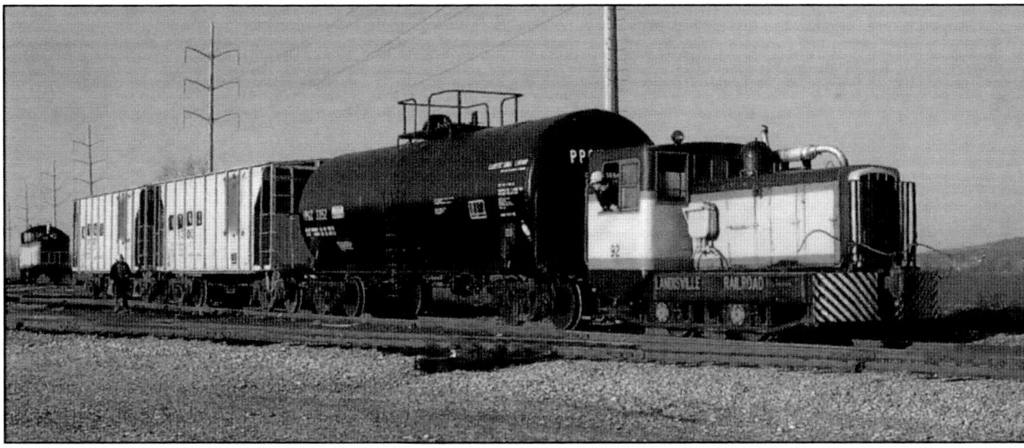

The railway's last engine was the gas-powered, 160-horsepower No. 2861, built by Fate-Root-Heath for delivery in 1928. Drawing good bids at the railway's dissolution, No. 2861 was photographed on the job by John Petko in 1990 as No. 92 (pictured) for Amherst Industries at Landisville Railroad in Lancaster, Pennsylvania. (*Railpace Newsmagazine*.)

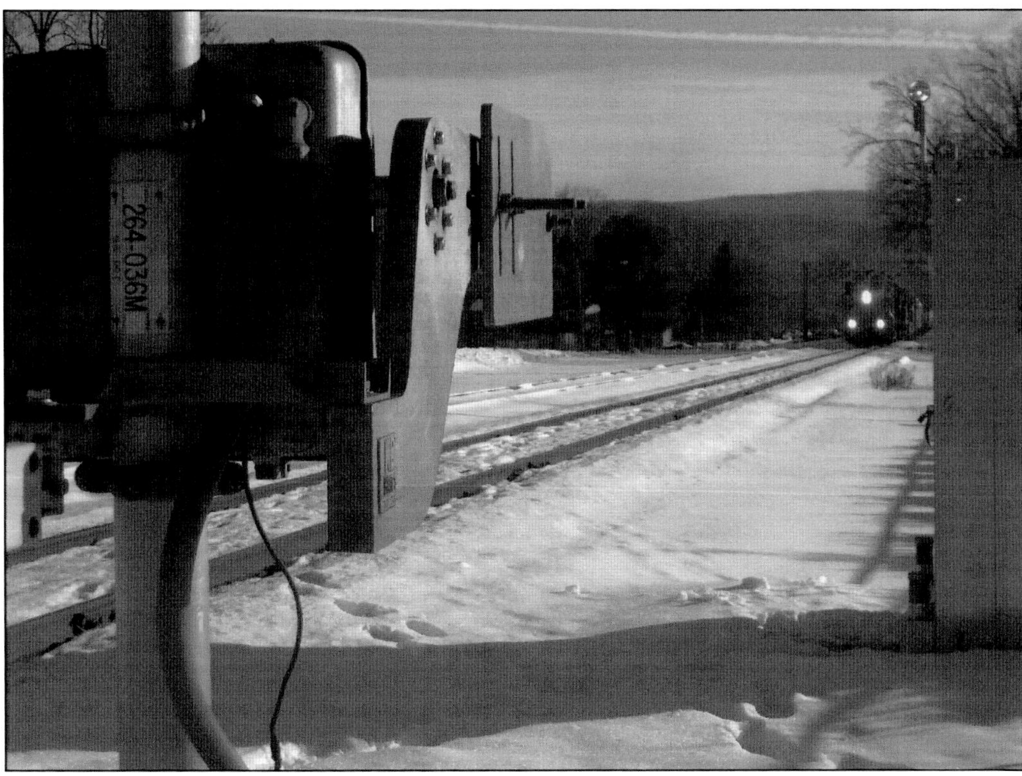

In 1970, the final passenger train from Scranton to New York called at East Stroudsburg. The DL&W's main line is down to one track used by freight trains a few times a week. An automatic gate (left) has replaced the shanty at Broad Street. Only an occasional excursion train brings passengers to East Stroudsburg now. (Authors' collection.)

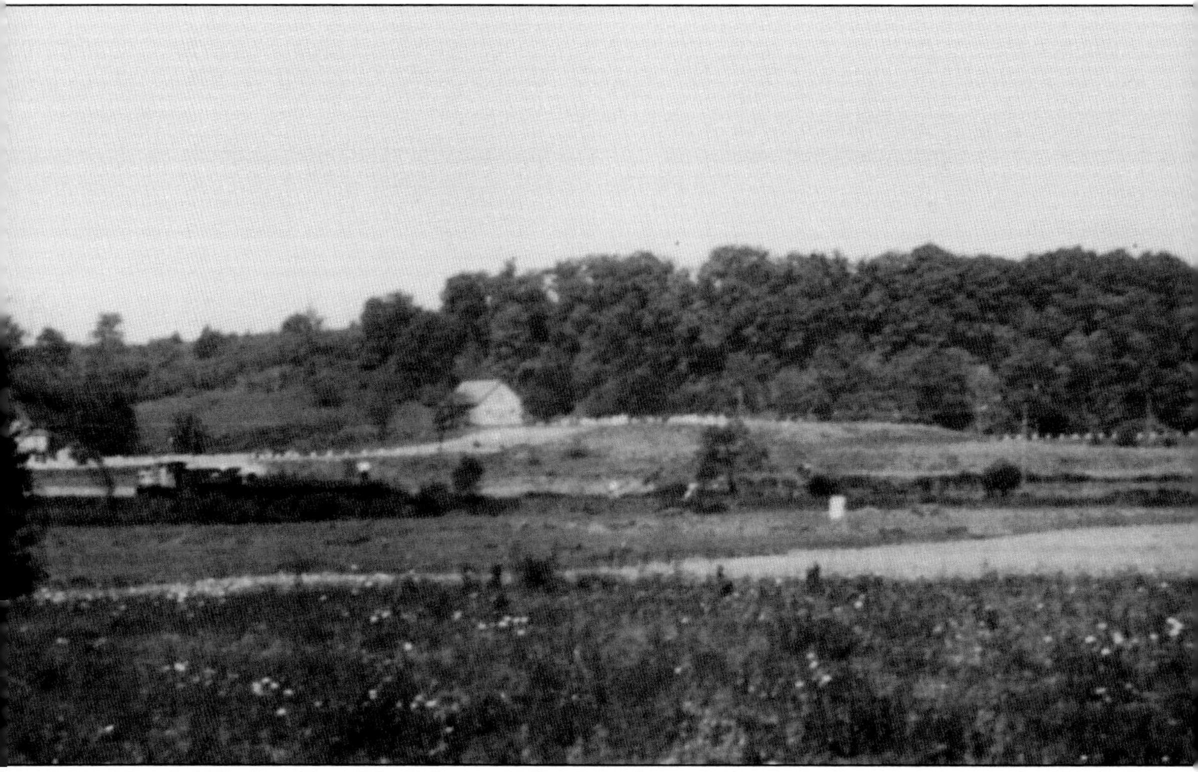

Entitled *The Last Trip of the Delaware Valley R.R.*, this snapshot was taken in June 1938 by Elizabeth Dimmick Walters, curator of Monroe County Historical Society from 1940 to 1979. She took the photograph near her home on the northwest side of Milford Road just north of Eagle Valley Corners. What appears to be a flatbed car with two men aboard and stacked with rails is pulled by the railway's Plymouth gas engine or a converted truck. Beakleyville Church on Route 447 is in the distance. Today, the train would be running through the parking lot of Eagle's Glen Mall, overlooked by Halterman's Toyota on the hill at the church site. A view of the same area in winter is seen on page 41. (MCHA.)

The Passing of the Dinkey

Across the meadow from our home rises the embankment of an abandoned railroad. A single-track line whose rolling stock has long since been consigned to the graveyard.

I occasionally walk along the track as its winds its way through the roads and across the fields at the end of the line twelve miles north. A few short years ago this short line boasted a thriving business in the movement of ice, coal, and mine props. From a connecting carrier, visitors from eastern cities were transferred and conveyed to the hotels and boarding houses in the river valley through which the railroad ran. Had it not been for the "dinkey" – we hardly knew it by any other name – many a country boy and girl would have been denied the advantage of a high school education.

When we were boys and visited Grandpa on the farm, we would race across the fields to the track when we heard "her" coming. The roadbed was not very straight and the train swayed from side to side like a bobsled in a crooked rut. We always expected the engine to jump the track and our only thought was to save the little brass Indian perched on top of the large square headlight.

Though we are no longer boys, we still remember the kindly old conductor who always waved to us as he went by. What an opportunity the railroad man has to promote good will for his company by being always courteous and thoughtful to the comfort of his customers.

But this has all changed. No longer does the sound of the shrill whistle echo through the valley. No longer do we hear the chug-chug of the little engine, as we heard it years ago, puffing along from station to station. The friendly crew knew everyone along their route; everyone knew them. Inability to hold to schedule never troubled them very much; but they were strong on helpful service – and conversation.

Now, buses transport the scholars and summer visitors. A motor truck has replaced the baggage car. It would be difficult to estimate the economic loss to our community from the substitution of the highway for the railway. Moreover, we shall not try to represent our concern in terms of revenue, but in the sense of losing an old and respected friend.

– Horace G. Walters

Horace G. Walters was president of the Monroe County Historical Society from 1968 to 1970. He and his wife, Elizabeth Dimmick Walters, lived near Eagle Valley Corners, and he is likely describing the right-of-way behind the house before Skyline Drive-In and Eagle's Glen Mall were built. The couple were married in 1925 in Shawnee-on-Delaware. (MCHA.)

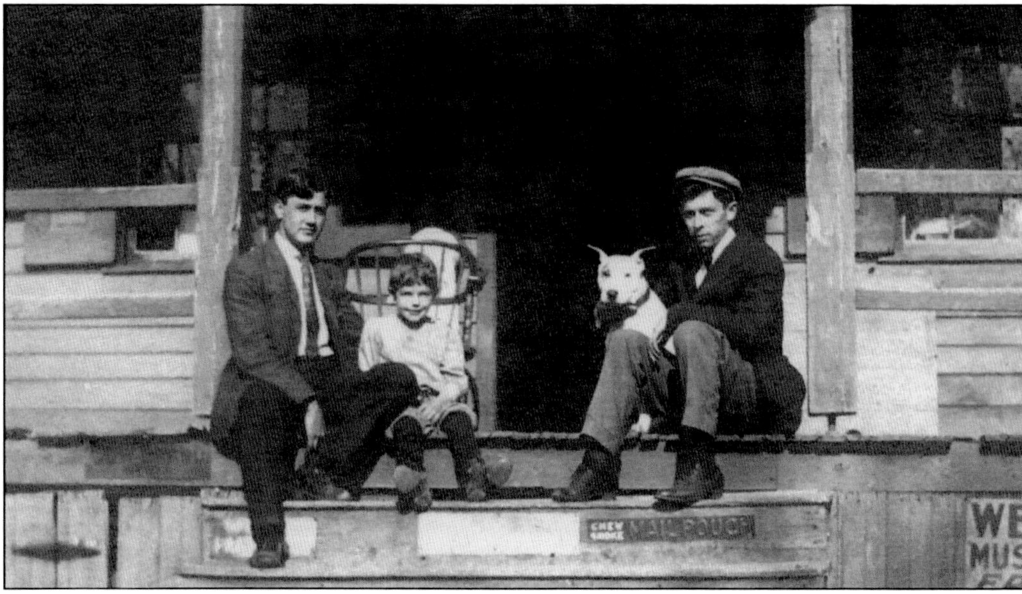

Melvin Huffman (right) sits with friends on the steps of his family's store in Marshalls Creek. In 1910, at the age of 30, Huffman became stationmaster of the railway's Marshalls Creek station, which still stands directly behind the store. (Bob Huffman.)

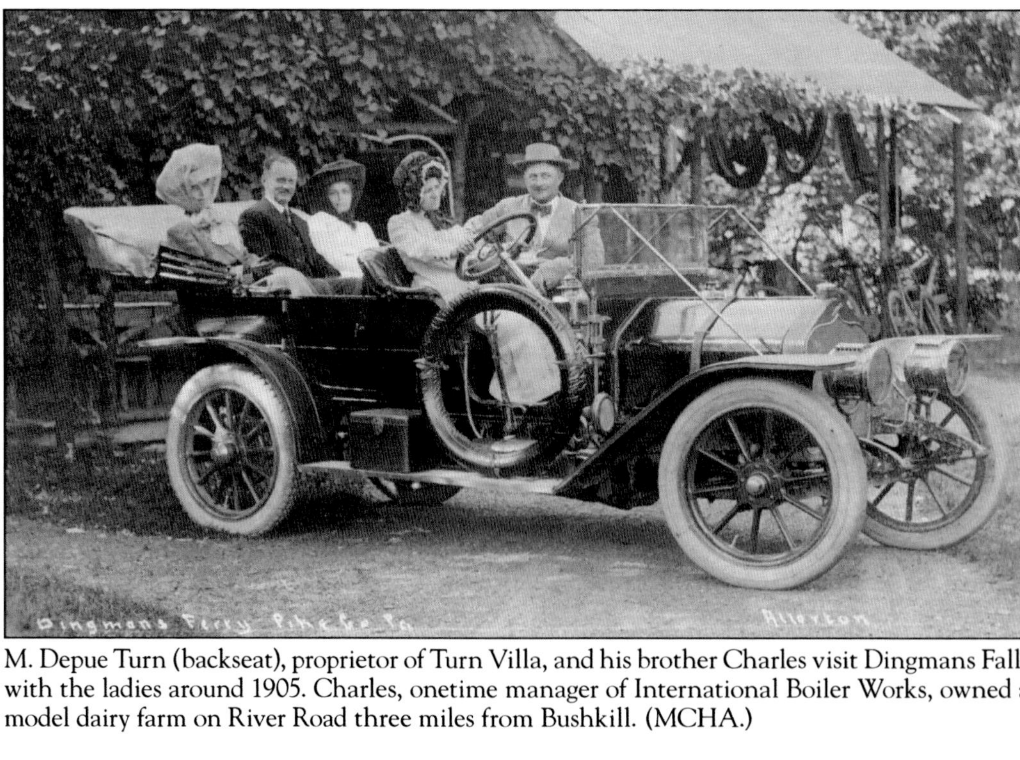

M. Depue Turn (backseat), proprietor of Turn Villa, and his brother Charles visit Dingmans Falls with the ladies around 1905. Charles, onetime manager of International Boiler Works, owned a model dairy farm on River Road three miles from Bushkill. (MCHA.)

Eight

The Right-of-Way

Engineering, enterprise, and sweat could not have made the railway a reality if property owners had not granted a right-of-way. For astute businessmen, the grant promised easier transport of their goods and more customers for their inns. Other grantors, homesteaders known only to their descendants, asked only access to a stream, a "good farm crossing" over the tracks, or a wire fence to spare livestock an untimely end on the engine's cowcatcher.

The total investment by the railway for land in Monroe County was just under $12,000, of which East Stroudsburg cost $3,350. The cost in Pike County was just over $2,500, of which $1,500 was for the station area in Bushkill. The costliest purchase was $2,000 for 140 feet at the Marshalls Creek station. Six deeds went for only $1, of which Oak Grove, Pardee's Loop, and Coolbaugh were notable bargains. An "X" signed one of the deeds.

Deeds required the railway to put in stations at Delaware Valley Junction, Oak Grove, and Turn Villa. The railway also built stations at Marshalls Creek (perhaps from an existing building), Frutcheys, and Bushkill and improvised with an old railcar for a station at Delaware Valley Inn and an old Lackawanna carpenters' shed, hauled in by four horses in 1903, at Shoemakers. Landowners provided a station at Echo Lake and probably Coolbaugh. The stops at Eagle Valley, Craigs Meadows, and Maples may have been just gravel platforms.

There are few images of the track. However, aerial photographs from 1939, a year after the rails were scrapped, clearly show the scar of the right-of-way. One can trace its path smack through markets (Weis, Miggy's); fields and forests that today are developed communities (Birch Acres, Lake of the Pines); and over and past land that is now covered by water at Lake Valhalla, Frutcheys Drive, Echo Lake Park, and Lake of the Pines. Repaving has smudged out the track crossings of Milford Road. Within the national park, a stretch of right-of-way can be walked, though even there the landscape has been altered by the regrowth of forest over farms and meadows that are still remembered but long disappeared.

Comparing the right-of-way to the scenes of today is a short lesson in local history. Walking a section of the railway's route is a longer contemplation on the effect of the automobile on the landscapes and lifestyles of today.

Grantor of Right-of-way	Feet	Approximate Premises Today
Wm. & Margaret HANEY; Samuel & Sarah HANEY	90	Birch Street at back of car wash
Oscar STEMPLE	2,865	Today's Oak Street
James & Elizabeth KINNEY	536	Weis Market
D. Porter & Mary Agnes ANGLE	2,255	Eagle Valley/Eagle's Glen Malls
James, Grant, Reeder & Frances POSTEN	1,153	Eagle Ridge housing
Jacob & Mary KAUL	1,914	Milford Commons community
Charles & Margaret KAUL	2,033	Lake Valhalla community
George BRUTZMAN	913	Stroudsburg Pocono Airport
H.O. & Jennie BUSH	1,085	Airport Road and northeast
Stephen & Georgiana HOLMES	2,514	Birch Acres community/St. Paul's
Austin& May BUSH; Emma BUSH;	3,465	Mt. Manor Golf Course, Craigs
Albina & Edwin BUSH		Meadow to Marshalls Creek
A.D. & Nellie MILLER	163	Bend of Marshalls Creek
J. Madison, R.V., Martin, Emma & Morris PLACE	255	West of Marshalls Creek Road
C.W. & Emma STONE	140	Marshalls to Pond Creeks
Lizzie & Charles PLACE	175	Huffman store parking
Eliza LANDER	374	Between lake and Milford Road
W.B. & Clara EILENBERGER & Harvey HUFFMAN	3,570	South bank of Lake Marshall
Edith & C.V. SMITH	800	Oak Grove
Jabez ANGLE	420	Mt. Nebo Road at Rt. 209
Charles & Mary ANGLE	2,197	Pardee's (Lakeview) Loop
John & Rosetta KINTNER	1,389	West of Frutcheys Drive
Stogdell WOLFE	1,980	East of Frutcheys Drive
Carrie & Ira STETLER	657	South of Wesley Church
Sarah& Andrew ALBERT; H. & L. FRANKENFIELD	2,220	Southwest end, Holy Cross Road
Josiah & Mary COLEMAN	1,440	Holy Cross and Hollow Roads
M. Frank & Martha COOLBAUGH	2,105	Middle Smithfield School
Charles & Annie VAN WHY	1,992	Former Blue Ridge Inn/Tru Value
Charles E. & Emma VAN ALLEN	1,997	Echo Lake Park
Oliver & Barbara MICHAEL	2,023	Maple Lane Townhouses
M. Depue & Sarah TURN	1,111	Turn Villa (Echo Lake Farms)
Edwin & Henry PETERS& Cornelia COOLBAUGH;	2,222	Lake of the Pines community
Aaron DREISBAUGH; Mary & W.T. LEAS;		
Frank Van GORDEN & wife; Sara HANNA	2,565	North of Sand Hill Road
Hannah OVERFIELD (Monroe County)	2,343	Winona Falls Road to Bush Kill
Daniel & Sarah CLARK (Pike County)	1,065	East of Bush Kill crossing
John H. & Charlotte COOK	4,499	Along Creek Road to The Maples
Charles & Emma WALLACE; Edwin PETERS;	1,495	Railway Avenue (Rail bed section
Lizzie & W. P. TOWNSEND		of Railway Avenue Trail)
J.H. SHULL (Railway Trustee), earlier Samuel PETERS	957	Behind "TheRoost"

These grantors of right-of-way have been recorded in Pike and Monroe Counties. (Authors' collection.)

In this aerial of Bushkill from Penn State University, the right-of-way is to the right (southeast and south) of the dotted white line. (Authors' collection.)

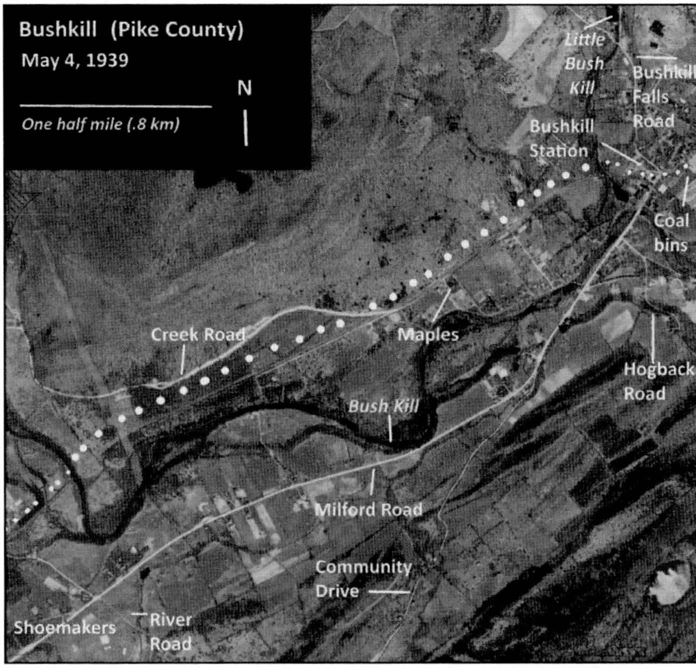

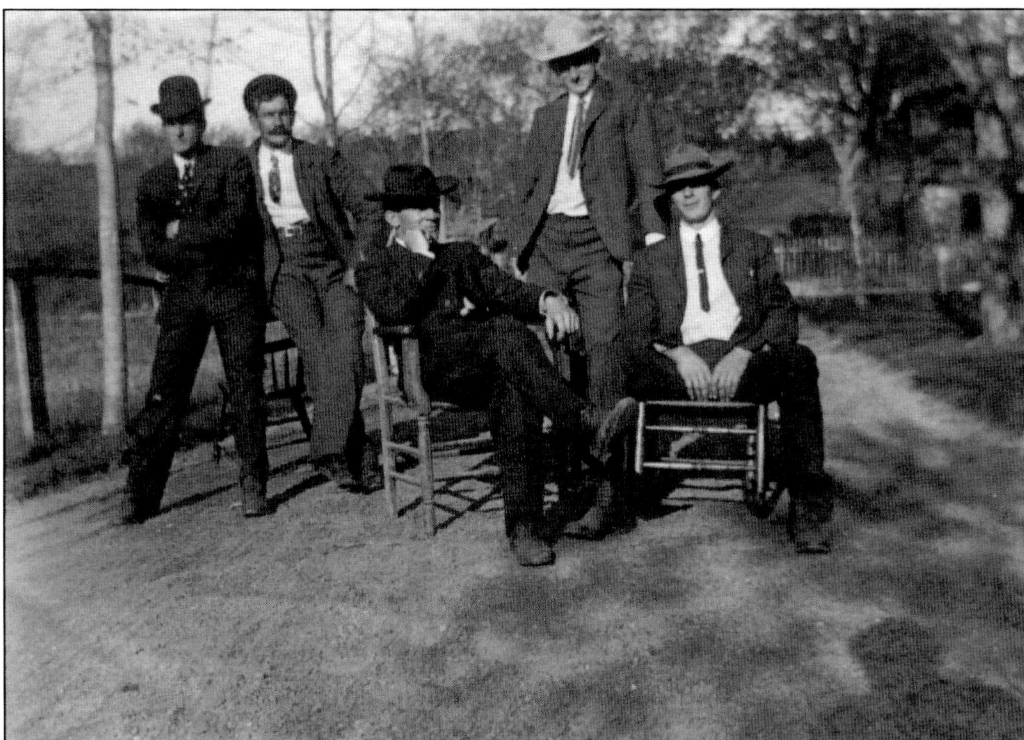

Railway-era scions of Bushkill (and the enterprises of their families) are, from left to right, either Peters (hotel, mill, land for Bushkill station) or Nyce (lumberyard at station); Clinton Guillot (poultry farm); Norman Guillot (stationmaster, coalyard manager); Ralph Turn (general store); and Bill Cook (land along Creek Road, garage/car service). (PCHist.)

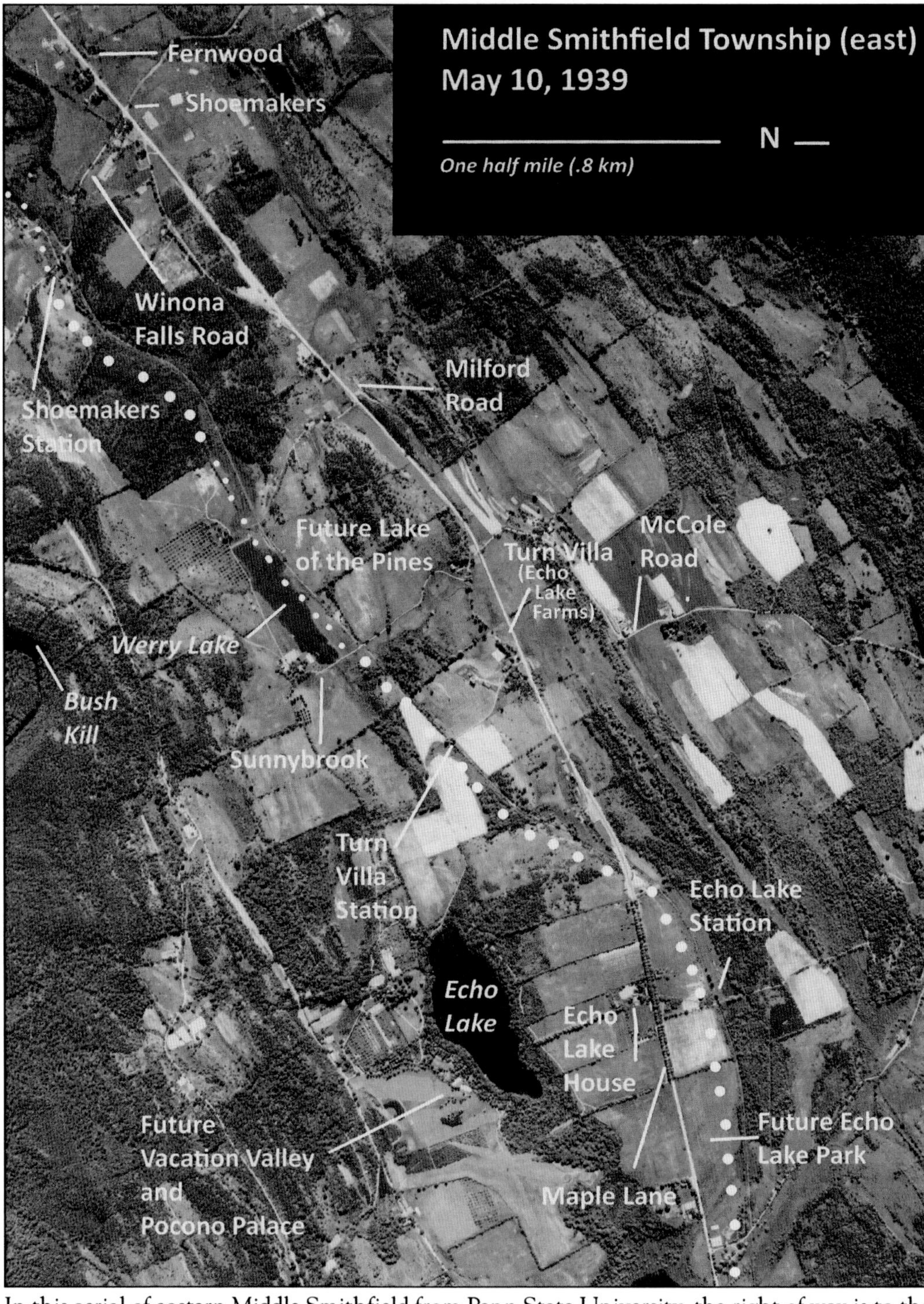

In this aerial of eastern Middle Smithfield from Penn State University, the right-of-way is to the right (southeast and south) of the dotted white line. (Authors' collection.)

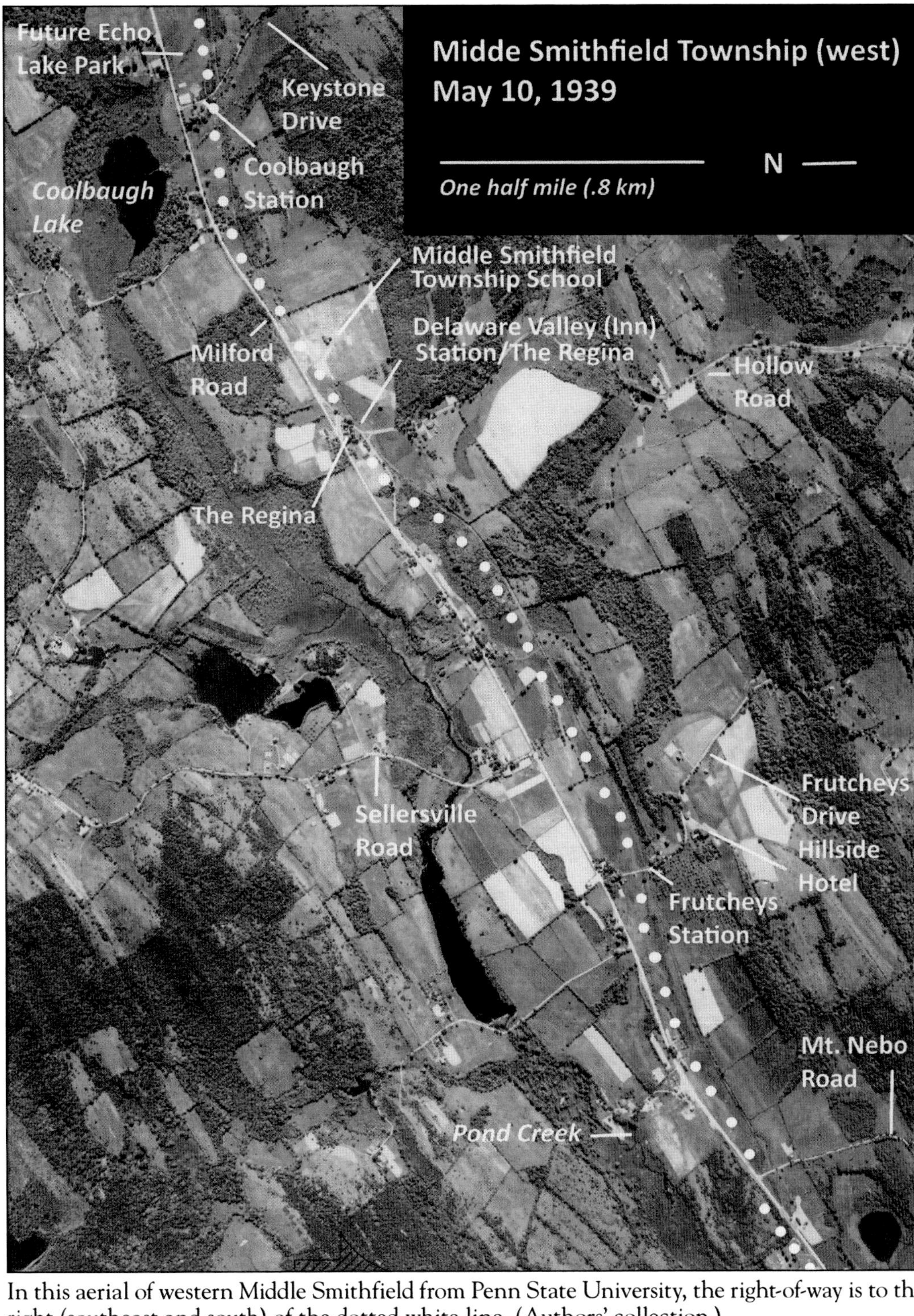

In this aerial of western Middle Smithfield from Penn State University, the right-of-way is to the right (southeast and south) of the dotted white line. (Authors' collection.)

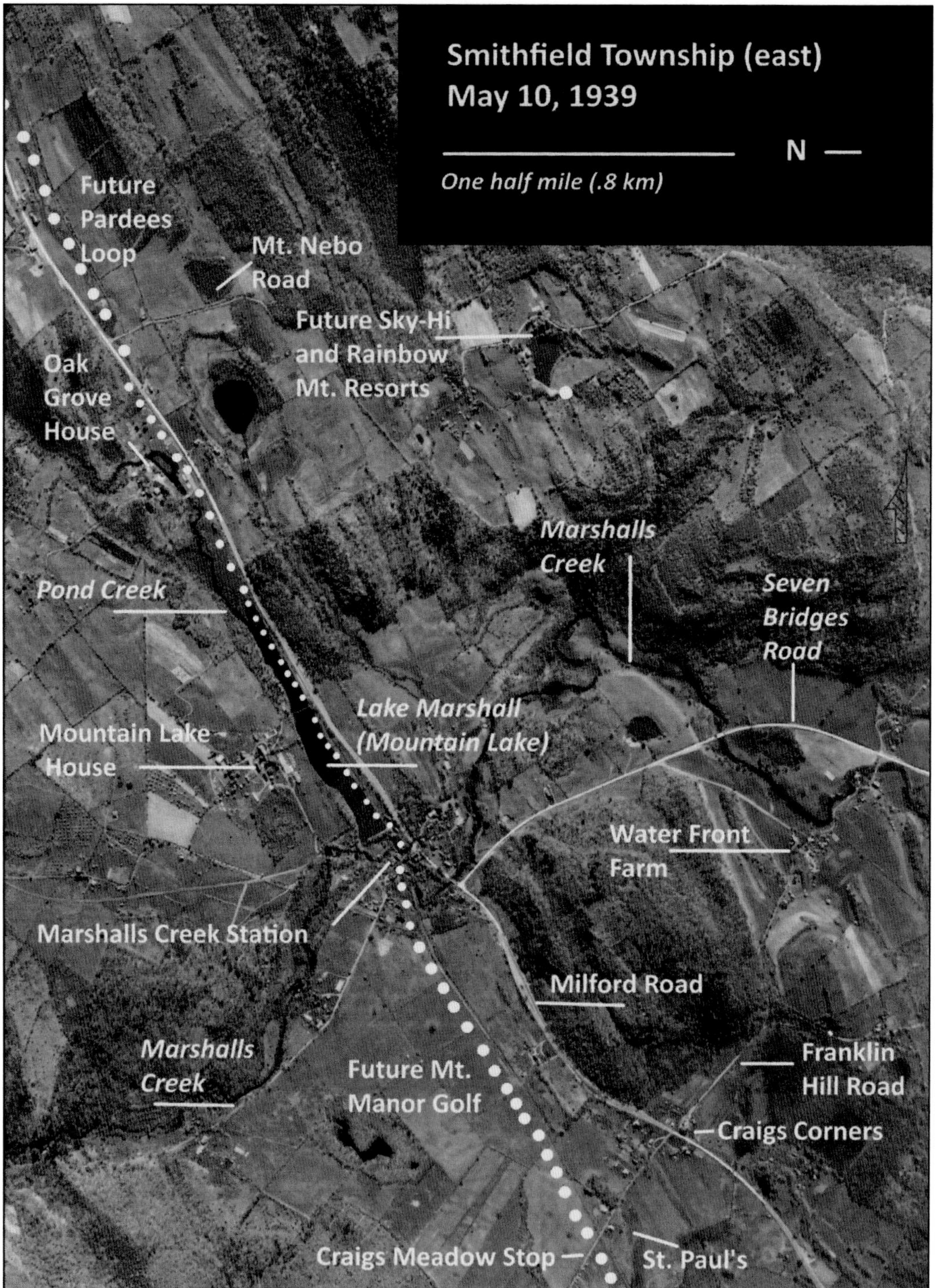

In this aerial of eastern Smithfield from Penn State University, the right-of-way is to the right (southeast and south) of the dotted white line. (Authors' collection.)

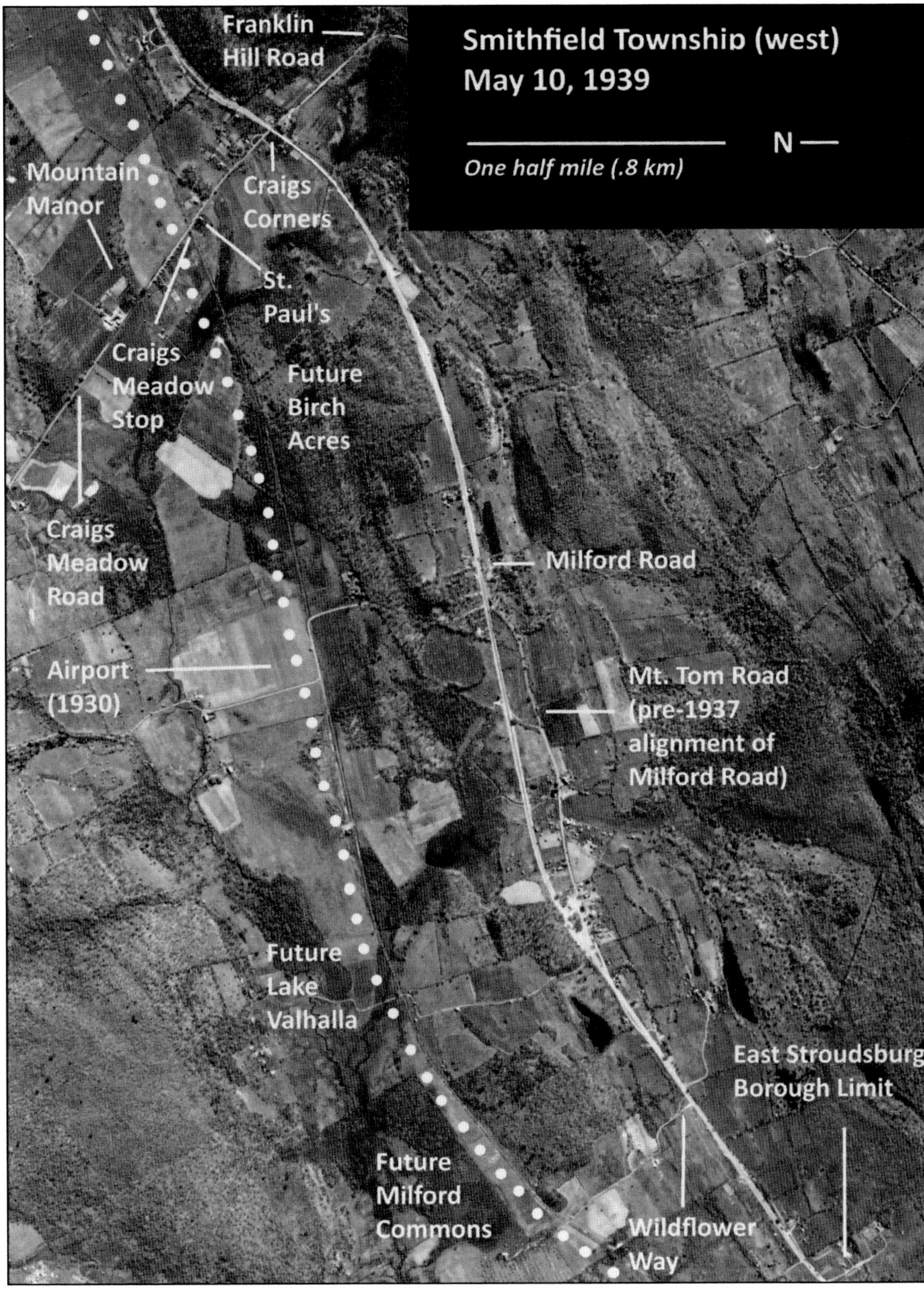

In this aerial of western Smithfield from Penn State University, the right-of-way is to the right (southeast and south) of the dotted white line. (Authors' collection.)

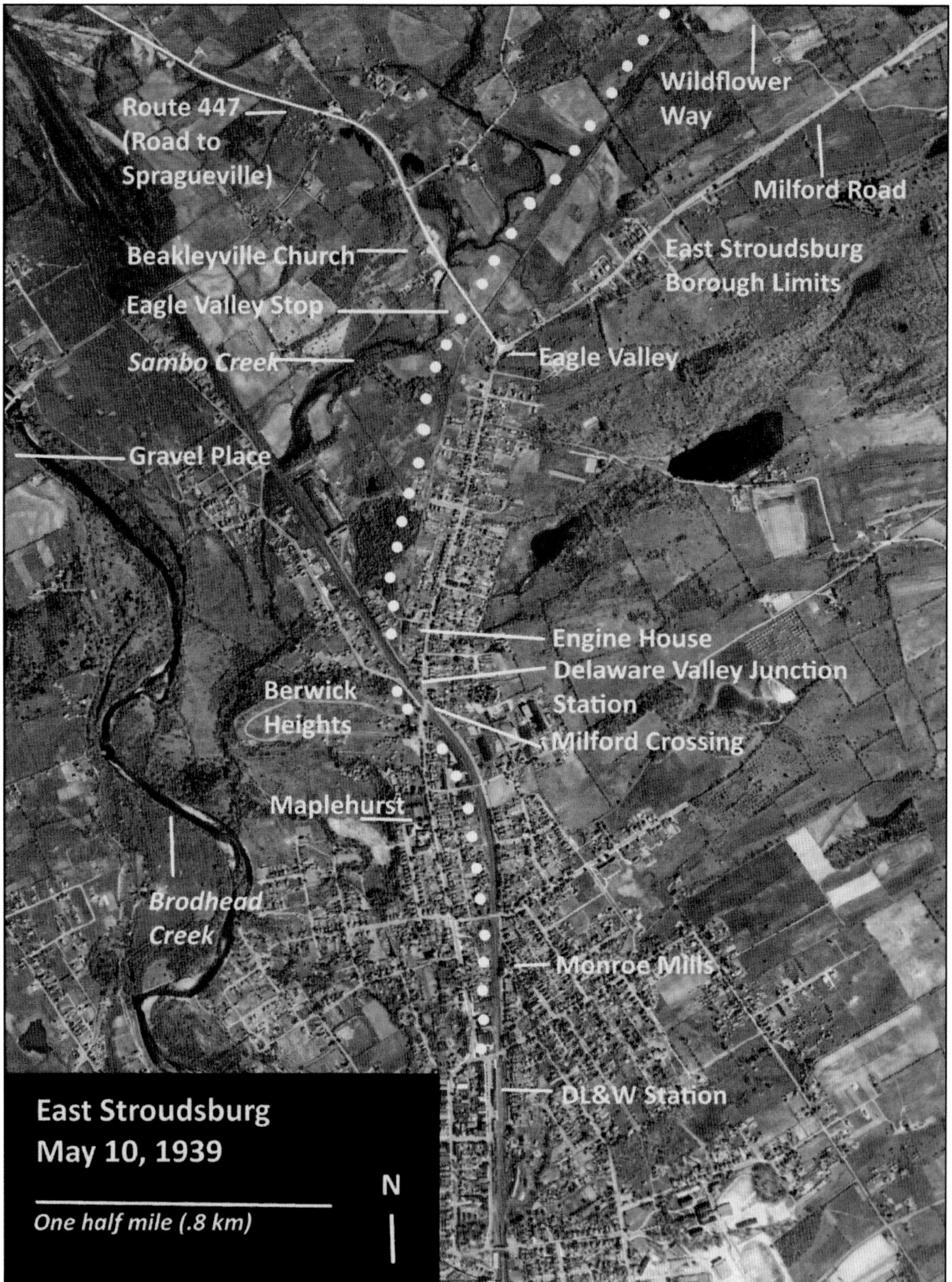

In this aerial of East Stroudsburg from Penn State University, the right-of-way is to the right (southeast and south) of the dotted white line. (Authors' collection.)

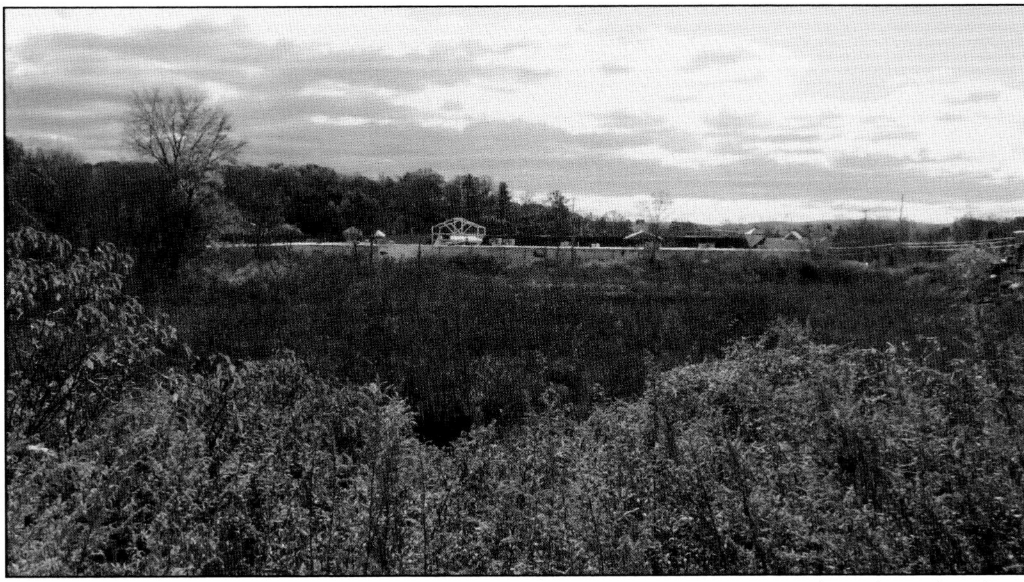

From today's Oak Street in East Stroudsburg to Jay Street near Craigs Meadow, the right-of-way was repurposed in the 1980s for a wastewater line. This view from Fawn Road south to Eagle Valley Mall (above) takes in the old right-of-way from Weis Market (peaked roof, far right) to Eagle's Glen Mall (far left). (Authors' collection.)

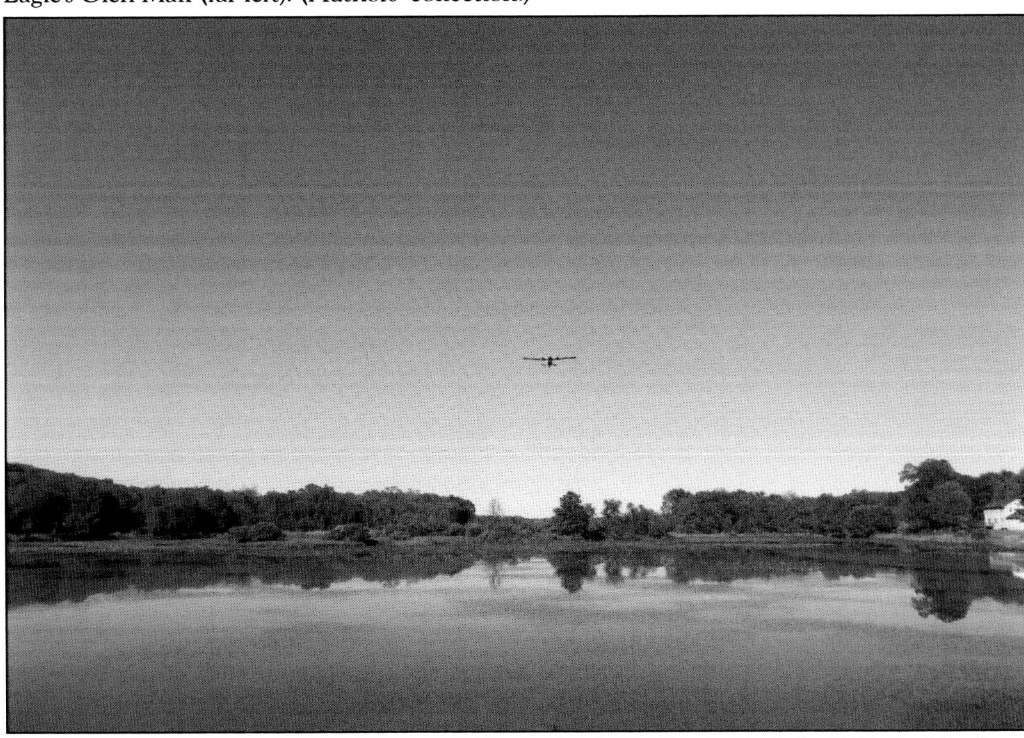

Leaving East Stroudsburg, the railway crossed boggy land now flooded by Lake Valhalla. Northeast of the lake, Pocono Stroudsburg Airport began as Pipher Airport in 1930. The railway ran on or along Airstrip Road, crossed Airport Road at a cut still visible today, and ran along what is now Delaware Avenue to Craigs Meadows. (Authors' collection.)

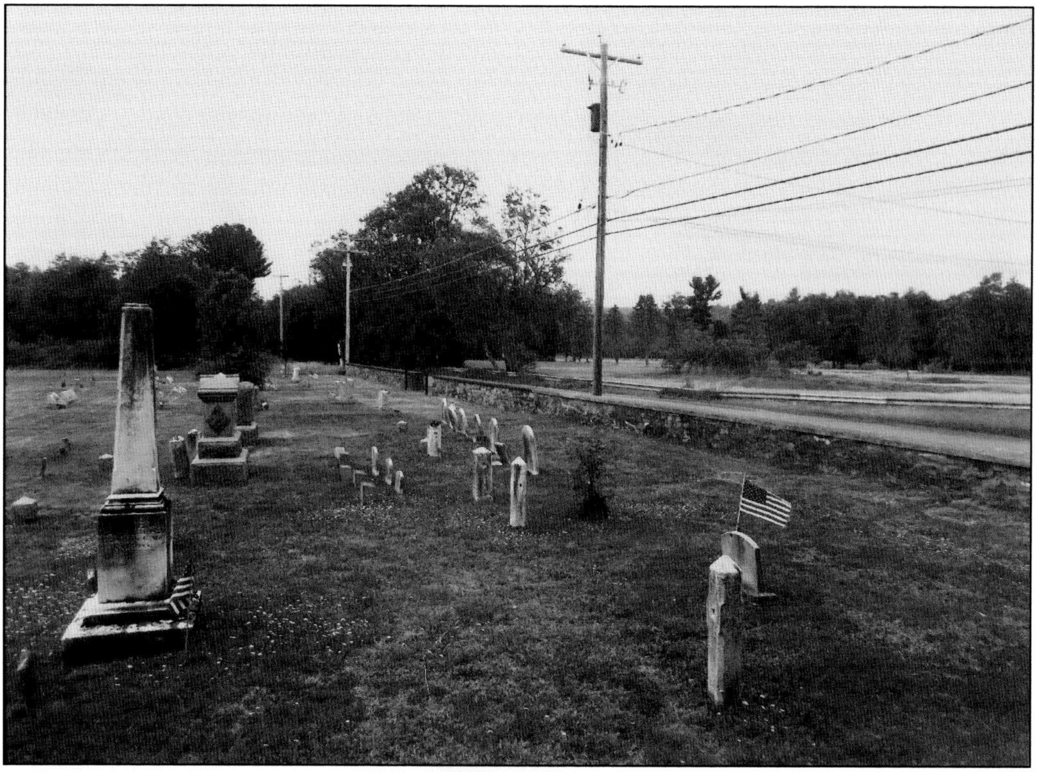

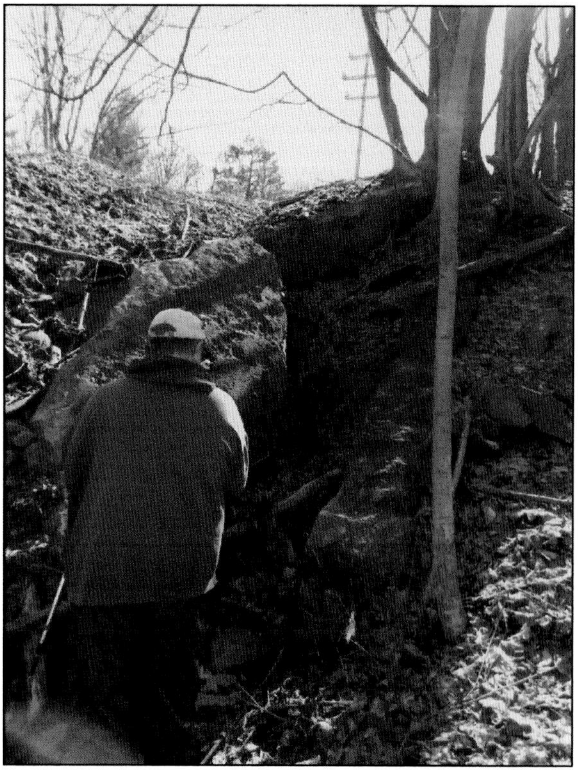

From Craigs Meadow northeast, most of the right-of-way has reverted to the original owners or their descendants. At St. Paul's Church, land donations in 1944 expanded the church's property north across the old railbed. (Authors' collection.)

Railroad historian Kim Williams photographs the rubble beneath the traffic on Milford Road in Middle Smithfield. The concrete walls and fill are the remains of a vehicle bridge built in 1937 over the railway's right-of-way. Perhaps only three runs of the railway ever used this detour off the old grade crossing nearby. (Williams obtained the landowner's permission to enter this area; please respect owners' rights when hiking.) (Authors' collection.)

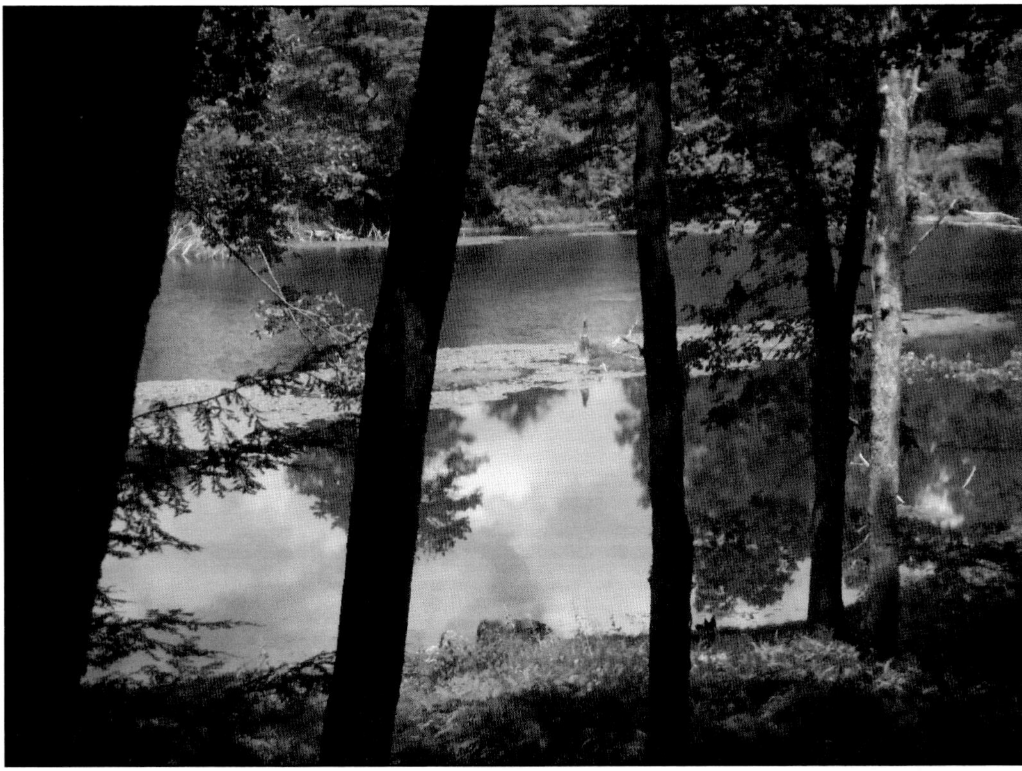

A section of railway embankment (above) still peeks out from the water northeast of the dam on Werry Lake in the Lake of the Pines community. (This is private property; do not trespass.) As drainages have been dammed one by one since the era of the railway, similar scenes have occurred at Frutcheys Drive and Echo Lake Park. (Authors' collection.)

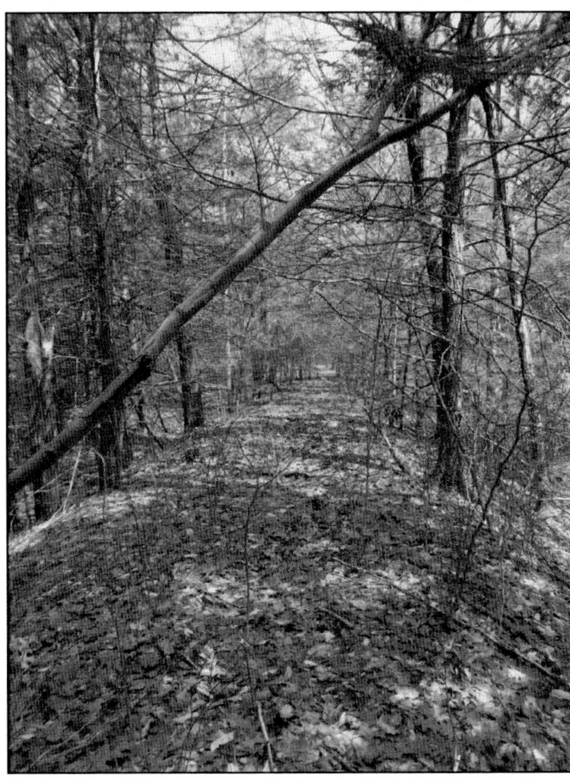

The return of the right-of-way to owners required a new survey in 1967 and ultimately took until 1969. John H. Cook was fortunate to get back almost a mile of the right-of-way between Bush Kill and his Maples guesthouse as early as 1944. At that time, the western half of the parcel was wooded, and the eastern half was fields. Today, it is entirely wooded. (Authors' collection.)

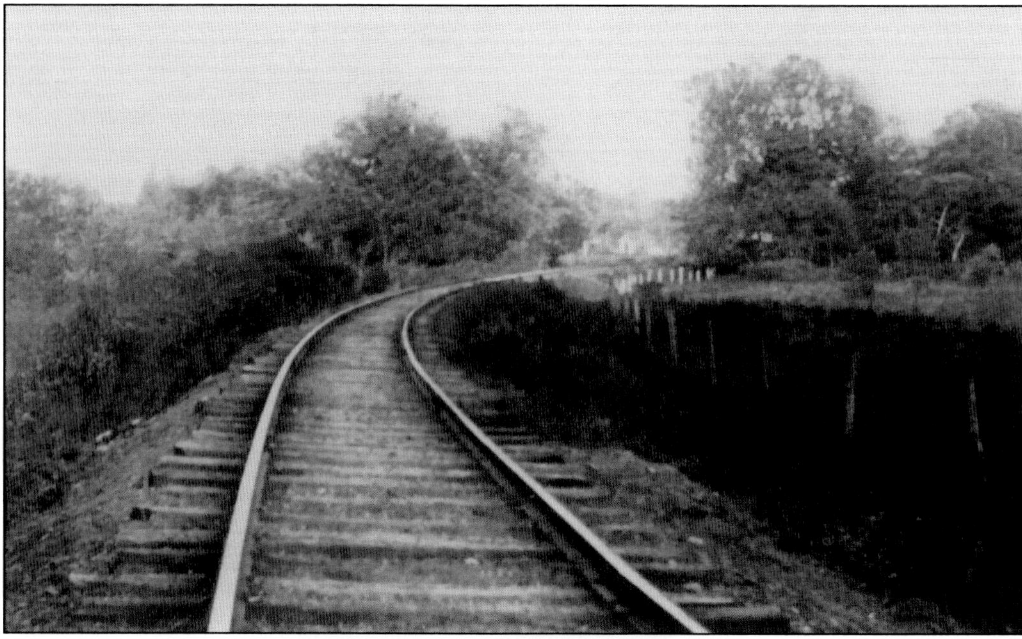

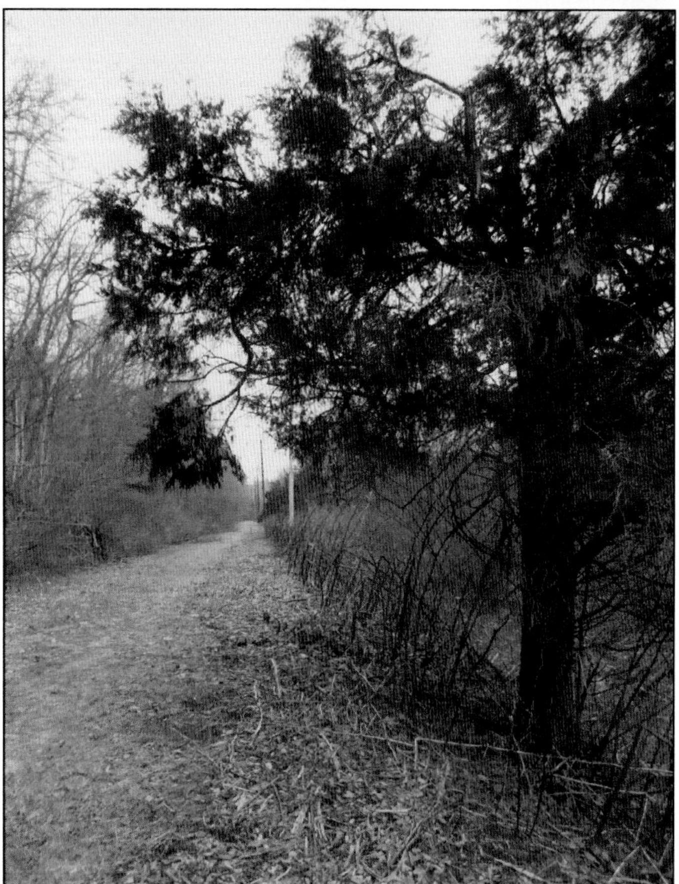

"The Turn of the Delaware Valley Road into Bushkill Pa" is just west of Little Bush Kill. The small structure in the distance is perhaps a maintenance building for the railway on a small expansion of the right-of-way alongside the stream. (Authors' collection.)

At the same location today, Railway Avenue Trail follows the old Railway Avenue east on the railbed for about a quarter mile from Creek Road. The trail then turns south to rejoin Creek Road. This view is at N 41 05.372, W 75 00.700. (Authors' collection.)

Nine

A Railway Visitors Can See

The idea for this book began with the goal of finding, and hiking where possible, the railbed of the Delaware Valley Railway. This final chapter is an armchair tour of the route and of the most significant locations of the railway.

In the borough of East Stroudsburg (see chapter 3), a level walk northward from the DL&W station to the enginehouse is a mile one way. Eagle Valley Mall, with limited bus service back to the start, is a half mile farther. Three miles north on Milford Road (Route 209), the Marshalls Creek station (see chapter 4) stands behind the 1836 Saloon at the turn for Route 402. Park at the shopping plaza on the right (southeast) side of Route 209 and cross carefully at the light to see this sturdy little wood building.

About four miles farther north on Milford Road, Echo Lake Park in Middle Smithfield Township (see chapter 5) offers a walk with smooth lawns, some damp footing and a short hill on the trails, and perhaps the dodging of a Frisbee or soccer ball. Look carefully for the park entrance on the right across from Middle Smithfield Presbyterian Church.

Delaware Water Gap National Recreation Area in Bushkill (see chapter 6) is a 70,000-acre national park open to hiking except where posted. Visit www.nps.gov/DEWA for information on the park, including hunting seasons. Search the site using the term "Railway" to find the Railway Avenue Trail. The three hikes described below are all within the park.

The right-of-way embankment from Shoemakers to Bush Kill is a rough, brambly quarter mile atop the embankment, best left to stronger hikers in the autumn. Park without blocking the driveway to Shoemaker House, which is on the west side of Winona Falls Road; the pull-off on the east side is private property.

The Railway Avenue Trail is a designated park trail that is .25 miles long, level, and cleared. Park at (but do not block) the pipe gates on the right of Creek Road either half or three-quarters of a mile from the traffic light in the village. The Maples guesthouse was located across Creek Road at the trail's west end. A hike to the east abutment is also possible—see below.

Exploring the village of Bushkill will involve about a one-mile level walk. There is a short, overgrown descent to the coal bins, best approached from the south and in the late fall. Park at the picnic area on Bushkill Falls Road just off Route 209 or at McDade Trail parking at Bushkill Visitor Center on Route 209 south of the bridge. Prior reading about the village or online exploring beforehand will certainly enhance the visit.

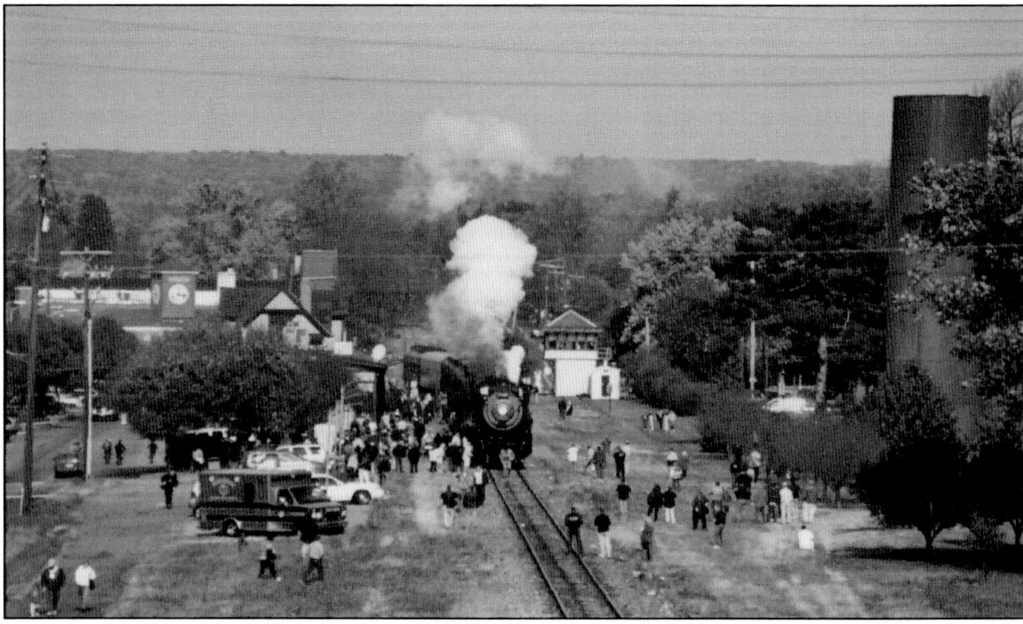

Pictured in East Stroudsburg from the Ridgeway Street Bridge in 2003, the DL&W Station (left) is in its original position east of the tracks, the 1908 switching station is in the center distance, and the metal water tower is on the far right. Engine No. 2317 visits from Steamtown National Historic Site. The bridge is at N 40 59.646, W 75 10.921. (Authors' collection.)

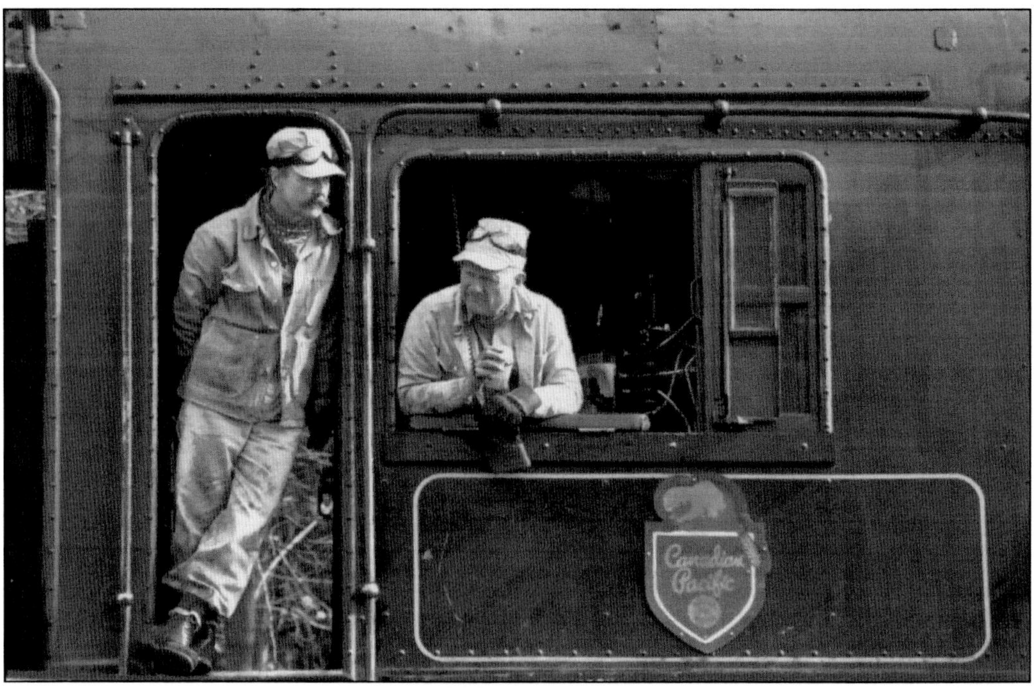

Costumed crew in East Stroudsburg help bring the era of the steam engine alive when an excursion train comes through. Often, the relocated DL&W station and the railroad tower (switching station) will be open for these events. (Authors' collection.)

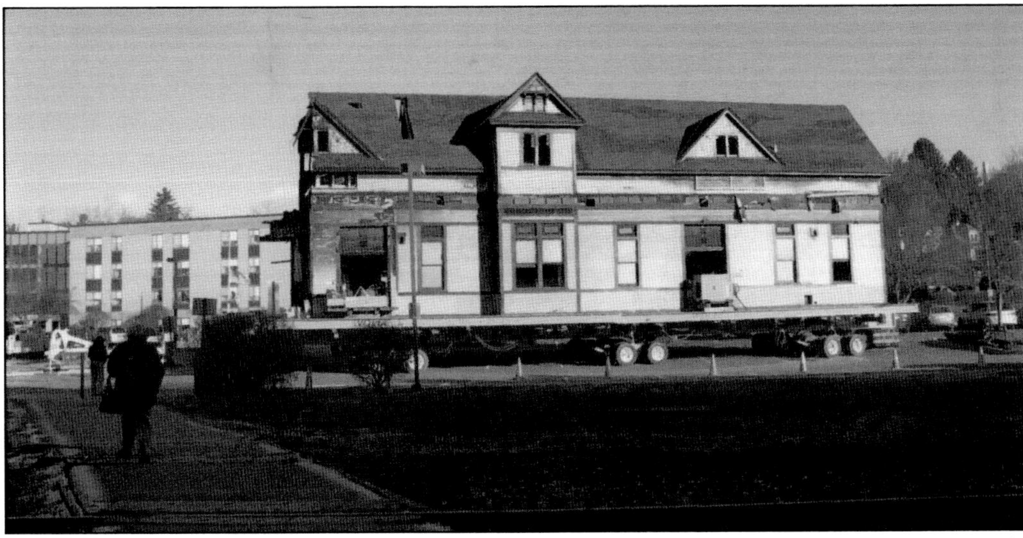

For years, the former DL&W station in East Stroudsburg was a popular restaurant called the Dansbury Depot, replete with model trains running on tracks close to the ceiling. The restaurant suffered a fire in 2009, and the main hall of the station was moved across to the east side of the tracks in 2010. (East Stroudsburg Community Alliance.)

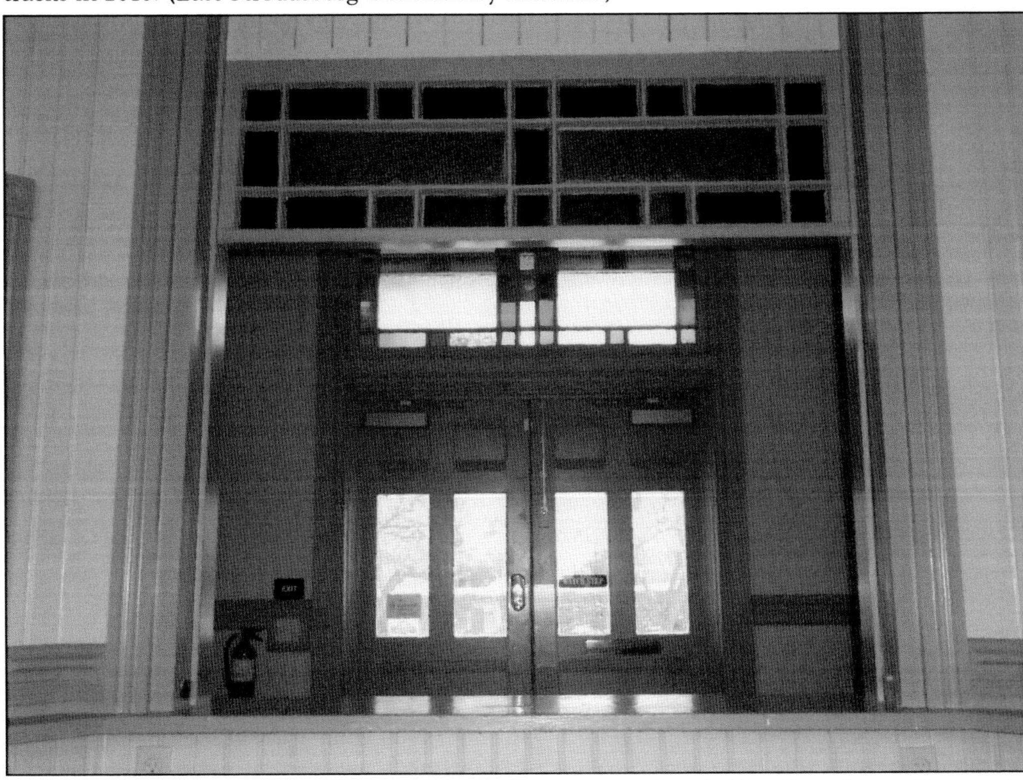

The refurbished DL&W station on South Kistler Street is rented out by East Stroudsburg Community Alliance for functions and meetings. Many details of the original station are preserved, such as the stained-glass transom above the entrance, seen here through the ticket counter. The station's coordinates are N 40 59.942, W 75 10.855. (Authors' collection.)

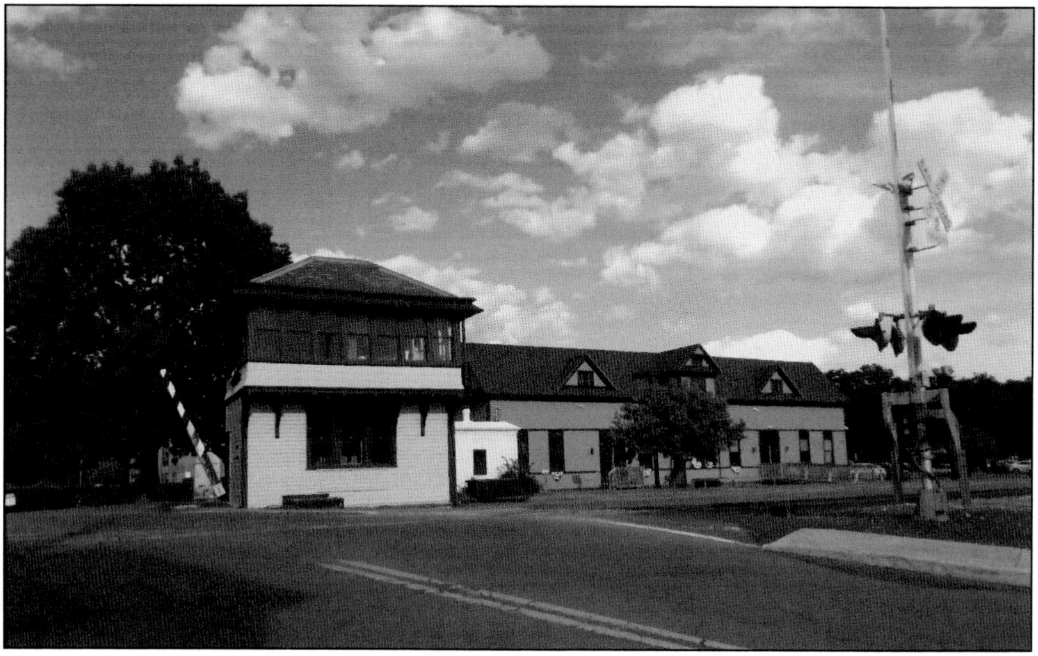

The East Stroudsburg railroad tower (switching station) at 31 Analomink Street and the relocated main hall of the DL&W station, now at 5 South Kistler Street, overlook the remaining DL&W track today. The tower is at N 40 59.961, W 75 10.883. (Authors' collection.)

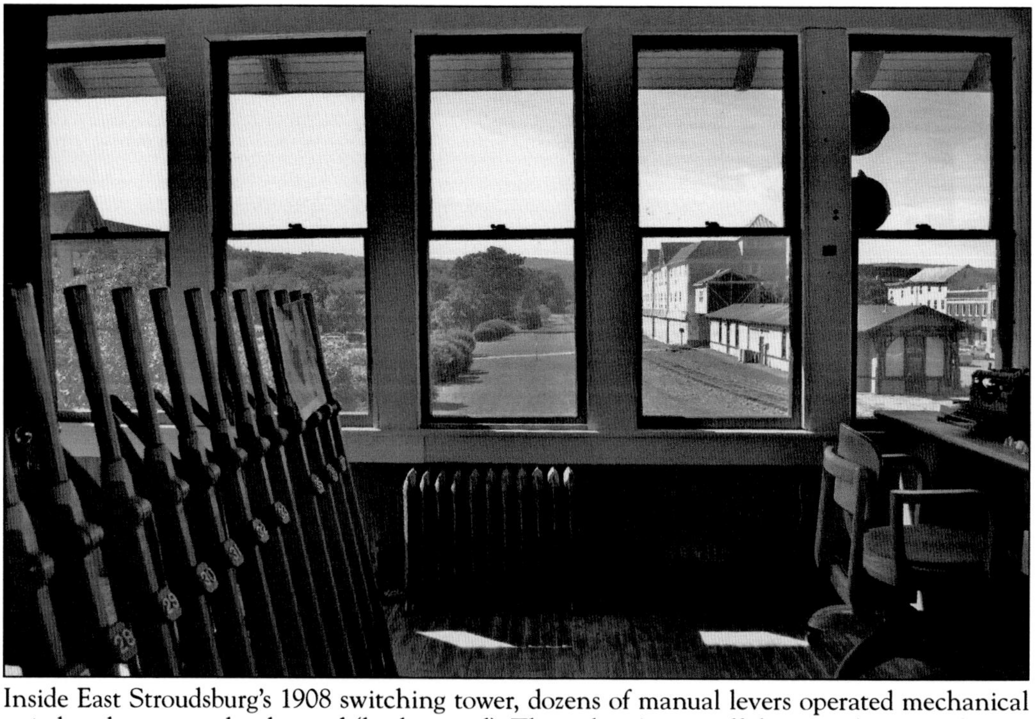

Inside East Stroudsburg's 1908 switching tower, dozens of manual levers operated mechanical switches that ran under the yard (background). The railway's turn off the main line at Delaware Valley Junction, nearly a mile to the north, is shown on the switch master's wall map but was not operated from here. (Kim Williams.)

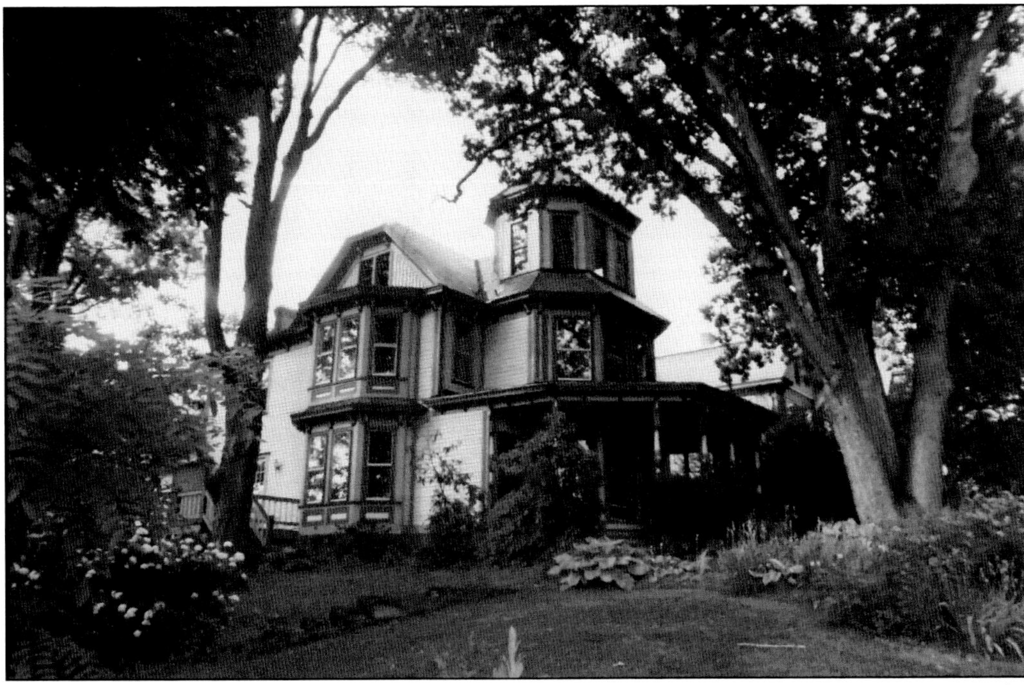

From his home on Analomink Street in East Stroudsburg, Milton Yetter could keep an eye on his railroad. As the impressive residence of a successful man, the house had modern appointments like a complete bathroom. This home is still a private residence; please do not trespass. This view is at N 41 00.002, W 75 10.816. (Authors' collection.)

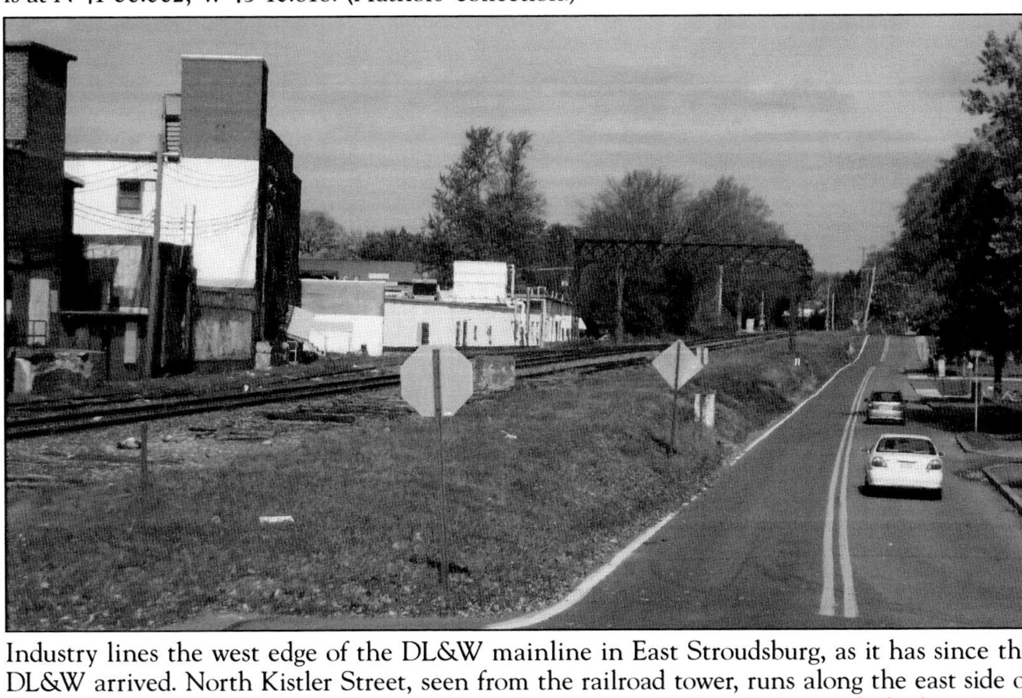

Industry lines the west edge of the DL&W mainline in East Stroudsburg, as it has since the DL&W arrived. North Kistler Street, seen from the railroad tower, runs along the east side of the tracks to join Lackawanna Avenue, where the remains of a foundation mark the location of Monroe Mills. (Authors' collection.)

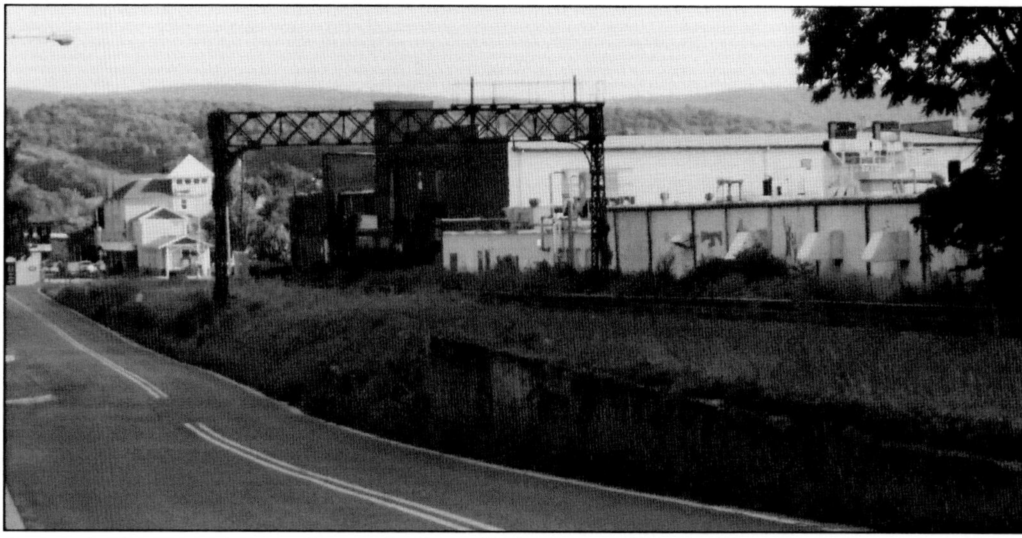

A view looking south over the trackside wall of Monroe (Wyckoff) Mills in East Stroudsburg, down North Kistler Street and the DL&W right-of-way, shows the station site (peaked roof) on Crystal Street. The dinkey would lay over on a rail stub just north of the mill. The wall is at N 41 00.097, W 75 10.898. (Authors' collection.)

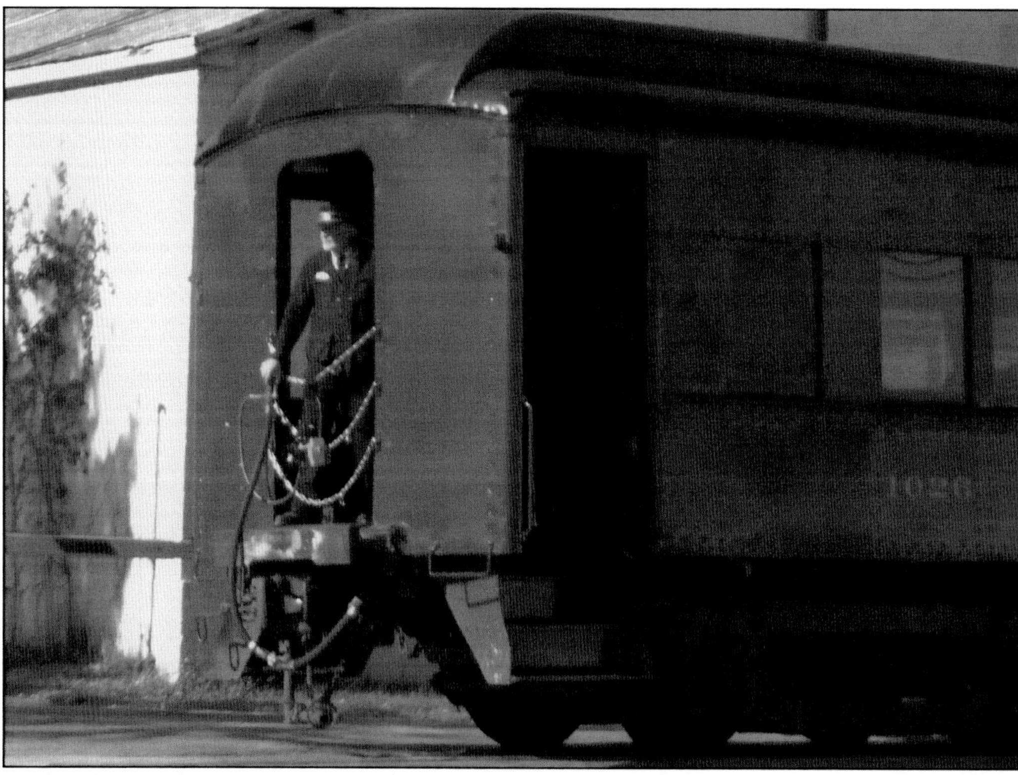

With a clang and a roar, an excursion train out of Steamtown National Historic Site slowly heads home north along Lackawanna Avenue at Burson Street in East Stroudsburg. Until 2016, the tracks of an industrial siding from the days of the DL&W still peeked through the asphalt here. The siding is at N 41 00.384, W 75 10.946. (Authors' collection.)

At busy grade crossings, rail employees monitored street and train traffic from elevated shanties. The DL&W built shanties at Broad Street and at Milford Crossing in East Stroudsburg that were identical to this one at Mount Pocono around 1915. They were demolished around 1980. All that remains of these picturesque structures is the stump of a support post at Lackawanna Avenue, which can be found at N 41 00.512, W 75 11.056. (Authors' collection.)

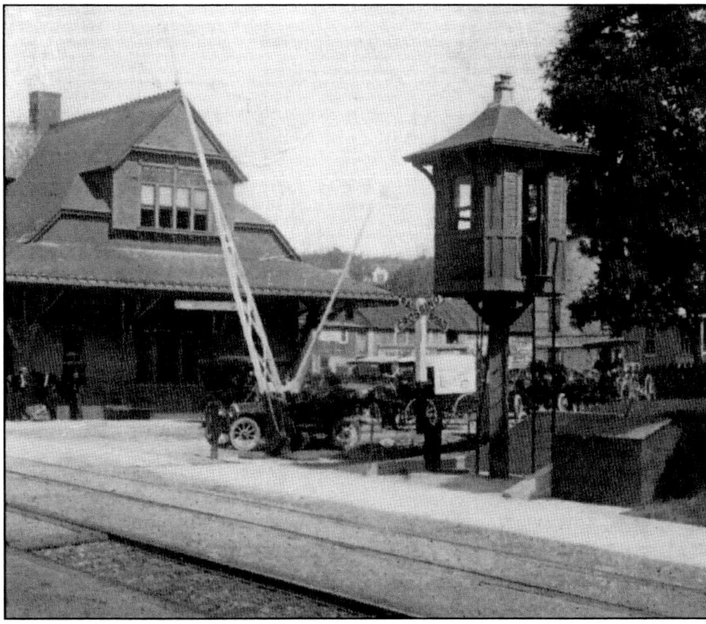

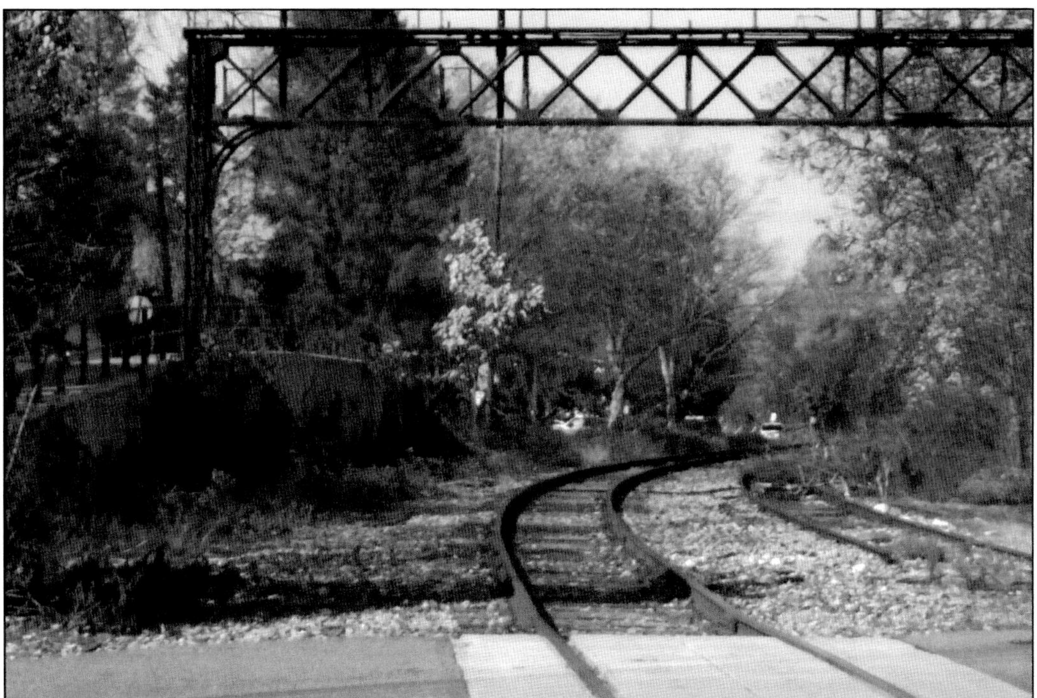

The signal bridge at Milford Crossing in East Stroudsburg still stands today, though with only one functioning track beneath it. The railway's Delaware Valley Junction station was at the far right, behind the shrubbery. King Street climbs along the DL&W mainline on the far left. The King Street sidewalk is at N 41 00.537, W 75 11.100. (Authors' collection.)

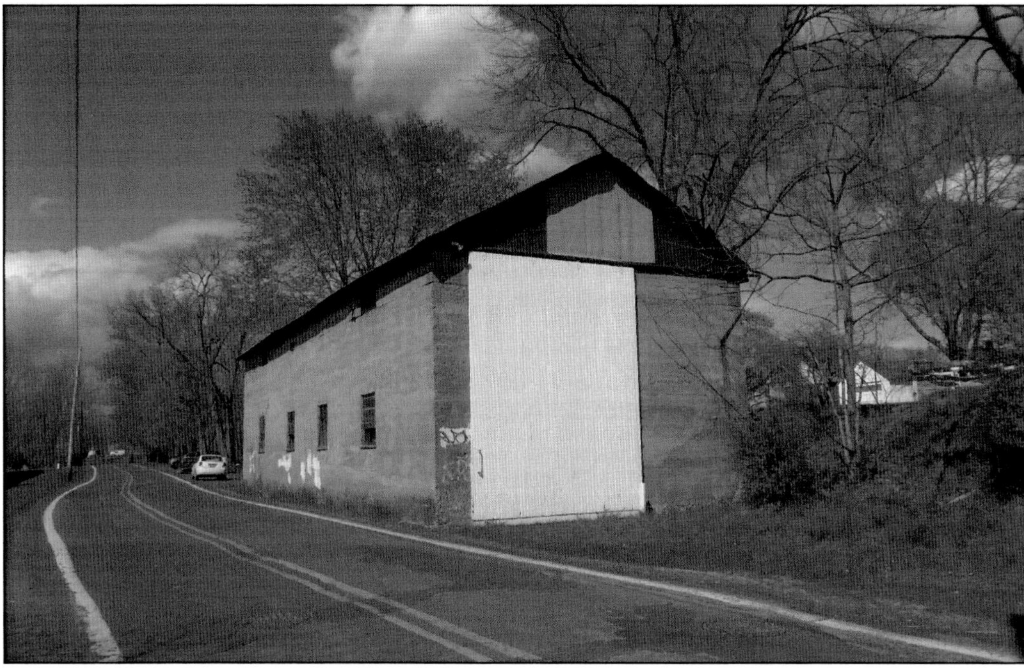

The railway's enginehouse is on today's paved Oak Street in East Stroudsburg, surrounded by houses and light industry. In the railway era, it stood in a field alongside the railway track. The building is now privately owned and has no rail equipment inside. Its GPS coordinates are N 41 00.696, W 75 11.114. (Authors' collection.)

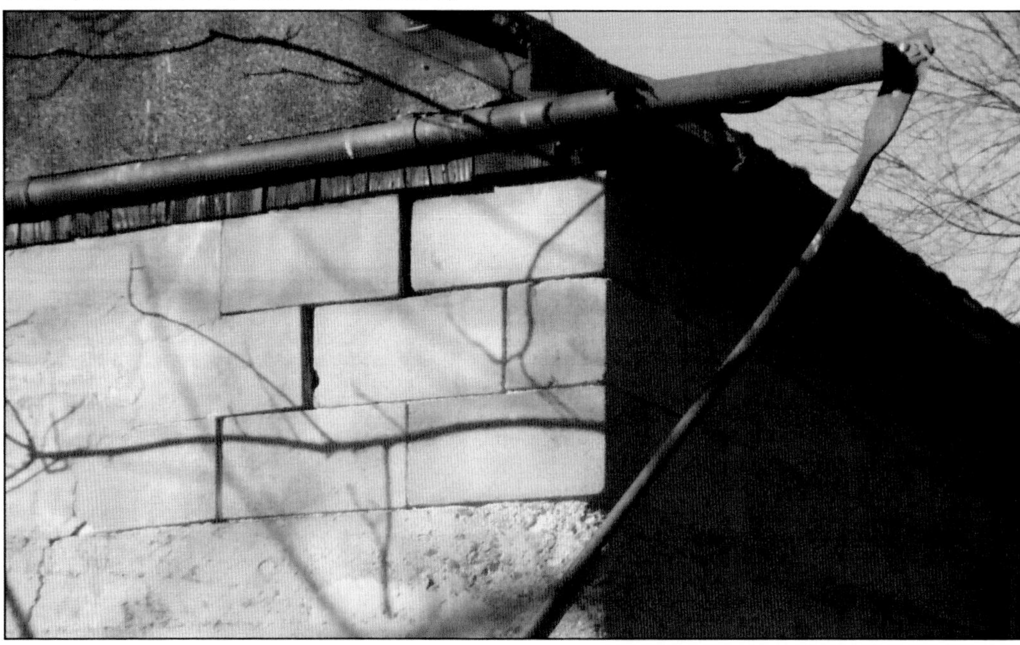

Three courses of concrete block above the original masonry work show where the roof of the East Stroudsburg enginehouse was raised in later years, perhaps to accommodate the No. 902 camelback engine. The north door is shorter than the south door; perhaps the 902 backed out southward when done. (Authors' collection.)

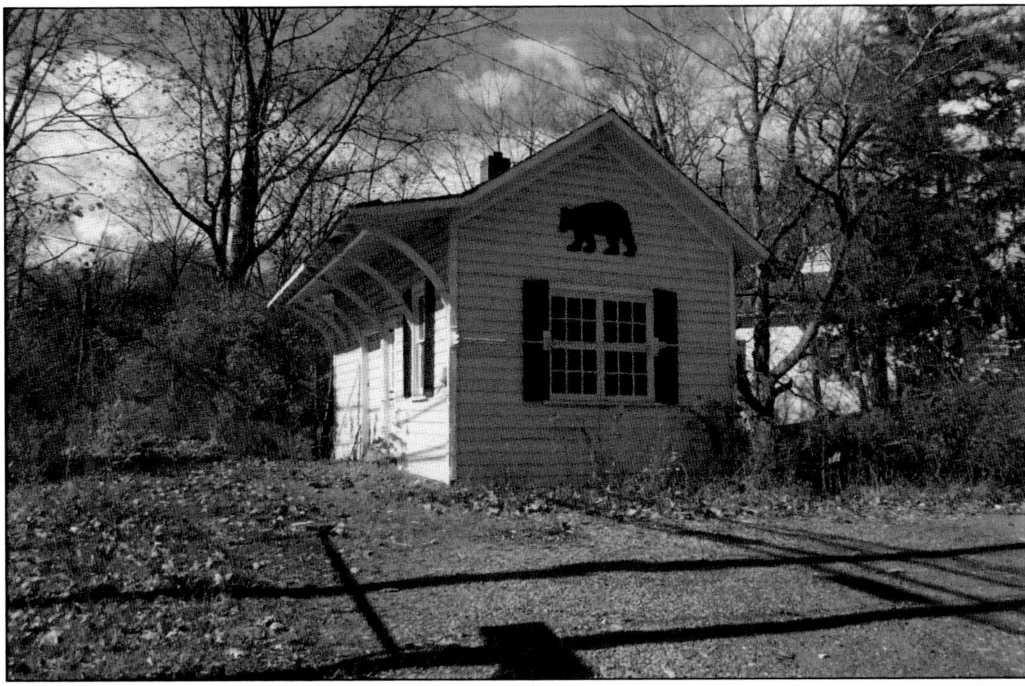

Still standing a century after it served the railway, the sturdy Marshalls Creek station has weathered valley floods, career changes, and being slammed into by a truck. The railbed is on the left of the station, and the bridge abutments at Marshalls Creek are just yards beyond the station, which can be found at N 41 02.594, W 75 07.684. (Authors' collection.)

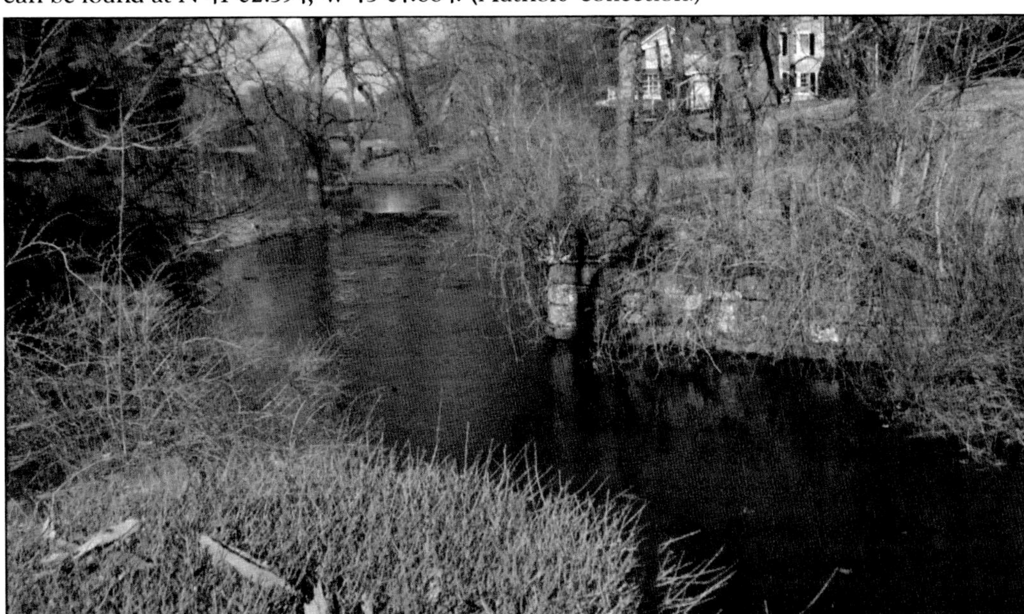

In fall and winter, the north abutment for the railway bridge over Pond Creek at Marshalls Creek can easily be seen from the north side of the automobile bridge, looking toward Lake Marshall. The track crossed here and then ran along the southeast bank of the lake. The abutment is at N 41 02.594, W 75 07.652. (Kim Williams.)

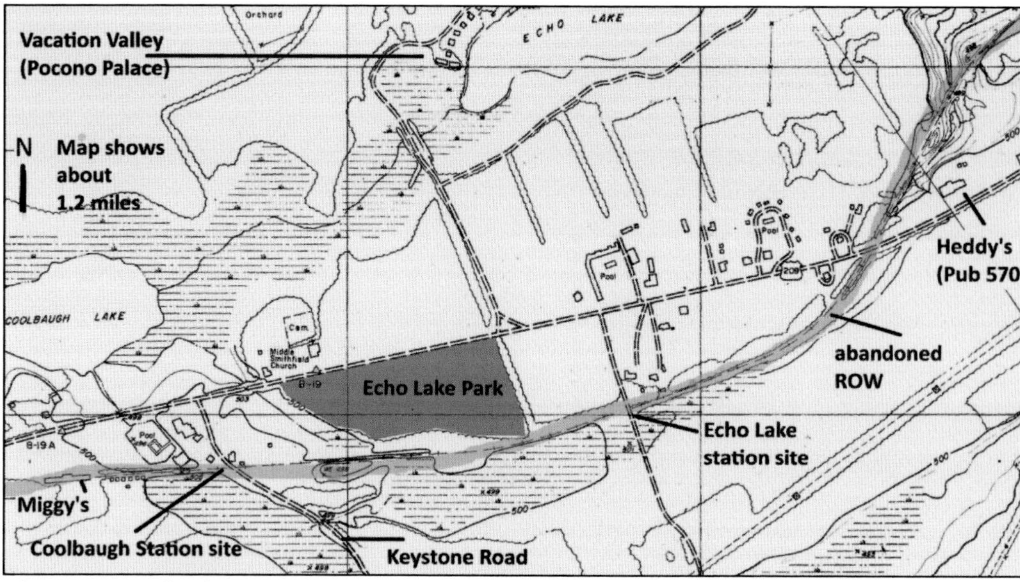

This 1967 map by the Army Corps of Engineers shows the area along Milford Road at Echo Lake Park and the abandoned railroad. Miggy's Market is directly in the footprint of the right-of-way. The Coolbaugh Station site is near N 41 03.743, W 75 04.116. (DEWA.)

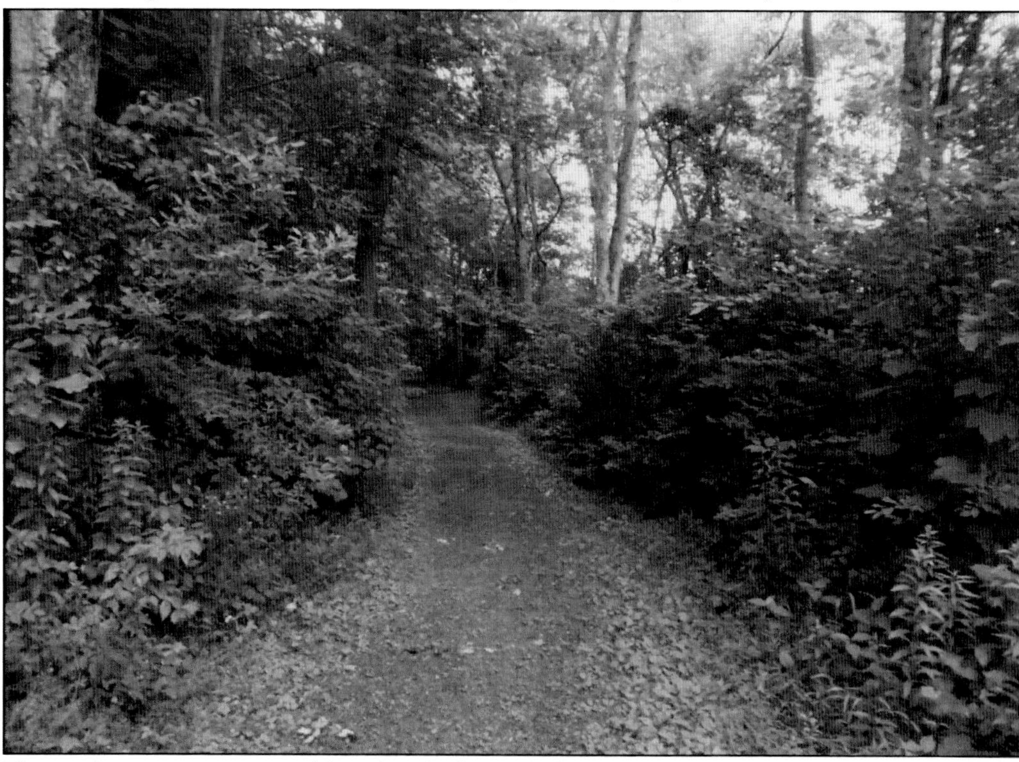

The track ran near or on an old road at the base of a low shelf along the southwest border of Echo Lake Park. It then continued along what is now a utility line cut to the Echo Lake station. (The cut is on private land; do not trespass.) No remnants of the station are visible today. This view is at N 41 03.748, W 75 03.736. (Authors' collection.)

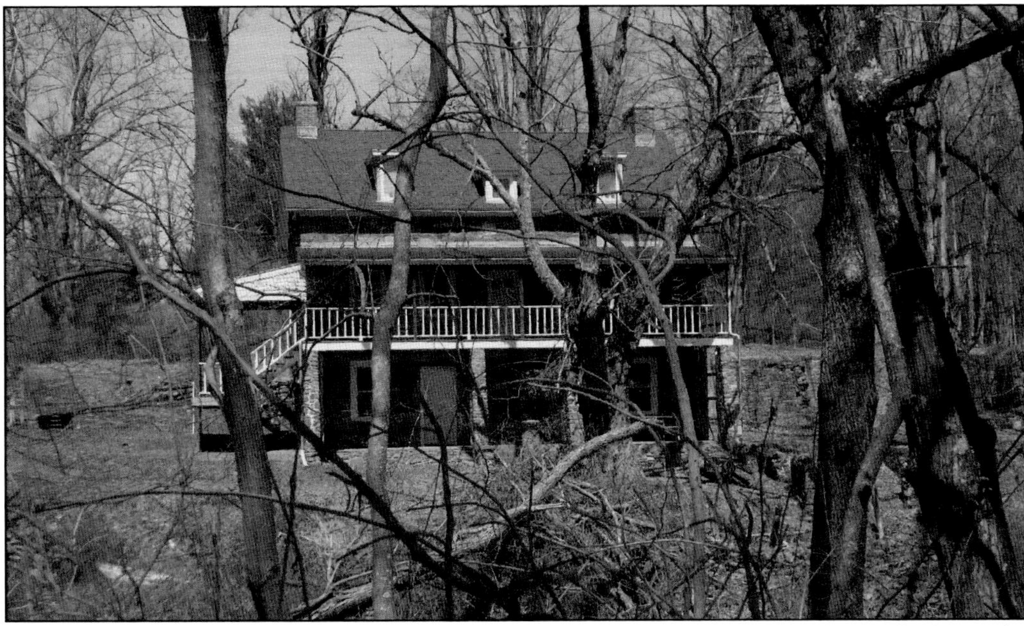

The 15-foot-wide railway embankment at Shoemakers is across the pond from the Jacob Shoemaker House, built around 1800. (It is a private residence; please stay clear.) Alongside the embankment, close to Winona Falls Road, are remains of a foundation, probably for the station. The foundation is at N 41 04.797, W 75 01.944. (Authors' collection.)

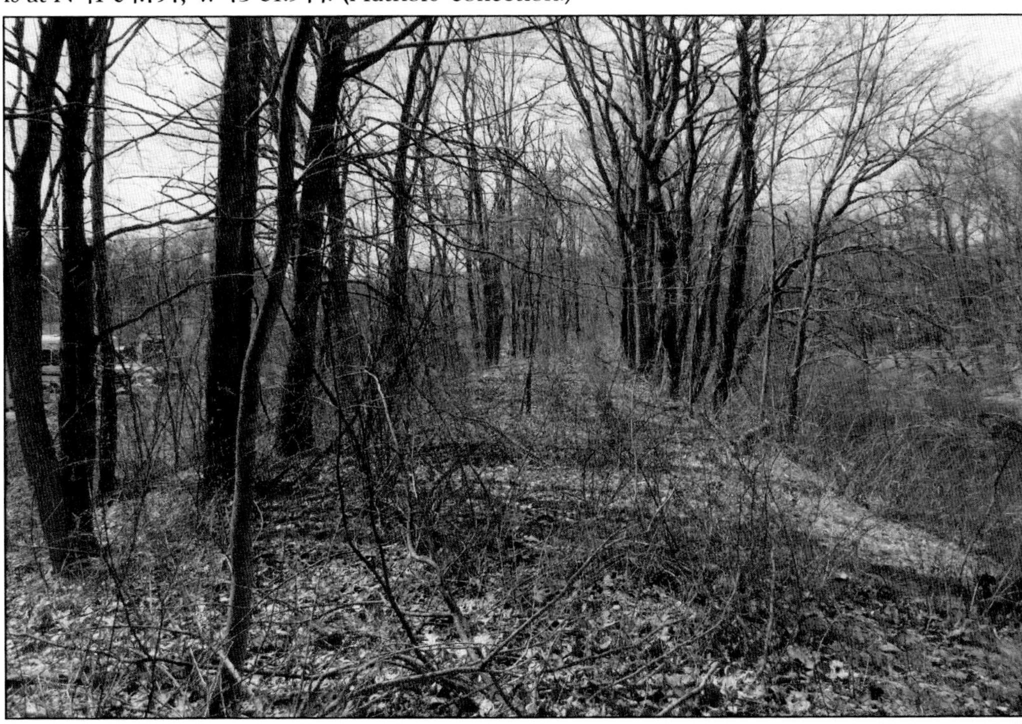

In this view looking west atop the rail embankment in Shoemakers back toward Winona Falls Road, just before the railbed dips at the old millrace, Shoemakers Pond is at the right and Fernwood warehouse at the left. The embankment is at N 41 04.871, W 75 01.828. (Authors' collection.)

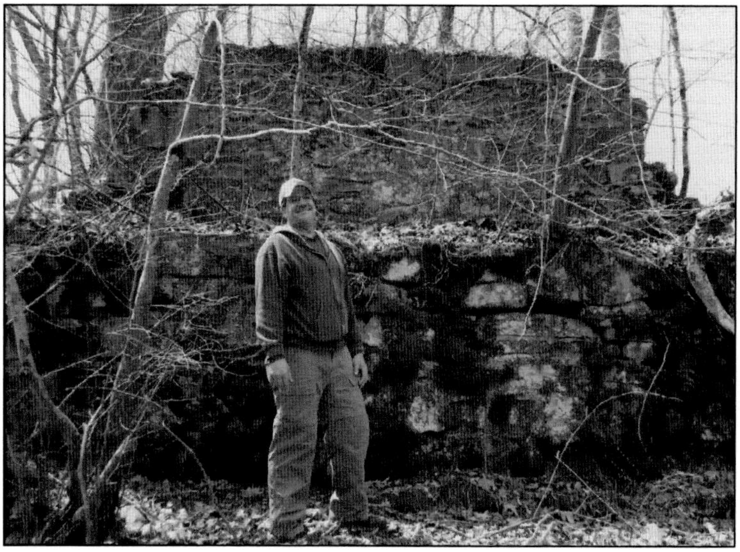

There is no substitute for the satisfaction of walking the landscape and discovering vestiges of the railway's passing for one's self. Seen from the edge of Bush Kill in Shoemakers, the height and solidity of the two-tiered west abutment are memorable. Please respect property rights when hiking. The abutment is at N 41 04.931, W 75 01.740. (Authors' collection.)

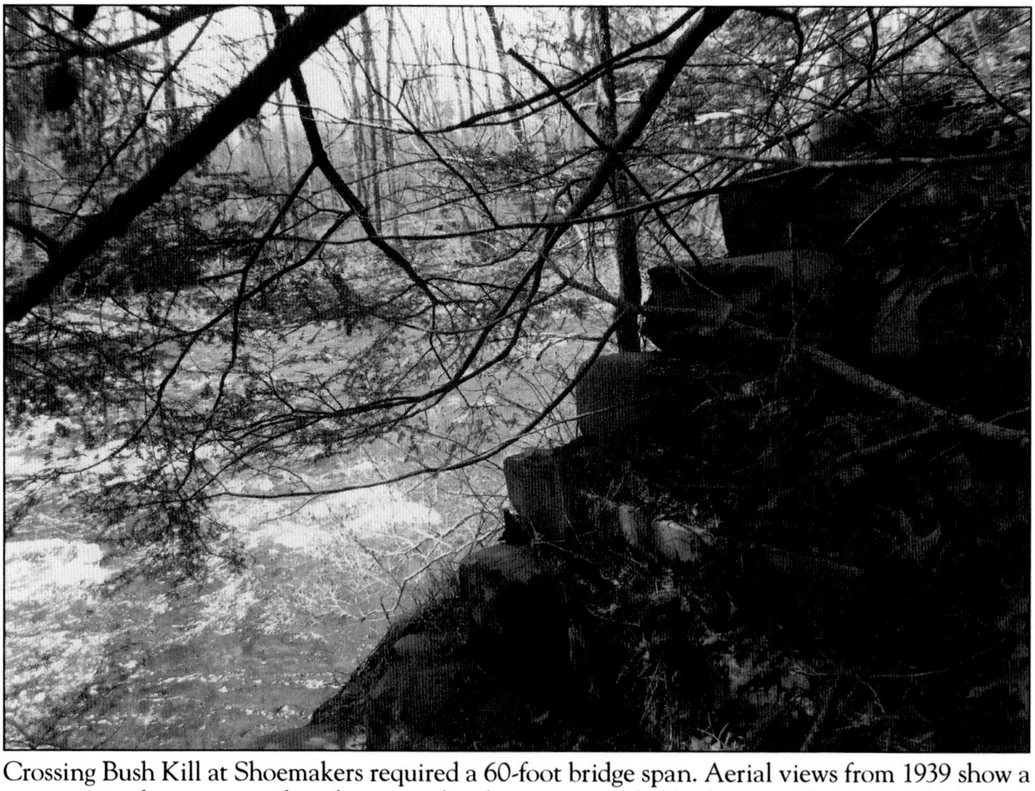

Crossing Bush Kill at Shoemakers required a 60-foot bridge span. Aerial views from 1939 show a structure in the stream midway between the abutments, probably the base of a pier for the bridge. The pier is no longer visible. This view looks upstream from the south flank of the east abutment at N 41 04.945, W 75 01.713. (Authors' collection.)

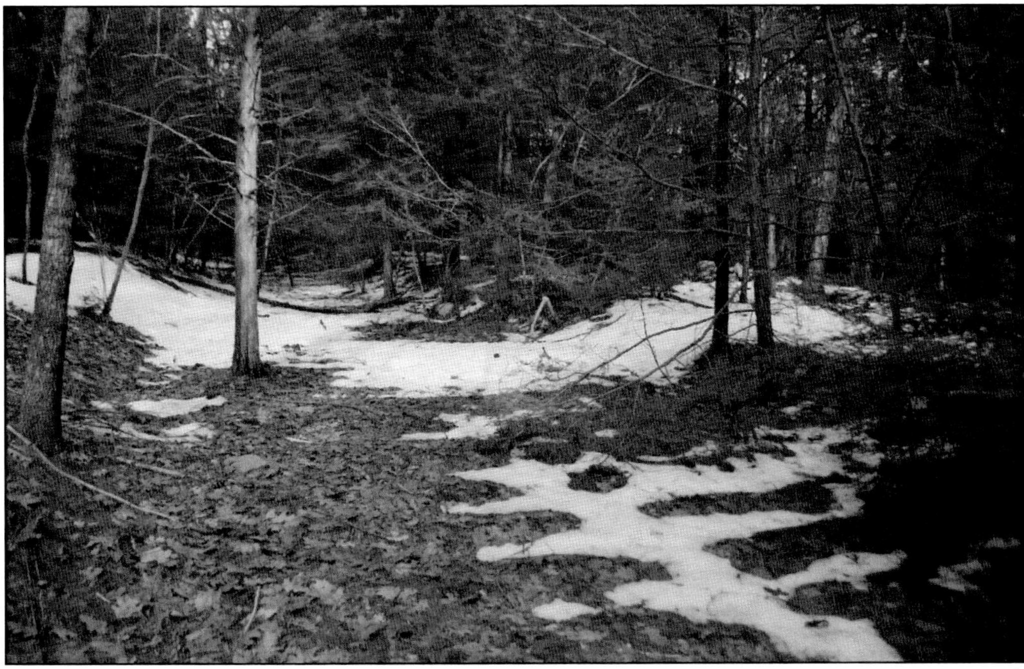

Hiking in late fall and early winter can reveal features that are hidden by summer growth. Could these snow-filled grooves in the railbed east of Bush Kill be indentations from rail ties? (Kim Williams.)

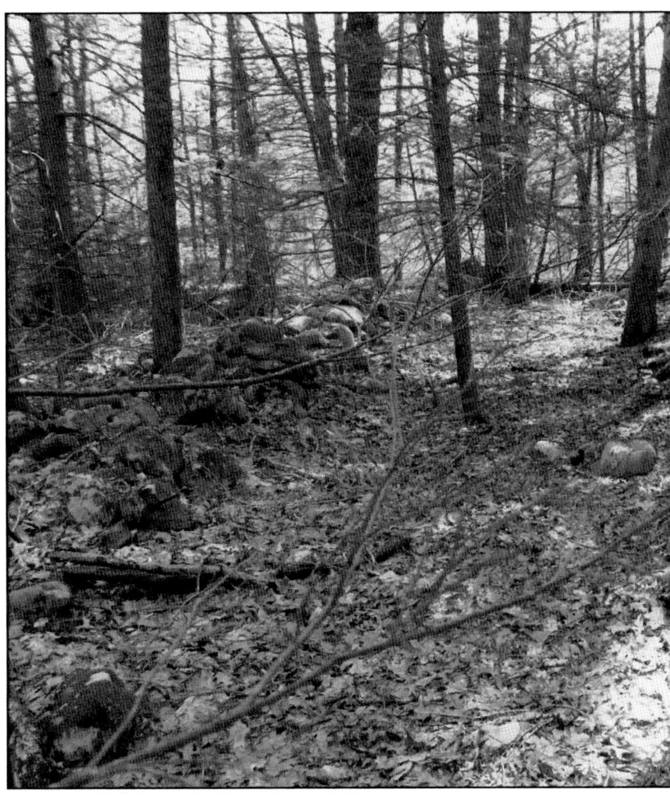

East of Bush Kill, the embankment runs through old farmland and over stone walls. To hike to the east abutment, follow Creek Road west .2 miles from the turn at the Maples to the telephone cut on the left. Walk the cut .4 miles until it turns sharp left (south). Continue straight west into the woods .6 miles to Bush Kill. The wall is at N 41 05.046, W 75 01.550. (Authors' collection.)

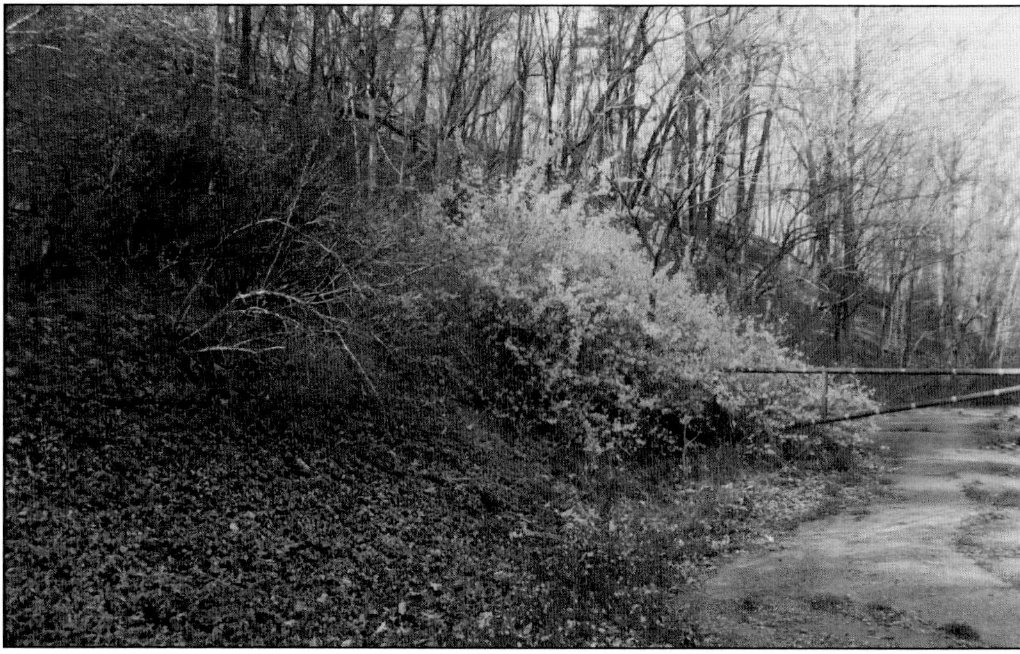

The west end of the Railway Avenue Trail is across Creek Road from the site of the Maples and a likely location for the Maples stop. The railway embankment descends here from behind and above the forsythia bushes on the left to the level of the paving at the pipe gate on the right. The embankment is at N 41 05.372, W 75 00.700. (Authors' collection.)

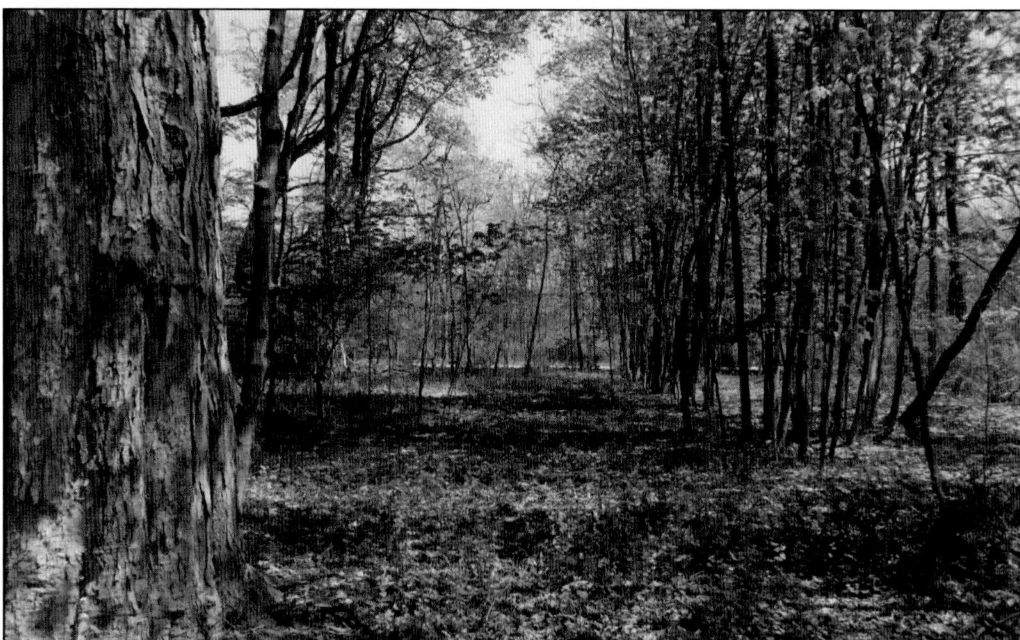

From the site of the Maples guesthouse, the tree-lined driveway is still clear eastward to Creek Road. Automobiles sometimes circled the drive on dark nights, perhaps probing for the turn in Creek Road. The house site is at N 41 05.335, W 75 00.698. (Authors' collection.)

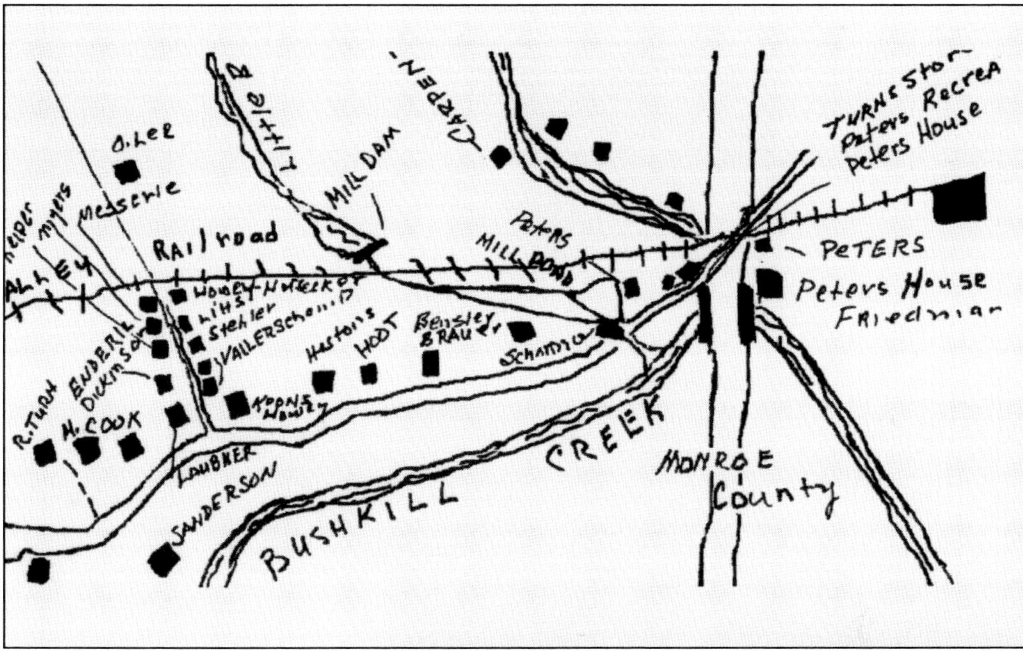

Lawrence Butz drew this map of central Bushkill from memory. The tracks, crossing, and coal bins figure large in recollection. Houses line Creek Road along Bush Kill and up Railway Avenue to the track. The coal bins are at the far right. North is to the upper left. (DEWA.)

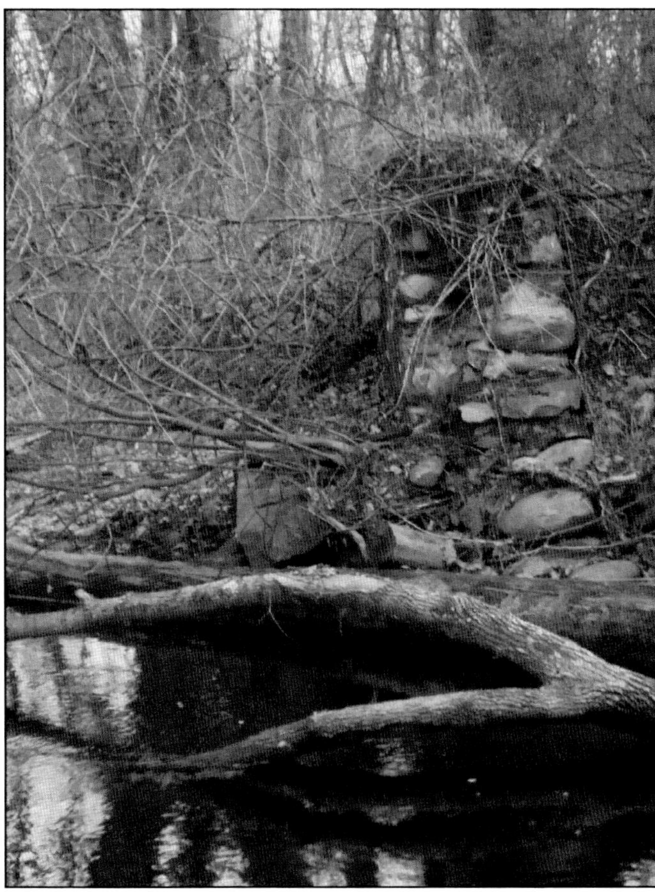

The abutments over Little Bush Kill, 150 yards west of the station in the village of Bushkill, have eroded severely. In 1955, Hurricanes Connie and Diane swelled Bush Kill, destroyed the Mill Pond, and tore out Milford Road bridge. Had the railway still been scraping by, this flood might have ended its career. The east abutment is at N 41 05.577, W 75 00.269. (Authors' collection.)

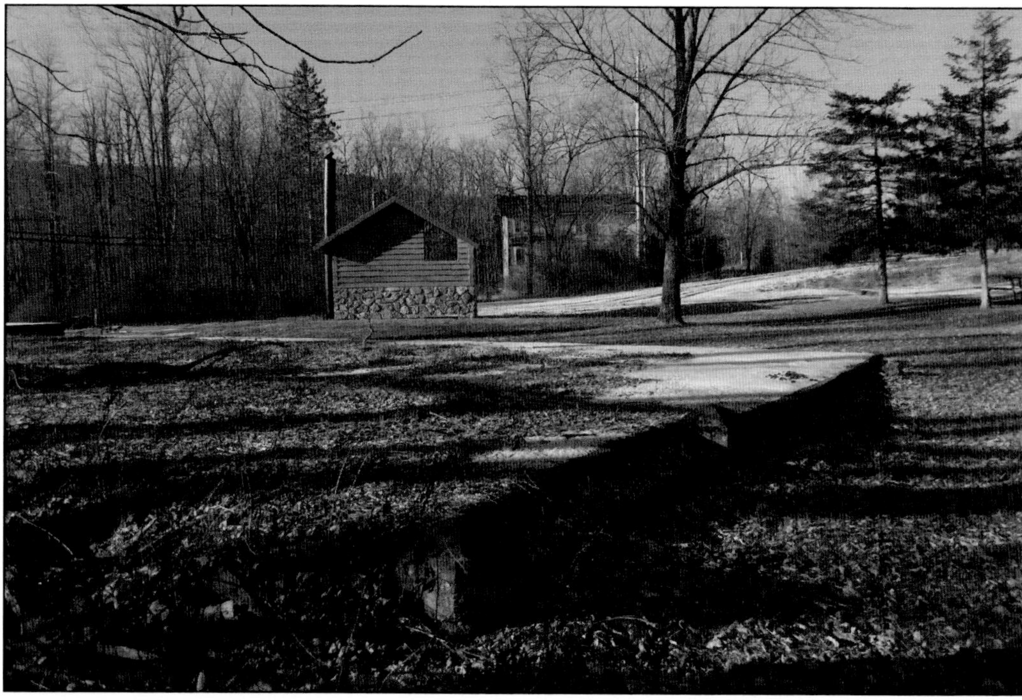

The view north over the foundation of the new station in the village of Bushkill shows the area of Nyce's lumberyard. Storyland, a children's park, was later built here. It closed in the 1970s. Carpenter House, in the distance, was Bushkill's post office from the 1930s until 2004. The small structure to the left is modern. (Authors' collection.)

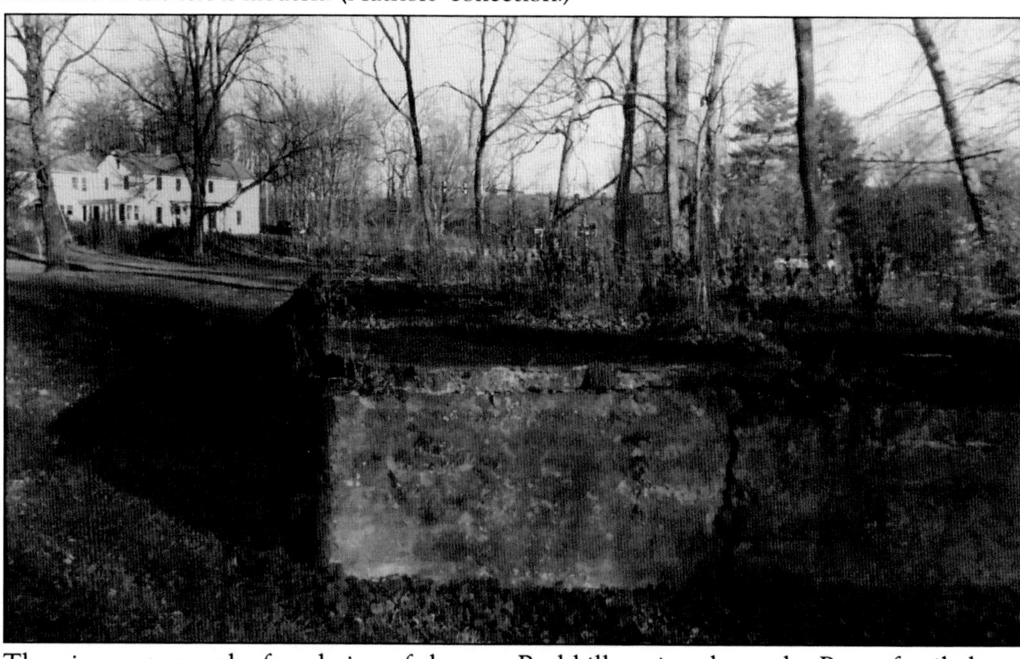

The view east over the foundation of the new Bushkill station shows the Peters family home at the left and the path of the railway to the coal bins across Milford Road in the center. The foundation is at N 41 05.591, W 75 00.142. (Authors' collection.)

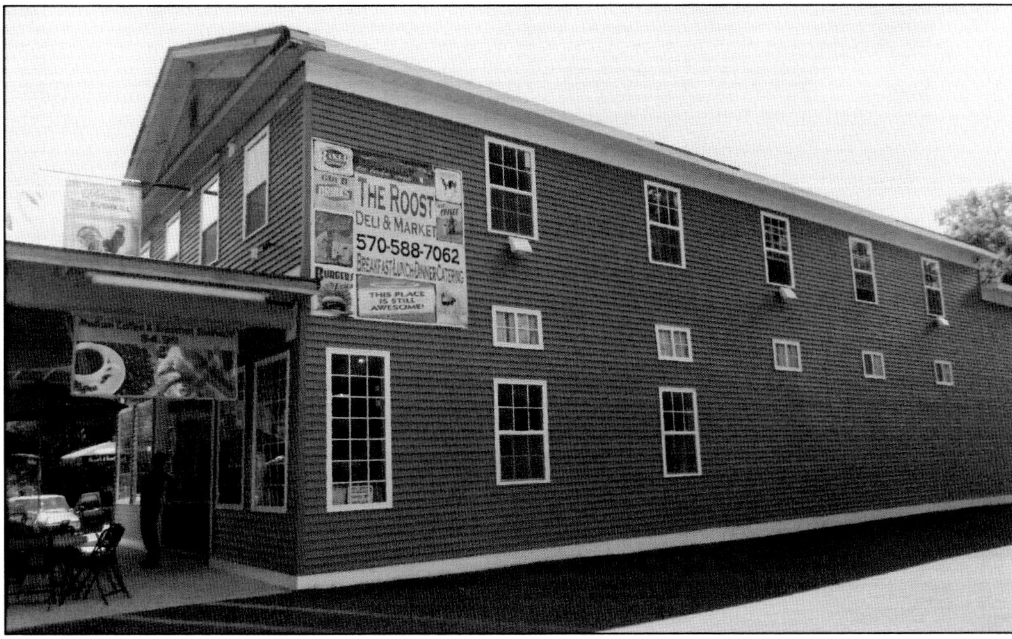

Bushkill's Nyce Brothers (later Turn & Cook) General Store from the railway era is now the Roost. The drop in the roofline at the far right shows the seam between the 1837 store in back and the large 1916 addition in front. The store backed onto the right-of-way and the station. It is at N 41 05.547, W 75 00.140. (Authors' collection.)

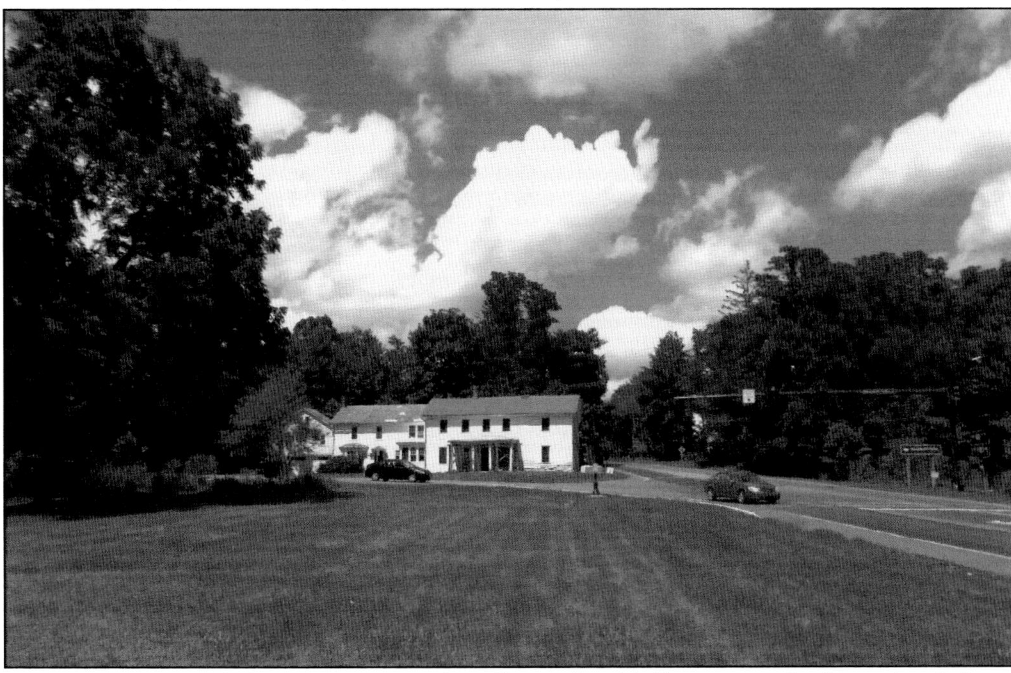

Today, the view north from the Roost in the village of Bushkill is open to the Peters family home on the north side of Bushkill Falls Road. The Peters grant of right-of-way stipulated that there be no buildings on the right-of-way within 115 feet of the intersection. The home is at N 41 05.594, W 75 00.114. (Authors' collection.)

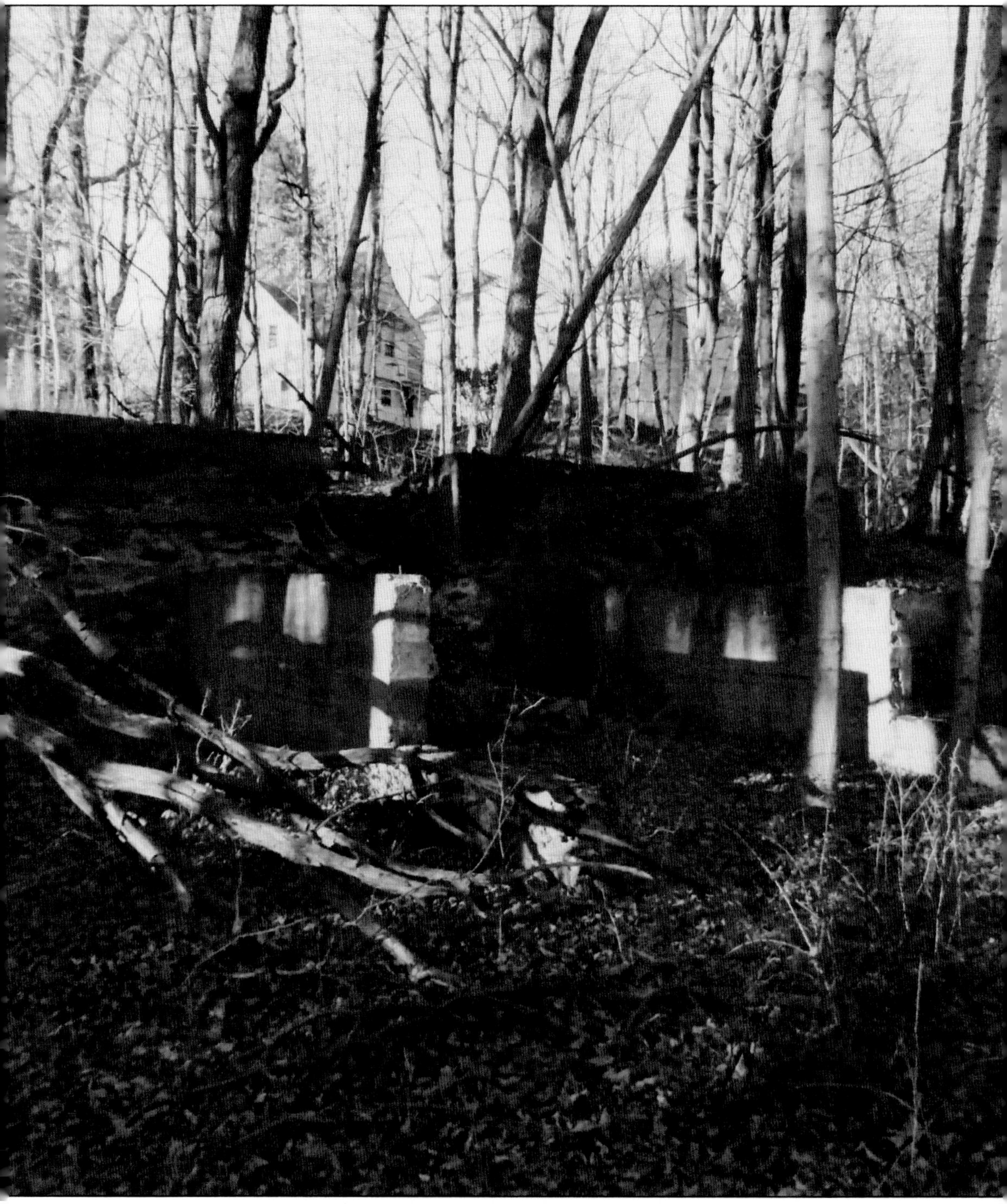

The northernmost reach of the railway, in the village of Bushkill, was the coalyard behind the Dutch Reformed church (visible in the background) on Milford Road. The train came in from the left at the top of the bins, and the floor of the coal hopper lowered to drop the coal into the pockets. The coalyard GPS coordinates are N 41 05.589, W 75 00.048. (Authors' collection.)

Bibliography

The Bells Ringing the Message of Progress in Monroe County, Pa. East Stroudsburg, PA: Hughes Press, 1915.

Cullen, George A. *Mountain and Lake Resorts on the Lackawanna Railroad.* New York: Lackawanna Railroad Passenger Department, 1909.

Henwood, James N.J. "Country Carrier of the Poconos: The Delaware Valley Railway." *Railroad History Bulletin* 174 (Spring 1996): 26–50.

Tebbs, Robert. "Along the Cinder Trail." Unpublished manuscript. Monroe County Historical Association, 1989.

US Interstate Commerce Commission. *Valuation Docket No. 864 Tentative Valuation Report on the Property of the Delaware Valley Railway Company as of June 30, 1919.* Washington, DC: Government Printing Office, 1926.

Walters, Horace G. *The Passing of the Dinkey.* East Stroudsburg, PA. Unpublished manuscript. Railroad Files, Monroe County Historical Association, no date.

About the Organizations

The Monroe County Historical Association in Stroudsburg is located in the 1795 Stroud Mansion. Its archives include photographs, postcards, and unpublished notebooks on the railway by Thomas T. Taber III and Robert Tebbs. The association also maintains the 1882 Driebe Freight Station (NYS&W) in Stroudsburg. The Pike County Historical Society in Milford holds photographs of Bushkill, the northern terminus. Housed in the Columns, a 1904 mansion, the society offers exhibits and collections for research. Year-round activities support these organizations.

East Stroudsburg Community Alliance maintains the former DL&W station, and East Stroudsburg Railroad Tower Historical Society preserves the switching station; both of these stations saw many a dinkey run by. The former station and tower open on occasion for rail excursions and special events. Steamtown National Historic Site in Scranton and the Railroad Museum of Pennsylvania in Strasburg have archives, exhibits, and rolling stock.